TECHNICAL VOCATIONAL EDUCATION AND TRAINING IN JAMAICA

TECHNICAL VOCATIONAL EDUCATION AND TRAINING IN JAMAICA

ACHIEVEMENTS, IMPACT, AND CHALLENGES

EDITORS
Disraeli Hutton, Ph.D
Hope Mayne, Ph.D
Raymond A. Dixon, Ph.D

University of Technology, Jamaica Press

First published in Jamaica 2024 by
University of Technology, Jamaica Press
237 Old Hope Road
Kingston 6
Email: utechjapress@utech.edu.jm

© 2024 Disraeli Hutton, Hope Mayne, Raymond A. Dixon, Editors

All rights reserved. Published 2024.

A catalogue record of this book is available from the
National Library of Jamaica.

ISBN: 978-976-8335-04-3 (print)
ISBN: 978-976-8335-05-0 (eBook)
ISBN: 978-976-8335-06-7 (Kindle)

The University of Technology, Jamaica Press has no responsibility for the persistence or accuracy of URLs for external or third-party Internet websites referred to in this publication and does not guarantee that any content on such websites is, or will remain, accurate or appropriate.

Cover and book design by Robert Harris
Email: roberth@cwjamaica.com
Set in Scala 11/15 x 24
Printed in Jamaica by Pear Tree Press.

Contents

List of Tables / vii

List of Figures / ix

Preface / xi

Acknowledgments / xiii

Introduction / xv

1. Early Development of TVET in Jamaica / 1
   CEDRIC McCULLOCH AND DISRAELI HUTTON

2. Technical High Schools and their Contribution to Advancing Technical Vocational Education and Training in Jamaica / 33
   MARCIA ROWE-AMONDE

3. TVET Rationalization in Secondary Schools / 57
   CAROLE POWELL

4. The Toolmaker's Institute, Supporting the Jamaican Industrial 89 Manufacturing Sector: Achievements, Impacts and Challenges / 80
   CHRISTOPHER O'COY BRYAN

5. Non-Traditional Skills Training for Career Development / 102
   DISRAELI HUTTON

6. TVET Policy Development and Implementation / 126
   GRACE McLEAN

7. Technical and Vocational Education and Training at the Tertiary Level in Jamaica: Achievements, Challenges and Impacts / **148**
HALDEN MORRIS

8. The University of Technology, Jamaica: Reflecting on a Model Institution for Workforce Development / **175**
HOPE MAYNE AND RAYMOND A DIXON

9. Workforce Training Readiness / **194**
RAYMOND A DIXON

10. Funding Strategies in TVET: Implications for Performance / **215**
DISRAELI HUTTON

Biographies / **239**

List of Tables

Table 2.1	Technical High Schools in Jamaica – Year of Establishment	/ **41**
Table 2.2	Enrolment for Academic Year 2014/2015	/ **44**
Table 3.1	Iterative Operation Model for Ten (10) Parishes	/ **74**
Table 3.2	Rating the Pilot Condition and labour Market Orientation Variables According to Indicator Scores	/ **76**
Table 3.3	Comparative Exam Data: CSEC & NVQ 2000–2007	/ **76**
Table 7.1	Tertiary Level TVET Programmes Offered in Jamaica (2006)	/ **158**
Table 8.1	Enrollment and Graduation at the University of Technology, Jamaica: 2011–214	/ **184**
Table 10.1	Categories of Training Funds Applied for TVET Countries in Latin American and African Countries	/ **218**
Table 10.2	Multi-dimension Questions regarding the Efficient and Effective Implementation of TVET	/ **220**
Table 10.3	Training Expenditure in the United States of America based on Company Size	/ **221**
Table 10.4	HEART NSTA Trust Enrolment, Completion, and Certification for the Period 1982/83–2022/23	/ **228**
Table 10.5	HEART NSTA Trust, Income and Expenditure for Operating Period 2016/17–2021/22	/ **229**

Table 10.6 Capital Expenditures for Secondary Schools in the Then Six Regions of the MoEY / **231**

Table 10.7 TVET and Non-TVET Expenditure in Selected Secondary Schools / **232**

List of Figures

Figure 2.1	Map outlining the location of Technical High Schools in Jamaica	/ **38**
Figure 3.1	Economic Justification of the Cluster System (Tomlinson, 2009)	/ **64**
Figure 3.2	School Clusters in Parish of Westmoreland (Pilot Report 1998–2005)	/ **65**
Figure 3.3	School Clusters in Parish of St Elizabeth (Pilot Report 1998–2005)	/ **66**
Figure 6.1	Integrated qualification framework displaying Jamaica's Framework	/ **134**
Figure 9.1	10-Year Enrolment Trend 2012/13–2021/22 (Heart Trust/NSTA, 2023)	/ **199**
Figure 9.2	Integrating STEM at the Primary level (Dixon & Hutton, 2015)	/ **208**
Figure 9.3	Integrating STEM at the Secondary level (Dixon & Hutton, 2015)	/ **209**
Figure 10.1	Sources of Funding for TVET	/ **219**

Acknowledgements

THE COMPLETION OF THIS BOOK ABOUT THE achievements, impact, and challenges of TVET in Jamaica, has been made possible by the contribution of several authors with expertise in TVET, business, and education. Their expertise spans all the levels of TVET. The editors express our sincere appreciation for their immense contribution to the development of TVET in Jamaica over the years and for their tireless effort to contribute their chapters to this publication.

The complex process of bringing together, negotiating, and editing submissions of authors recognized as experts in TVET, nationally and internationally, is only possible with committed and enthusiastic individuals. While this book has been long in the making, the perseverance of Dr Disraeli Hutton in seeing it to its completion is noteworthy. We thank the various individuals who served as resource persons for this publication and the publisher and editorial personnel who provided feedback to improve the quality of each chapter.

The Editors.

Introduction
Overview of the Book

IN CHAPTER ONE, *Early Development of TVET in Jamaica*, the authors divide the history of the offering of TVET programmes into two periods, pre-HEART Trust/NTA and post-HEART Trust/NTA eras. In chronological order, they describe the contributions made to develop TVET from as early as 1843, covering initiatives and policies such as the Lump report and other State initiatives, practical training at the post-elementary level, the establishment of technical schools in selected parishes, and early technical education at the tertiary level. **Chapter two**, *Technical High Schools and Their Contribution to Advancing Technical Vocational Education and Training in Jamaica*, examines in more detail the contribution of technical high schools to TVET, government project such as the Basic Skills Project, and the Technical High Schools Development Project that targeted the improvement of technical high schools. The upgrading of secondary schools to technical high schools, and the evolution and expansion of their curriculum are also covered. The author also addresses some of the challenges technical schools presently face. In **Chapter three**, *TVET Rationalization in Secondary Schools*, the author gives an in-depth description of the phases of the TVET Rationalization Project, described as a "one of a kind" as it utilized a unique model to share TVET resources across technical schools and institutions. The project emerged out of efforts by the Ministry of Education and other stakeholders to address the failure of the school system to prepare its leavers for the world of work, a finding by the Ministry of Education that was consistent with UNESCO's findings.

Chapter four, *The Toolmaker's Institute, Supporting the Jamaican Industrial Manufacturing Sector: Achievements, Impacts and Challenges*, provides an assessment of the impacts and challenges of the Toolmaker's Institute, now the National Tool and Engineering Institute (NTEI), particularly during the period 1969 to 1984. **Chapter five**, *Non-Traditional Skills Training for Career Development*, shifts the focus from the traditional areas and institutions which offer TVET, and makes the argument that with the emphasis on Science, Technology, Engineering, Arts, and Mathematics (STEAM), TVET needs to embrace other occupational areas within the arts, as offered in programmes at Edna Manley College of the Visual and Performing Arts (EMCVPA); athletics, such as programs offered at G. C. Foster College; and maritime, such as programs offered at Caribbean Maritime University (CMU). **Chapter six**, *TVET Policy Development and Implementation*, focuses on the development and implementation of policies in TVET over the last 60 years in Jamaica, examining significant policies that were enacted during the 1960s, 1970s, 1980s, 1990s, 2000 and beyond. A comparison is made of the TVET policy model used in Jamaica with the TVET policy models used in Finland and Singapore. Lessons than can be learned in Jamaica from both systems are highlighted. **Chapter seven**, *Technical and Vocational Education and Training at the Tertiary Level in Jamaica: Achievements, Challenges and Impacts*, provides a brief synopsis of TVET at the tertiary level in Jamaica prior to 1970 and a comprehensive account of what took place after 1970. It explores new developments in TVET in Jamaica at the tertiary level providing a description of the development of TVET leadership graduate programs at the University of the West Indies and the University of Technology, Jamaica. **Chapter eight**, *The University of Technology, Jamaica: Reflecting on a Model Institution for Workforce Development*, covers the University of Technology, Jamaica (Utech, Jamaica), formally the College of Art, Science and Technology (CAST), academic excellence in TVET, specifically up to when the institution celebrated its 50-year anniversary. It provides a description of programmatic achievements, followed by specific programmatic development in response to workforce needs after it transitioned from a college to a four-year degree granting university and the offering of post-graduate programmes. Insightful interview with a past president provides insight on how Utech, Jamaica has contributed to workforce development.

In **Chapter nine**, *Workforce Readiness*, an argument is made for educational frameworks that integrates TVET and STEM at the primary and secondary levels of the education system to deliver the types of competencies that will produce a workforce that is innovative and competitive globally. Finally, **Chapter ten**, *Funding Strategies in TVET: Implications for Performance*, describes different models that are used to finance TVET, with special focus on the benefits of the model that has been used in Jamaica since the establishment of the HEART Trust Act.

CHAPTER 1

Early Development of TVET in Jamaica

CEDRIC McCULLOCH AND DISRAELI HUTTON

THE DEVELOPMENT OF TECHNICAL VOCATIONAL EDUCATION AND Training (TVET) in Jamaica may conveniently be divided into pre- and post-HEART Trust/NTA (1982) periods. The early period is designated pre-HEART Trust/NTA. This division is made as it is safe to assert that The Human Employment and Resource Training Act, 1982 (HEART Trust), with its three per cent tax dedicated to TVET, was the 'game changer' for the TVET sector of the education and training system. In 1991, the name of the organization, then known as The HEART Trust was changed to The HEART Trust/National Training Agency (HEART Trust/NTA).

There is little evidence to show that there was any systematic approach to training in Craft before the abolition of slavery. Artisans would be trained on the job and "the education required to work on the plantation would have been acquired through a crude form of apprenticeship or on-the-job training. And the jobs required labourers with the physical capacity for endurance under inhospitable working conditions" (Hutton, 2016, p. 57). The establishment of the Negro Education Grant in 1838[1] was the impetus for an education system that had significant government input (Campbell, 1968). But the context for this initiative by the Imperial Government was, in part, as a result of the decision by the Whigs[2] of 1833 to make a grant available for popular education in England. The concern of skills education came out of the action of some local assemblymen to provide support for education to the churches involved in the education of ex-slaves. In particular, there was one set who felt that the ex-slaves should be provided with the "kind of education that would be of service to the plantations" (Campbell, 1970, p. 17). Campbell (1970) pointed out: "At best the talk about agricultural education meant schools in which pupils would be taught scientific agricultural skills; at worst the assemblymen simply had in mind the conditioning of children at an age to agricultural grind" (p. 17).

EARLY PROGRAMME INITIATIVES

Two clusters of initiatives emerged during the pre-HEART Trust/NTA period with a stronger emphasis on Agriculture and Home Economics Education and Training. But, as the influence of agriculture receded, Technical Education and Training became more dominant in the latter period.

The early initiatives in TVET started immediately after emancipation in 1838. A few persons should be credited for the early attempts to establish technical education in Jamaica. For example, a bill proposed by Mr Orrett in 1843 provided 30 pounds per year over two years for any schools which were involved "in agricultural work for twelve hours a week" (Gordon, 1970, p. 18). There was another initiative by Lord Elgin who, in a Bill in 1844, established Jamaica's first Board of Education. The purpose of the Board went beyond the proposal for the teaching of agriculture in schools, and one of its first tasks was the establishment of a teacher- training college for the training of students in the area of scientific agriculture (Gordon, 1970). According to Gordon, the Board was instructed to give special consideration to schools which had agriculture as part of their curriculum. Although the establishment of the Board of Education represented a significant development in education at the time, its impact was marginal because it did not have the power to influence the Assembly which was the real decision-making entity of the local authorities.

The other actors who were in support of some form of technical training included Governor Sligo "who felt that schools should operate as schools of industries as well as provide for the mental development of students. A school of industry was interpreted as one that taught agriculture several hours per day" (Whyte, 1977, p. 80). In fact, the Governor felt that skills training should not be limited to agriculture but industrial training should be pursued at the same time. James Phillippo, a Baptist missionary, also advocated for "industrial training which would include job training in trades" (Whyte, 1977, p. 80). So, the concept of schools for industry-related training was promoted by both Governor Sligo and James Phillippo during the early post-emancipation period. (Incidentally, James Phillippo was credited for establishing the Phillippo Baptist Church in Spanish Town, which is still in use today.) But, essentially, agriculture-related training remained the focus after the ending of the Negro Education Grant in 1845.

The first venture into teacher training was the establishment of a normal school of industry, specifically to train teachers of agriculture who operated in elementary schools. The need for this entity became even more important when it was determined by the Inspector of Schools in 1847 (Whyte, 1977) that industrial training was being retarded because of the poor physical conditions of schools and inadequate attendance. The poor attendance was associated with the parents' use of their children to pursue income-earning activities. The normal school operated for five years, from 1847 to 1852. One of the reasons for its early demise was that the programme drifted into the traditional mode of teaching academic subjects and the real aim of preparing teachers for industry was sidelined.

The thinking in the late 19th century was that training in agriculture should be central to the operations of elementary schools. Millicent Whyte (1977) expressed the opinion that the emphasis on training in agriculture was related to the perception that students in elementary schools were destined to be workers of the soil. This line of thought continued into the 1950s. For example, on the plains of Westmoreland, in the 1950s, on a Thursday afternoon, boys attending elementary school also went to the Extended School Garden, while girls remained in the school building and did sewing and other home economics-related subjects (Whyte, 1977). This practice remained in the primary all-age schools in the 1960s and beyond.

THE LUMB REPORT AND OTHER STATE INITIATIVES

The central role of agriculture in the curriculum of educational institutions dominated discussions in the 1890s. These discussions received support in the report of the Lumb Commission of 1898. Overall, the report was critical of the quality and effectiveness of the education system, which included the areas related to skills acquisition. Gordon (1968) indicated that the Report was in favour of training elementary school children in general manual skills and not the trades. The Lumb Report recommended the continuation of the teaching of sewing and domestic science, but it should be limited to "plain sewing, cutting and repair of garments and knitting of useful articles" (Gordon, 1968, p. 122). The Report cautioned that these skills should not be taught if a registered female teacher was not available at the school. In addition, it recommended that agricultural skills should be taught in order to prepare the school graduates to earn a living by working off the land they occupied and also, importantly, to encourage a love for agriculture by the children of the ex-slaves. It should be noted that, even in those early days, there was a resentment for agriculture. One obvious reason would be the need to toil in the hot sun daily, although they were working for themselves and their families. As presented by Gordon (1968):

> The opinion seems to be held that the present system of education tends to encourage a distaste for manual labour in favour of clerkships and such occupations, and to create an exodus from country into towns. . . . Any such general distaste for manual and agricultural labour must be felt to be an evil, and we believe that, to whatever extent it may exist in Jamaica, the carrying out of our recommendation will tend to check it. (p. 125–126)

The development of technical education received greater support with the establishment of the Board School, which was later named "the Government Model School or Continuation and Commercial Education which was established in 1896" (Whyte, 1977, p. 84). The concerns of the Lumb Report regarding the ineffectiveness of the manual skills teachers were addressed by the training of these teachers in the newly established Manual School. This was the genesis of the technical schools, starting with Kingston Technical, which was the only one up to the 1950s.

TECHNICAL AND VOCATIONAL EDUCATION

With the expansion of the industrial sector and the arrival of the bauxite industry, Kingston Technical School was the only such institution providing a level of skills training that would be consistent with the skills required. A technical Exploratory Committee was appointed in 1949 to advise the Consultative Committee on Education on the type of technical education that would be required in Jamaica. Among the recommendations were the establishment of a technical institute in the vicinity of Kingston; technical high schools adjoining or in close proximity to industrial and occupational areas; and technical departments in secondary schools. It was further recommended by the Exploratory Committee that technical education should be linked with the apprenticeship programme being carried out in industry, trade and other occupational areas (Whyte, 1977).

TRANSITION FROM PRACTICAL TRAINING CENTRES

The establishment of four Practical Training Centres, including Holmwood, 1936; Carron Hall, 1937; Dinthill, 1938; and Knockalva, 1940 was a precursor to the upgrading to technical schools. While there was a need for technical skills training, as noted earlier, Kingston Technical School was the only technical school in place up to the 1950s. The Kendal Report of 1943, for example, did not support the upgrading of the Practical Training Centres to play a similar role as the Kingston Technical School. The view, as presented by the report, was that these schools should continue to provide training in agriculture and domestic skills. Institutions such as The Carron Hall specialized in Home Economics, while Holmwood, Dinthill and Knockalva were essentially agricultural institutions with minor offerings in auto mechanics and woodwork. Real change in the offering related to technical education came about after the Advisor of Technical Education to the Secretary of State for colonies was asked to advise the government on the matter in 1959. According to Whyte (1977), the advisor indicated that Jamaica would not be able to compete in the 'modern competitive world' if the workforce is not prepared with the appropriate skills that are underpinned by general education. Today, these training institutions are still in operation and are making a significant contribution to skills development for economic growth and development. Over a period of 100 years, they have made the transition from practical training centres to trade training centres, to technical schools to technical high schools.

THE PRACTICAL TRAINING AT THE POST-ELEMENTARY LEVEL

It was around the beginning of the decade of the 1950s that Jamaica turned its attention seriously to the development of technical education, although technical education in Jamaica started around 1866 in Industrial Schools. These schools devoted three hours per day, for three or four days per week, to subjects like Agriculture, Manual Training, Sewing and General Home Economics. The emphasis, however, up to the beginning of the 20th century, was on agricultural education.

With the new impetus for technical education and skills training generated after advisory missions to Jamaica and the West Indies, Jamaica began to respond with greater urgency to the strengthening of technical training. This led to the establishment of technical schools across the island including in St Elizabeth, St Andrew, Vere and Frome, and Titchfield Technical Schools across the parishes of Jamaica. With an increased number of technical high schools in Jamaica (over 12), concerns are expressed if some of these schools are adhering to their technical education focus. Presented in the following section are five of the institutions which played a pivotal and historical role in skills development in the Jamaican educational sector. These include Kingston Technical High, Dinthill Technical High, Holmwood Technical High, Carron Hall High, and Knockcalva Agricultural.

KINGSTON TECHNICAL HIGH SCHOOL

The first major response to Governor Sligo's and James Phillippo's thinking of providing training in trades and related skills came to fruition with the establishment of the Kingston Technical High School. However, the origins of the school began with the Board of Education in 1892, which had the responsibility to find space for the training of some 3,000 students who were located mainly in Kingston. Started as an elementary facility for boys and girls, the objective was that "the school is to gradually grow into a centre for specialized manual instruction, [and] children from other Kingston schools are . . . the first to benefit by the training afforded by the Board School" ("The First Government", 1911). As further clarified by Sangster (2016), "The School was designed to be a model elementary school offering advanced manual training and it was hoped that it would develop into a centre of good general and technical education" (p. 5).

Under the headship of Mr J. G. Peet, who was a trained and certificated English teacher, and also a qualified woodwork instructor, the name was changed to the Manual Training School for boys in January 1896. The School was located at the same site on Hanover Street where The Mico Teachers' College was first established. Initially, it was accorded the name Board School because the Board of Education was responsible for supervising its operations (Kingston Technical High School, 2020).

The school went through several changes during its early years regarding its location and programme offerings. So, in fulfilling that hope of becoming a premier technical programme, the curriculum underwent major changes which evolved into the present Technical High School programme. This upgrading of the school also marked the beginning of the formal offering of technical subjects which led to certification at the level of City and Guilds. The school has remained a major provider of skills training for the Jamaican workforce. However, it was not until 1913 that the school was revamped and relocated for the second time to 82 Hanover Street in Kingston (Kingston Technical High School, 2020). The training provided in its early years was limited to woodwork and domestic science but, with a more innovative thinking, the programme now "included structural engineering, machine shop practice, welding, electrical installation, commercial subjects and handicrafts" (Sangster, 2011). Efforts were also made to ensure that certification was provided by world-recognized examination bodies from Britain. Accordingly, the students were prepared for examinations conducted by "the Royal Society of Arts in commercial subjects and for the City and Guilds of London Institute in the technical and domestic science subjects. The school was then known as the Government Commercial, Technical and Continuation School" (Sangster, 2011, p. 4).

The school celebrated its 124 years of existence in 2020, and it remains committed "to the original purpose . . . which is to equip Jamaicans with an education which produces students with skill sets that are needed for the job market (locally/globally) now and in the future" (Kingston Technical High School, p. 1). Despite the historical role that the school has played in advancing technical and vocational education, there are some, including parents of students, who desire to have a more traditional high school. However, the school is committed to continuing on a path that prepares students who will make a direct contribution to the development of the Jamaican economy. And, in so doing, the school will provide training which reflects the needs of the workforce.

The determination of the school to become a certification centre for technical vocation education is consistent with the stated goal of ensuring that each graduate leaves the institution with two or more certifications in NCTVET, City and Guild, CVQ, and NVQ as well as five or more CXC, CSEC, and CAPE subjects. Further, based on the historical relationship with The Mico University College and the University of Technology (UTech), Kingston Technical will forge meaningful relationships by twinning the school with these tertiary institutions (Kingston Technical High School, 2020).

Like the other early established technical schools, Kingston Technical High produced some of the outstanding academics, entertainers, sportsmen and women. Some of the alumni include "Headley Brown, former Governor of the Bank of Jamaica (November 1985–March 1989), Jimmy Cliff, actor and singer, and George Rhoden, Olympian (Helsinki, Finland 1952)" (Kingston Technical High School, 2020, p. 2). But while every effort is being made to continue the noble tradition of technical and vocational education; the reality of training and education and the needs of the workplace, the long-term vision of the school is at risk. As asserted in the Kingston Technical High School (2020) publication, "we still remain the school of choice for an alternative approach to education and an institution that is constantly re-imaging education. We are gradually moving away from the traditional approach to education" (p. 2).

DINTHILL TECHNICAL HIGH SCHOOL

The establishment of Dinthill High School came out of the concern of the Governor of Jamaica from 1934–1938, Sir Edward Brandis Denham, that the disadvantaged of the country did not have an opportunity to receive a worthwhile education. As a result of the Governor's effort, the school began operation on property owned by Dinthill, for whom the school was named. The school started on April 1, 1938 as one of the practical training centres for boys only (Dinthill Technical High School, 2008). It was given the name Dinthill Youth Centre for Boys. The school catered for boys between 15 and 17 years old who were not allowed to attend elementary school beyond the age of 15. So the school provided them with the option of continuing their education at the practical training centre instead of just joining the workforce as was the case before. Under the leadership of Superintendent A. G. Foster, who was the first principal, Dinthill started as a boarding school with 33 students. Seven of the children boarded on the campus and the others lived in the neighbouring communities (Dinthill Technical High School, 2008).

The whole thrust of the school was to prepare graduates for a career in the field of agriculture. As such, the training programme was focused on preparing students in the basic areas of agriculture, but they were also trained in the related skills areas such as carpentry, welding, motor mechanics, shoemaking, tailoring and upholstering (Dinthill Technical High School, 2022A). The students were therefore trained in the jobs that were necessary to maintain activities in the agricultural sector, which was the dominant source of employment and economic activities. In order to entice graduates from the programme to remain in agriculture, each graduate was provided with between 5–15 acres of land to start their own farm. Of course, they were required to pay for the land in scheduled instalments over a number of years (Dinthill Technical High School, 2008).

The design of the curriculum allowed for a type of work-study training programme. Each year, the cohort was divided into two groups and while some were involved in hands-on field work training, the other group pursued classroom activities. This was similar to what is widely known as an apprenticeship programme which allowed for both classroom activities and on-the-job skills training. The students were also involved in extra-curricular activities, including cadet training, which remained an important element of this programme.

The school has gone through a number of changes in response to the needs of the country. With a greater emphasis on the development of the rural areas of the country, in 1950, the school was changed from a practical training centre to a rural secondary school. The official name was Dinthill Rural Secondary School. In 1959, the school facilities were significantly improved and expanded as a result of a government grant of 10,000 pounds. This allowed the school to admit children, aged 13–14, therefore, younger students from the surrounding area were able to gain an education. And, for the first time, the school permitted students who were not boarding to be admitted (Dinthill Technical High School, 2008).

In 1961, the school was further upgraded to become a technical high school to cope with the increased need for persons trained in technical skills and, for the first time, female students were admitted to the school. Dinthill has remained a school which emphasizes training in agricultural skills but it has broadened its curriculum to include subjects in the arts and sciences. It has also excelled in sports and continues to make its impact at the local level and also internationally.

The programme offerings at Dinthill now fully represent that of a 'comprehensive technical high school'. Agriculture remains a major focus and there are two programmes – Agricultural Technology and Agricultural Business. There is also Business Education which comprises Secretarial Skills, Clerical Skills and Information Technology. The Industrial Technology programme includes Auto Mechanics Building Technology, Mechanical Technology, Technical Drawing and Electrical/Electronics Technology. The Home Economics programme involves Food & Nutrition, Clothing & Textiles, Home Management, and Cosmetology. The core courses offered are just as comprehensive and include Mathematics and English, Computer Literacy, Physics, Biology and Chemistry (Dinthill Technical High School, 2023).

The mission of the school is to develop graduates who are sociable, responsible, committed, and can efficiently contribute to the social and economic well-being of self and community" (Dinthill Technical High School, 2022B, p.1). The underpinning vision seeks to maintain "an ethos that facilitates order, harmony, discipline, co-operation and thereby ensuring that the opportunity is provided for the timely and orderly growth for our teachers and our students (Dinthill Technical High School. 2022C, p. 1).

HOLMWOOD TECHNICAL HIGH SCHOOL

Holmwood Technical School was the first vocational school to be established in Jamaica in 1936 under the headship of Superintendent Edgar Rogers. It had an enrolment then of 50 male students. In keeping with the trend in training at that time, the programme was focused on agriculture, but the school provided training in areas such as woodwork, bookkeeping, shoemaking, auto mechanics, tailoring, building construction and carpentry (Holmwood Technical High School, 2023). Holmwood operated under the same principles as the other agricultural-based schools such as Dinthill but, in addition to providing trained persons for the agricultural sector, its graduates were also prepared to continue their education at the Jamaica School of Agriculture, a tertiary institution.

The school was converted to a practical training centre in 1938, in keeping with the policy of government then to strengthen training in agriculture. Holmwood also became a boarding school and it admitted children from the Turks and Caicos Islands. (Jamaica was designated the protectorate of the Turks and Caicos Islands by the British who continued to own the country.) The school was designated a Technical High school in September 1960 and it began to admit female students in 1961. With the decline in emphasis on training in agriculture, the school abandoned its farm programme and began to operate in the same mode of a traditional high school. This was concretized with an expansion and diversification of the subject offerings to include Agricultural Science, Chemistry, Physics, Biology, Art, Geography, History, English Language, and Spanish. Practical subjects such as Metalwork, Auto Mechanics,

Technical Drawing, Cookery, Dressmaking, Accounts, Typewriting, Shorthand, Office Practice, Surveying, and Electrical Installation were also offered (Holmwood Technical High School, 2023). The school continues to make great strides in sports and the academic areas, and it boasts a strong vocational education programme.

Regarding its exploits in the sports arena, the school has been involved, both at the national and international levels, in areas such as athletics, cricket, and football. In athletics, the school has had representatives in the Jamaican Olympic team in the areas of long-distance running and the shot-put. At the regional level, the school has had representatives participating in the CARIFTA games. For the areas of football and cricket, the school was represented in the Under-19 football game held in Guatemala and the Junior Games in cricket on a number of occasions. At the local level, the school dominated the Headley Cup from 2002 to 2007 and was winner of one of the One-Day Cricket Competitions. In the Girls Athletics Championship, the school was the winner each year from 2003–2011. This feat was repeated in 2013. The school also had success in other areas such as netball, swimming and basketball (Holmwood Technical High School, 2019).

Currently, the school is poised for the expansion of its facilities to remove it from the shift system and to accommodate more students. Based on Cabinet approval, an amount of J$184m was made available to complete the construction. With this investment, they moved from the limiting shift system. Addressing the strategic importance of this planned expansion, Principal Hidran McKulsky pointed out: "Instead of giving us 300 students each year, at the end of construction, the Ministry of Education may give us 350 or 375 and reduce from Christina and other schools 75 or 50 students" (Anderson, 2023, p.1).

CARRON HALL HIGH SCHOOL

Carron Hall, like many other institutions of learning, was established as a result of the philanthropic effort of money left for the building of a home for orphaned children. This responsibility was taken on by Mrs. Gellaty, the daughter of Presbyterian Minister, James McNee. The building was completed in 1921 and named the Girls' Home. The institution admitted girls who were older than 15 and had passed the age for attending the elementary school. There were also children attending from Haiti, Cuba and Hispaniola. The curriculum was limited to cooking and sewing, in keeping with the role designated for females which was largely that of the homemaker.

With a rethinking of how development should proceed for the school, the following was captured by Dotlyn Dawes (1996), Principal from 1995 to 2014, who said:

> In the 1930s, the importance of vocational education was the focus of government of the day. Vocational education was aimed at training the youths of the country to appreciate the rural economic environment, make use of natural resources at hand, develop various forms of manual skills, thus raising their standard of efficiency, and improving their economic position, and developing strength of character. (p. 2)

Within this context, the role of females naturally expanded, and the nature of training would change. So, "girls were encouraged to become good homemakers and receive practical training in housecraft, needlecraft, farming and other practical avenues for individual and communal improvement" (Dawes, 1996, p. 2). The Girls' Centre was established at Carron Hall in response to the new attitude and outlook towards development and training, but also a response to the success of the Holmwood venture in establishing a vocational training centre. Mrs. Gellaty continued to play a significant role in the life of the institution as she was the person who leased the property for establishing the Centre to the Government. The government took over the ownership of the school in 1937 and it was renamed Practical Training Centre (PTC). The name of the school was changed twice between 1937 and the 1950s, from PTC to Rural Secondary Technical School, to Jamaica School of Home Economics. The school was closed briefly in July 1962 and it was reopened in October 1962 under a new name: Vocational School for Girls.

With the government assuming responsibility for the school in 1937, the programme was extended to three years, with some students going on to do four years of training. The first year of the programme included basic subjects and vocational subjects. This was in keeping with the principle that skills training had to be underpinned by basic learning skills in the form of English and Mathematics. The vocational areas included subjects such as Food and Nutrition, Home Management, Woodwork, Dressmaking, Gardening, Dairying and Home Nursing. For the second and third years, the students began to pursue more specialized areas of interest. And only those who received scholarships had the opportunity to pursue the fourth year of the programme (Dawes, 1996).

The school made further strides in the latter part of the 1960s when the students were introduced to regional and international examinations. Students then were required to do regional examinations in CXC subjects, but they also had the opportunity to do overseas examinations such as the UCLI, RSA, and GCE. The Jamaica School Certificate (JSC), the local examination, was also an available option for the students. With the new examinations available, students were exposed to new courses such as Mathematics, English, Agricultural Science, Beauty Culture, Biology, Art and Craft, Clothing and Textile, and business courses including Office Practice, Typewriting, and Principles of Business.

The school maintained a tradition of providing training and education for the poor and economically challenged children. Its basic philosophy from the inception of the school was to "care for the unfortunate girls in the Carron Hall District and its environs" (Dawes, 1996, p. 5). The philosophy retained its guiding light until the 1970s. The philosophy has since been modified to emphasize foundation skills such as "creativity and technological exposure which are necessary . . . to become well-rounded citizens with respect for God, self and others to foster good interpersonal relationships, and to prepare them for the world of work . . ." (Carron Hall High School, 2022, p. 2).

The school currently has over 244 students. While it started as an all-female school, it is now a coeducational school with 60 per cent of the students being males. The current principal, Carlington Johnson, pledged that along with the teaching staff he will work "to transform the school into true academic excellence. This will enable our students to maximise their true potential" ("As Carron Hall High Turns 100", 2022). The principal also pledged to maintain its 'vibrant agricultural production programme' with the school ranked third in the parish. Also, the school and its current leadership have pledged that the school will continue to provide schooling and skills training for the citizens of the immediate and surrounding communities.

KNOCKALVA AGRICULTURAL SCHOOL

Based on the recommendation of the Lumb Commission of 1898, the Knockalva Agricultural School was the fourth to be established in 1940, preceded by Holmwood, Carron Hall, and Dinthill. The school is located in western Jamaica and its name was taken from the community which is a part of the district of Ramble. The school was first named the Knockalva Training Centre and only boys attended then. The curriculum was limited to practical training in agriculture and woodwork, and students did courses including English, Mathemetics, Chemistry, Bookkeeping and Spanish (Knockalva 75th Anniversary, 2015).

During the year of Jamaica's Independence, 1962, the curriculum was revamped to become an agricultural training centre which offered a two-year programme in vocational agriculture (Gardner, 2016). The objectives of the school then included the provision of agricultural and technical training for students between 15 and 17 years; training of agricultural leaders who would be better equipped to train neophyte farmers in the practice of farming; and the provision of trained students for the farming community (Knockalva Agricultural School Profile, 2017). The centre was upgraded further in 1980 to assume the status of the primary agricultural school in Jamaica, offering a three-year programme to students between the ages of 15 to 20. As confirmed by Gardner (2017, p.4), "Currently, the school offers two- and three-year programmes in general agriculture at the semi-tertiary level and core subjects at the CXC level to youngsters . . ."

The impact of the institution was not limited to training in vocational agriculture and related skills, but it was also associated with persons involved in extracurricular activities at the highest level. One such person was Samuel Benjamin Francis, the superintendent, who was credited for guiding the school in making significant contributions in the areas of sports, 4-H clubs and cadet training. Samuel Francis went on to become the first principal of Vere Technical, located in the parish of Clarendon, which he served from 1960 to 1983. George Kerr was a product of Knockalva and he went on to represent Jamaica in the Olympics of 1956, 1960 and 1964, running in the 800 metres race and winning a bronze medal in 1960 and placing fourth in 1964. The school's prowess in sports and cricket, in particular, was legendary. In fact, in the area of cricket, it is reported that, in the 1950s, the majority of the Hanover cricket team comprised players from Knockalva (Knockalva 75th Anniversary, 2015). The 4-H club became a driving force in the extracurricular activities of the school and, as reported: "Knockalva had the reputation of being the most prominent school in Jamaica to win medals in all categories of the 4-H parish finals and at the 4-H National Achievement Day in Denbigh, Clarendon" (Knockalva 75th Anniversary, 2015, p. 16).

Although Knockalva is operated as a post-secondary school since its inception, one of its academic goals is "to reclassify Knockalva Agricultural School as a community college focusing on agriculture, science and entrepreneurship with a curriculum based on 21st century agricultural practices . . ." (Knockalva Agricultural School Profile, 2017, p. 1). As one of its primary objectives, the institution is planning to take the bold step to establish a private-public partnership relationship to give the agricultural training programme national prominence. So, as Knockalva positions itself to face the new challenges of training and education, its revised vision is to make the programme available to the rest of the Caribbean countries, and its mission is to upgrade offerings and reposition its presence to become the national training institution for agriculture, serving the country at large, but also providing training for students in the Caribbean.

THE BIG, BOLD MOVE – TECHNICAL VOCATIONAL EDUCATION AND TRAINING

With the exception of the Apprenticeship Programme (Act of 1955), Technical Vocational Education and Training in Jamaica up to 1960 was, essentially, school/institution based. Although the imperative link with firms/industry and employers was recognized, these entities were not important contributors to programme development and execution. In short, TVET programme development was not driven by Labour Market Information.

By the early 1960s, the Government of Jamaica (GoJ) recognized, beyond doubt, that a national co-ordinated vocational training programme was necessary. The two driving forces were (a) inadequate supply of trained and certified workers to satisfy the needs of industry, and (b) high rates of unemployment among young people below the age of 30 years, (most of these young people being low achievers in the formal education system).

In 1966, a Vocational Training Working Group was established comprising a tri-partite representation of Government, Employers (industry) and Trade Unions. The Working Group recommended a Crash Programme of training in the following occupational areas: Building Construction, Electrical Trades, Automotive Trades, and Mechanical Trades. The Crash Programme was implemented by the Ministry of Labour in Industrial Training Centres (ITCs). By the early 1980s, there were some 31 Industrial Training Centres in Jamaica. Clearly, a Crash Programme with ITCs in the parishes could not provide industry with the required skilled and certified manpower. As a result, in 1967, the Government requested the assistance of the United Nations Development Programme (UNDP) in the establishment of a National Industrial Vocational Training Programme. A project was approved by the Governing Council of the UNDP in 1969. The objective of the GoJ/UNDP project was to assist the Government of Jamaica in the definition and initial implementation of a National Industrial Vocational Training Programme. In so doing, the following activities were identified, (a) completion of the necessary preparatory work, (b) creation of an advisory committee, (c) organization of a training department, and (d) establishment of a vocational training development centre (McCulloch, 1997).

THE INTERNATIONAL LABOUR ORGANIZATION (ILO) TEAM IN JAMAICA

The International Labour Organisation (ILO) was designated the Executing Agency and, by April 1970, the ILO team, headed by Project Manager, Mr W. Beck, was in place in Kingston, Jamaica. The ILO experts and their Jamaican counterparts concentrated on two main objectives, which were the establishment of a National Industrial Training Board, and the Vocational Training Development Centre (Institute).

The ILO team of experts reported to the Permanent Secretary, Ministry of Labour and National Insurance. The Ministry, with inputs from the ILO team, established a Provisional National Industrial Training Board in July 1970. It appears that the National Industrial Training Board was initially conceived as an Advisory Board. However, by 1971, a draft bill was prepared by the Ministry in consultation with the ILO Project Manager and was being referred to as the National Industrial Training Act, 1971. This was to be a Statutory Body. Paragraph 24 and extracts from the Draft National Industrial Training Act, 1971, which are contained in the ILO team Technical Report No. 1, September 1971, are in harmony with the contents of The Human Employment and Resource Training Act, 1982, The HEART Trust, (International Labour Organization, 1971).

EARLY TECHNICAL EDUCATION AT THE TERTIARY LEVEL

The development of tertiary technical education was realized with (a) the formation of the Jamaica Agricultural Society in 1895; (b) the establishment of the Farm School at Hope, St Andrew in 1910; and (c) upgrading and changing the name of the Farm School to the Jamaica School of Agriculture (JSA) in 1939. As would be expected, agriculture was the primary source of economic activity, thus requiring the need to introduce more technological-type training to improve and maintain quality output and satisfy the international market.

College of Arts, Science and Technology

The College of Arts, Science and Technology (CAST) and the Jamaica School of Agriculture were the two tertiary institutions, at the outset, to deliver technical training at the tertiary level. The Jamaica School of Agriculture was established as a farm school 48 years before the Jamaica Institute of Technology (JIT), which preceded CAST and was formed in

1958. The JIT was designated to provide both part- and full-time training in technical courses. Based on the advice of the Technical Education Advisor to the Secretary of State for the Colonies, the JIT was renamed the College of Arts, Science and Technology. The change of name occurred in 1959 when "it became incorporated in the College of Arts, Science and Technology (CAST) Scheme of 1959. This was validated by an Act of Parliament in 1964" (University of Technology, Jamaica 2017, p. 1). In 1986, the College was designated a degree-granting institution after a revision of the CAST Scheme, thus empowering it to operate as a tertiary institution that is governed by a Council and an Academic Board (University of Technology, Jamaica 2017).

CAST was elevated to university status in 1995 and was renamed the University of Technology, Jamaica. The institution was formally accorded University status on September 1, 1995, as the University of Technology, Jamaica. This status of University was formally established by The University of Technology, Jamaica Act 27 of 1999 and the Act, which is the legal document establishing the permanency of the University, was approved by the Parliament of Jamaica on June 8, 1999 and it became one of the laws of the country with the signature of the Governor-General on June 29, 1999 (University of Technology, Jamaica 2017).

CAST started with four academic programmes and 50 students but, by 2017, the student population had grown to 12,000, which was second only to The University of the West Indies, Mona, Jamaica. The University has grown from four academic programmes to having three colleges and five academic programmes (University of Technology, Jamaica 2017). The colleges include the College of Health Sciences, the College of Business and Management, and the Joint Colleges of Medicine, Oral Health & Veterinary Sciences. The faculties include the Faculty of Education and Liberal Studies (FELS), the Faculty of the Built Environment (FOBE), the Faculty of Engineering and Computing, the Faculty of Law and Faculty of Science and Sport (FOSS) (University of Technology, Jamaica 2023B). Although a technical tertiary institution, the University is "renowned for providing quality education, incorporating art, culture, sports, and technology to enhance the academic experience" (University of Technology, Jamaica 2023A). In fact, the University has ventured into the delivery of non-technical areas such as law, which has raised concerns in some areas of the higher educational fraternity.

The University has positioned itself to strengthen its role as a regional tertiary institution by emphasizing "high-quality learning opportunities, research and value-added solutions to government, industry and communities" (University of Technology, Jamaica, 2023C, p. 1). This mission will be powered by a vision of preparing "work-ready leaders, committed to transforming students and society through high-quality teaching, research and value-added services" (University of Technology, Jamaica, 2023C, p. 1).

Jamaica School of Agriculture

The Jamaica School of Agriculture is best known as the foundation of tertiary-level agricultural education and training in Jamaica. But tertiary-level agricultural education and training did not begin under the umbrella of the JSA, nor is it conducted today under the JSA umbrella. There have been several name changes, which were indications of the development stages of agriculture in the country, thus the need to keep the discipline current and in line with international practice.

The name changes were instituted over the past 85 years. The JSA was initially called The Government Farm School, the first of its kind in Jamaica, and was established at Hope, St Andrew, in 1910. The School was later upgraded to become the Jamaica School of Agriculture in 1939 and, in 1957, it was relocated to Twickenham Park, St Catherine. In 1981, the JSA was closed at Twickenham Park and a Teacher Training College was established at Passley Gardens in Portland. "The college initially offered the Diploma in Primary Education and late in 1994, the Diploma in Secondary Education with special emphasis on Science, Mathematics and Computer Studies" (College of Agriculture, Science and Education, 2020, p. 1).

Following the closure[3] of the JSA at Twickenham Park in 1981, the College of Agriculture (COA) was established at Passley Gardens, Portland and the Twickenham Park students were transferred to the College of Agriculture at Passley Gardens. There was a further upgrading of the curriculum as the new College offered an Associate degree in Agriculture.

The life of the COA was short. Student enrolment declined between 1982 and 1995. The College of Agriculture and the Passley Gardens Teachers' College were merged in 1995, based on the recommendation of the Sherlock Report. This newly merged institution became the College of Agriculture, Science and Education (CASE). The College is the only one of its kind in Jamaica and the rest of the English-speaking Caribbean to offer skills training in agriculture, science and education.

CURRICULUM CHANGES

The curriculum at the Government Farm School at Hope in St Andrew was primarily practical hands-on training. The need at the time was to train farm overseers and technicians for the many crop and livestock estates. Enrolment at the Government Farm School fell during World War I, as both staff and students joined the armed forces overseas and some students found it impossible to pay their fees. After the war, admission requirements were raised, scholarships were offered to entering students, and the physical facilities were improved. All of these changes led to the name change from Government Farm School to Jamaica School of Agriculture in 1939. A curriculum was then introduced which embraced a scientific approach to agriculture. Basic and applied science subjects, as well as farm machinery, were added to the curriculum. Practical training was enhanced by the establishment of Agricultural Experiment Stations by the Ministry of Agriculture. These stations provided exposure for students to best practices in modern agriculture. The stations were located at: Grove Place, Manchester; Orange River, St Mary; Caenwood, Portland; Irwin, St James; and Bodles, St Catherine. It has already been noted that the Jamaica School of Agriculture was relocated from Hope, St Andrew to Twickenham Park, St Catherine in 1957. A major curriculum change was effected, starting around 1957. The shift to a scientific technology-driven agriculture was, essentially, Government policy. The curriculum was strengthened in the areas of Chemistry, Physics, Botany, and Zoology. These curriculum improvements ushered in matriculation arrangements for entry to the Bachelor of Science degree in Agriculture at the Trinidad, St Augustine campus, University of the West Indies.

Women at the Jamaica School of Agriculture

After many years of non-representation, 40 women were enrolled at the JSA, Twickenham Park, St Catherine campus in August 1968. There was clearly a demand for teachers of agricultural science and agricultural extension officers. The representations were spearheaded by the National Agricultural Extension Service, Jamaica Agricultural Society, and the 4-H Clubs. The enrolment of women at the JSA was consistent with Government policy. An all-male institution since 1910, the break with tradition was resisted by the male students. E. Gidden, a member of the 1968 class, stated that (personal communication, June 15, 2016) by the end of the first year the presence of female students brought a transformation of refinement and a more sobering character to the once male-dominated community. The women pursued programmes in general agriculture and home economics. Members of the first graduating class of August 1971 joined the Ministry of Agriculture as Home Extension Officers in the newly created Farm Family Development Programme of the Agricultural Extension Service.

Women are now an equal partner in the Faculty of Agriculture at the College of Agriculture, Science and Education. In fact, they are a majority in the faculty. For the 2015–2016 academic year, female registered students were 242, while male registered students were 206. Like their male counterparts, female graduates of JSA/CASE have received certification at the undergraduate and postgraduate levels in agriculture and are significant contributors to the ongoing development of agricultural enterprise in Jamaica.

Streamlining Training and Education in Agriculture

The pursuit of scientifically driven agriculture is, indeed, a profession which involves the acquisition of knowledge, skills and appropriate attitudes. The tradition of the PTCs, and more so of the JSA, has been critical in the preparation of technical functionaries for the agricultural sector. This tradition is the much-heralded combination of theoretical classroom learning and the practical hands-on acquisition of skills. As such, the six years, comprising three at a PTC and three at the JSA, is adequate time to develop the scientific technology-driven culture required for a modern agricultural enterprise. Clearly, the PTC and JSA nexus has been a success in moulding a cadre of technical personnel for the agricultural sector. Some of the outstanding graduates of the JSA entered the JSA through the route of the PTCs, therefore, it would be reasonable to argue that the JSA/PTC linkage has been beneficial to the agricultural sector.

The integration should be consolidated by formally linking the various institutions including Knockalva, Sydney Pagon, and Ebony Park HEART Academy with CASE. This vertical integration has been attempted with some success between the National Tool and Engineering and Institute (NTEI) and UTech. There are existing arrangements between CASE and the three named institutions in a number of areas. It is, however, recommended that the Ministry of Education should take the initiative and formalize these arrangements, thus creating clear pathways to CASE, including Advanced Placement into specified programmes.

THE COLLEGE OF AGRICULTURE, SCIENCE AND EDUCATION

The College of Agriculture, Science and Education is a publicly owned tertiary, institution of the Ministry of Education and Youth (MoEY). The CASE scheme order was granted in 1995 which established the legal order basis for the existence of CASE as a legitimate degree-granting tertiary-level educational institution. CASE has experienced growth and transformation over the last century and, before it was established, its rich history was rooted in the Government Farm School which at the time was located in Kingston. This initiative of having an agriculture conservatory started in 1910 when "approximately 12 young men enrolled at the time in the art and science of agriculture" (College of Agriculture, Science and Education, 2020, p. 1). The purpose of this effort was to train persons in the art and science of Agriculture, therefore equipping them with the skills that can be used to create employment opportunities. Today, skills in the art and science of agriculture are needed for career development. According to CASE (2020), the school produced the likes of Dr T. P. Lecky, who was born in the parish of Portland. Among his many contributions to national development, this late Jamaican Animal Scientist developed the Jamaica Hope and Jamaica Black breeds of cattle. In 1942, the Government Farm School was renamed the Jamaica School of Agriculture. It was then relocated in 1957 from the Hope Estate on the site that currently houses the University of Technology, Jamaica to Twickenham Park, Spanish Town, the old capital of Jamaica. In 1968, the first batch of female students was admitted. Today, more than half of the students attending CASE are females (University of Technology, Jamaica, 2023).

The Jamaica School of Agriculture was closed due to a Bill that was tabled in 1981 to revoke JSA Act. This led to the establishment of The College of Agriculture. This institution was granted the acquiescence to carry out teaching, research, and extension programmes in agriculture. In that very same year, the Passley Gardens Teachers College (PGTC) was established. The PGTC offered training in teaching and a diploma at the primary level of the education system; however, in 1994, the PGTC started to offer a "Diploma in Secondary Education with special emphasis on Science, Mathematics, and Computer Studies. 1984 saw the College graduating its first cohort of students. The College subsequently went on to deliver the Post Certificate Programme to teachers possessing the Certificate in Teacher Education, who desired to upgrade their qualification to the Diploma in Education (College of Agriculture, Science and Education, 2017).

The CASE institution is guided by philosophy, vision and mission that have contributed to the development of its programmes and the building of traditions. The philosophy emphasizes the commitment of the institution and its leaders to build and sustain a "democratic atmosphere in which our students can develop maturity, responsibility and self-discipline ... [thus enabling] creativity, entrepreneurial potential, and desire to respond to the challenges of nation-building" (College of Agriculture, Science and Education, 2009, p. 8). Its vision is that the institution "will become a university recognized for outstanding scholarship, applied research, and innovation in a learner-centred environment that prepares its graduates for global leadership and impact". The supporting mission is that CASE "will contribute to the sustainable development of society through the pursuit of excellence in teaching, applied research, and collaborative engagement in local and global communities" (College of Agriculture, Science and Education, 2020, p. 1).

INSTITUTIONAL COLLABORATION – INTERNAL AND EXTERNAL

CASE has forged relationships with external entities as well as made it their responsibility to develop internal relationships with critical public entities. They have partnered with entities such as Hi-Pro Feeds, Nutramix, Seprod, Fersan, and Interlinc Communication in the private sector (College of Agriculture, Science and Education, 2020). This collaboration is a part of their core values to achieve their mission of creating opportunities and growth within the society. The institution has a strategic plan on how they propose to move forward. This plan outlines the vision, mission, and core values; in addition, it provides a systematic structure on how they envision achieving their goals. The institution has developed critical activities on how to achieve global development. They have not only collaborated with the public and private sectors, but with other institutions that may foster learning and an increase in the knowledge and skills to continue education in agriculture, science, technology, and education. The University of Technology and CASE have an agreement to admit students from the CASE to UTech; however, in the meantime, CASE is putting plans and measures in place to be upgraded to a University (Davis, 2011).

ACADEMIC PROGRAMMES AND FACULTIES

According to the College of Agriculture, Science and Education Students' Handbook 2014–2015, there are three Faculties and two Departments. The faculties focus on different areas of study. The first faculty is the Faculty of Agriculture which offers a Diploma in Agriculture Programme; an Associate of Science Degree in General Agriculture; a BTech Degree in Agri-Food System Management; and a Bachelor of Science Degree in Agriculture Education, Plant Science, and Animal Science. The second, the Faculty of Science, has two departments, namely the Department of Biological and Physical Science and the Department of Mathematics and Computer Science. Within this department there are also offerings of associate and bachelor's degrees in areas such as Natural Science, Environmental Science, Education (Maths and Computer Science). The third faculty is the Faculty of Education which comprises the Department of Humanities and Aesthetics, and the Department of Educational Studies. The departments offer programmes in Primary Education, a Postgraduate Diploma, and a Master's in Education (College of Agriculture, Science and Education, 2020, p. 1).

Other academic areas are the Community College and Continuing Education Programmes, which offer the Associate of Science and Bachelor of Science Degree in Business Studies, Hospitality and Tourism, and Social Work. The institution also offers consultancy services, and Extra-Mural Studies in in collaboration with other institutions. The purpose of this Department is to target the primary geographic market to CASE's main and satellite campuses and to cover all or portions of the 14 parishes, as well as regional integration across the Caribbean. This includes government departments; non-government organizations (NGOs); educational institutions; commerce and industry-specific entities; as well as the general public (College of Agriculture, Science and Education, 2016, p. 5).

FUTURE PERSPECTIVE OF THE INSTITUTION

The College aspires to transform into a university. In doing so, a strategic plan has been formulated to achieve the objective of the institution becoming an outstanding university that will impact economic development. As an institution that focuses on agriculture, CASE plans to acquire property through leasing and establish a greenhouse for marijuana and other plants. Furthermore, in their plans to realign, three faculties have been proposed, namely the Faculty of Agriculture, the Faculty of Applied Sciences, Engineering and Technology and the Faculty of Liberal Arts and Management. This has seen the restructuring of academic programmes leading to each faculty having its own objectives and blueprint.

As the College moves forward, the external impact will also be re-envisioned, and new relationships will be explored and created. Under the Continuing Education and Extra-Mural Studies (CEMS) programme, existing centres such as the Brown's Town Centre, Ebony Park, and the Portmore Centre, will be upgraded. The new centres that will be explored and developed are Kingston (Salvation Army), Moneague Teachers' College, among other institution and centres (College of Arts, Science and Education, 2017). In addition to future prospects and developments of the institution, CASE aims to develop a series of short-term courses which will be offered both face-to-face and online. The purpose of this is to target persons that are practising farming, as well as persons from other professions who are interested in agriculture (College of Arts, Science and Education, 2017).

The growth of the student body has been favourable. While CASE seeks to expand its services to the wider society, in June 2016, the college saw an increase of 30 per cent in the number of students. The majority was registered for the Faculty of Agriculture (Williams, 2017). In 2022, the student population rose to 1,500 despite the impact of COVID-19 on the education system.

Impact of the College on Agriculture and the Wider Society

The focus on non-traditional skills for career development is of paramount importance, especially as the country is moving towards achieving Vision 2030 and providing employment opportunities while aiming to improve economic growth and development. In targeting the goal of having an impact on national development, CASE is embarking on current opportunities that present themselves in society. A prominent example is that of the Cassava Project "as the college is cognizant of the tuber's culinary versatility and its potential to earn money for the college" (Williams, 2017, p. 3). Furthermore, Williams (2017), quoting Monique Oates who was speaking on behalf of CASE, said, "We are pushing out cassava. You know that Red Stripe is now using cassava in their production, and a lot of people are now moving from white flour and moving on to cassava flour, breadfruit flour, and so we are pushing the cassava" (p. 3). This is imperative for national development.

In today's society, farmers and persons who have vested interest in the agricultural sector are being encouraged to learn the art and science of agriculture, especially in the area of career development. The use of technology in the education system and technological introduction by CASE is relevant in contemporary society; this has resulted in greater impact on the agriculture sector and the wider society. According to Wedderburn (2017) of the Communication and Public Relations Department, Ministry of Industry, Commerce, Agriculture and Fisheries, one of its key priorities is to continue to promote the use of technology as a critical tool in growing the agricultural sector. Currently, CASE is offering academic programmes in the related academic areas in preparation for this venture.

At all stages of its development – The Farm School, College of Agriculture or College of Agriculture, Science and Education – CASE has been the primary source of tertiary-level agricultural education and training in Jamaica. Before the establishment of the St Augustine campus of the University of the West Indies in Trinidad, JSA graduates proceeded to universities in the USA, Canada, United Kingdom, and Europe to receive degree-level certification – BSc, MSc, and PhD. JSA graduates with degrees, diplomas and certificates provided the human capital for the agricultural sector. In addressing the flexibility of the CASE graduates, Monique Oates indicated that they were the functionaries in several organizations including the National Agricultural Extension Service and, later, the Rural Agricultural Development Authority (RADA) and field staff of the Jamaica Agricultural Society and Jamaica 4-H Clubs (Williams, 2017). The future of a scientific technology-driven agricultural enterprise in Jamaica depends on an educated, trained and certified agricultural workforce. The institutions to prepare such a workforce must always be at the top of the national development agenda.

CONCLUSION

While deliberate attempts are now being made to mainstream TVET, the history of technical education has had a parallel path to general education. The approach of separating learners of general education from learners of technical and vocational education has placed TVET at a disadvantage.

Technical schools must be of the highest quality with a strong general education component. The current practice has encouraged the placement of strong students in liberal arts or traditional institutions and weaker students in vocational-oriented schools. An integrated school system, especially at the secondary level, would ensure that all students are equally exposed to both general and technical vocational education. The skills training, which received significant attention after emancipation, was focused mainly on job preparation and not the development of the learner. Our modern economy requires an educated workforce, but the tradition of separating skills development from general education has remained with us over the last 185 years. It should be noted that this experience is similar in most developing countries but, in the case of developed countries such as France, England, and Germany, skills training was never separated from general education (Hutton, 2016).

Another area of concern is the disjoined development of technical vocational education. There was some level of disagreement regarding training in skills for the trades versus training in domestic science such as sewing; training in agricultural skills versus training in skills for industry; and the integration of academic and practical education. While there was a view that black people needed enough education to take care of their daily needs, factors such as the (a) cost of setting up the training facilities, (b) unavailability of competent teachers, and (c) lack of a coordinated and national approach to the problem of training were debilitating. Notwithstanding the challenges with the development of technical education, the evidence suggests that the country has made steady progress. Technical vocational education is offered at all of the 176 public secondary schools and even the traditional high schools have opted to offer skills training, even if it is limited in comparison to the upgraded secondary schools. But, as indicated earlier, 15 of these secondary schools are technical high schools, which are specialists in offering technical and vocational education. The fact is that some of these technical high schools have taken on a more general education posture. While Kingston Technical High School does not occupy the same level of recognition as before, it continues to operate as one of the country's major technical high schools. The four schools which came out of the recommendation of the Lumb Report of

1989 – Carron Hall, Holmwood, Dinthill and Knockalva – continue to play their roles, some more significant than others, in the development of technical and vocational education and training.

NOTES

1. An amount of 30,000 pounds was made available annually by the British Parliament for the education of ex-slaves including their children. The grant allocation was reduced gradually, starting in 1840 and finally ending in 1845.
2. The Whigs were a political party of the Parliaments of Great Britain which played a significant role in the development of the political structure and economic affairs of the country.
3. Student unrest at the Twickenham Park campus in St Catherine led to the removal of the Principal, Mr Granville Gayle, in 1969. The JSA at Twickenham Park experienced some difficult years, resulting in the repeal of the JSA Act and the closure of the institution.

BIBLIOGRAPHY

Anderson, M. (2023). Expansion of Holmwood Technical will benefit neighbouring schools. https://jis.gov.jm/expansion-of-holmwood-technical-will-benefit-neighbouring-schools/

As Carron Hall High turns 100, principal gears up for change. (2022, August 29). *The Gleaner*, p. 1. https://jamaica-gleaner.com/article/news/20220429/carron-hall-high-turns-100-principal-gears-change

Campbell, C. (1968). *Towards an imperial policy for the education of Negroes in the West Indies after emancipation*. UWI Department of History

Campbell, C. (1970). *Social and economic obstacles to the development in post-emancipation Jamaica*. UWI Department of History.

Carron Hall High School. (2013). *History of Carron Hall High School*. https://www.workandjam.com/bl/education/carron-hall-high-school.htm

College of Agriculture, Science and Education (CASE), Department of Registry. (2016). *Enrolment data, academic years 2015–2016*.

College of Agriculture, Science and Education. (2016A). *Our History*. https://case.edu.jm/web/?q=our-history

College of Agriculture, Science and Education. (2016B). *Ownership and Governance*. https://case.edu.jm/web/?q=ownership-governance

College of Agriculture, Science and Education. (2016C). *CEMS* https://case.edu.jm/web/?q=cems

College of Agriculture, Science and Education. (2016D). *Vision and Mission* https://case.edu.jm/web/?q=vision-and-mission

College of Agriculture, Science and Education. (2020). *Our partners and stakeholders.* https://case.edu.jm/partners/

College of Agriculture, Science and Education (CASE). (2024, January 12). About us. [Image attached] [Post]. *LinkedIn.* https://jm.linkedin.com/company/college-of-agriculture-science-education

Cross, A. (2010, March 21). Lack of education is affecting productivity. *The Gleaner.* https://jamaica-gleaner.com/gleaner/20100321/focus/focus7.html

Dawes, D. (1996). *A historical background of the institution now known as the Caron Hall High School.* Caron Hall High School.

Davis, G. (2011, June 4). CASE is on a quest. *The Gleaner.* http://jamaica-gleaner.com/gleaner/20110604/business/business4.html/

Dinthill Technical High School. (2008). *The chronicles of Dinthill Technical High School.* Author.

Dinthill Technical High School. (2022A). *About us.* https://dinthilltech.org/about-us/

Dinthill Technical High School. (2022B). *Mission statement.* https://dinthilltech.org/mission-statement/

Dinthill Technical High School. (2022C). *Our vision.* https://dinthilltech.org/our-vision/

Dinthill Technical High School. (2023). *Academic programmes, Grades 7–11.* https://dinthilltech.org/programmes/

Deslandes, D. (2016). *Strategic realignment of the College of Agriculture, Science and Education.* CASE

Gardner, C. (2016, September 22). Knockalva: Agriculture powerhouse. *The Gleaner.* http://jamaica-gleaner.com/article/western-focus/20160927/knockalva-agricultural-powerhouse

Gordon, S. (1968). *Reports and repercussions in West Indies education, 1835–1933.* Ginn Publishers.

Holmwood Technical High School (2019). *About our school.* https://holmwoodtechnicalhigh.org.jm/main/index.php/about-our-school/

Holmwood Technical High School. (2023). *History of Holmwood.* www.holmwoodpsany.org/News_and_Events.html

Hutton, D. M. (2016). Education from emancipation to the Morant Bay Rebellion: Some lessons for today's Jamaica. *Jamaica Journal, 36* (3), 57–63.

International Labour Organization. (1971). *National Industrial Vocational Training Programme, JAM11, technical report.* Geneva

Kingston Technical High School. (2020) *Training and character*. Retrieved on November 16, 2023 from http://kingstontechnicalhighschool.edu.jm/kths-then-and-now/

Knockalva 75th Anniversary. (2015). *An Historical Account of Knockalva Agricultural School*. Author.

Knockalva continues to prepare young people for agriculture. (2017, February 20). *The Jamaica Observer Company*. https://www.jamaicaobserver.com/news/knockalva-continues-to-prepare-young-people-for-agriculture/

Lamey, J., Fraser, H., McCulloch, C. & Sayers, J. (2009). *A Historical Perspective on Agricultural Education in Jamaica*. Unpublished notes.

McCulloch, C. S. (1997). *The changing landscape of vocational training in the Caribbean and challenges for the future*. Paper presented at the ILO Conference, Curacao.

Sangster, A. (2011). *The Making of a University: From CAST to UTech*. Ian Randle.

The first government continuation school in Jamaica. (1911, September 30). *The Daily Gleaner*, p. 1. https://jamaica-history.weebly.com/kingston-technical-high-school.html

University of Technology, Jamaica. (2017). *History*. https://www.utech.edu.jm/about-utech/history-1

University of Technology. (2023A, December 12). *Info*. https://at.linkedin.com/school/university-of-technology-jamaica/

University of Technology, Jamaica. (2023B). *Academics*. https://www.utech.edu.jm/academics

University of Technology, Jamaica. (2023C). *Mission and Vision*. https://www.utech.edu.jm/about-utech/vision

Wedderburn, S. (2017). Technology to drive the agricultural sector. https://www.miic.gov.jm/content/technology-drive-agricultural-sector

Williams, P. (2017). A CASE for Agriculture. http://jamaica-gleaner.com/article/art-leisure/20170611/case-agriculture

Whyte, M. (1977). *A Short History of Education in Jamaica*. Hodder and Stoughton.

CHAPTER 2

Technical High Schools and Their Contribution to Advancing Technical Vocational Education and Training in Jamaica

MARCIA ROWE AMONDE

THIS CHAPTER EXAMINES THE ORIGIN AND DEVELOPMENT of technical high schools in Jamaica and their contribution to technical vocational education. These schools are located throughout the island and are defined by an emphasis on technical vocational education and training programmes which equip students for work, entrepreneurship and further education. As technical and vocational education developed in Jamaica over the years, significant investments have been made in expanding their programme offerings to include new and emerging areas and well-resourced laboratories.

BACKGROUND

The establishment of Kingston Technical High School in 1896 marked the origin of technical high schools in Jamaica. As the first technical high school, it was established in recognition of the need for training in the technical skills at the secondary level. This was a need that was echoed since emancipation in 1838, even though education and training was offered at the primary level. Both the 1879 Report Upon the Condition of Juvenile Population in Jamaica and the Lumb Report on the Jamaica Education System in 1898 called for the introduction of skills training as an integral part of the curriculum of schools (Gordon, 1968). The report on the Condition of Juveniles (1879) recognized that persons employed in rural agriculture saw little prospects in terms of upward mobility, so this fuelled the desire to find employment in towns and cities, such as Kingston. However, many of these workers lacked basic skills and had very little training. Often, this lack of the necessary skill set resulted in difficulties in finding employment, even though jobs were available.

Skills training was therefore considered a priority in equipping individuals with the competencies they needed for employment. However, the supply of competent individuals could not address the demand as there was a lack of skilled workers, resulting in a mismatch between demand and supply. Millicent Whyte (1983), recognizing this, argued for the need to add practical subjects to the curriculum when she spoke about the reform of teacher training in 1967 to include more teachers for the practical areas. It was during this time that subjects such as Woodwork, Metalwork, Arts and Crafts, Home Economics, Mathematics, and Science were added to the curriculum.

There was a recognition from this period that education and training needed to prepare individuals for employment. This was evident in discussions and drives to focus on skills training that will lead to social and economic development and individual empowerment. Technical and Vocational Education and Training (TVET) was seen as the driver for a qualified and competent labour force. There was also the recognition that TVET needed to be complemented by general subjects such as Language, Mathematics and Science in order to provide students with a solid general education background that would result in greater success in skills training and workers who would be able to perform at a higher level. In more recent times, this focus has resulted in an increased thrust to integrate subjects such as Science, Technology, Engineering and Mathematics (STEM) into the TVET curriculum in Jamaica to better prepare students for new and emerging jobs in the digital age.

In speaking about the Government's policy that directed technical and vocational education and training from 1900 to the 1960, the Technical and Vocational Unit in the Ministry of Education, Jamaica, describes the policy direction as a departure from educational provisions fashioned and adopted under colonial rule (Undated paper from the Technical Vocational Unit, Ministry of Education, Youth and Information [MoEYI]). This view is also reflected in Jamaica's TVET policy (2014) where the focus on TVET has been described as largely a post-Independence thrust by the Government of Jamaica, through the initiatives of the MoEYI, and supported by its former agency, the HEART Trust NTA. This is an indication that the Government of Jamaica took leadership after Independence for its education system, moving away from that of the colonial powers. This resulted in a curriculum that is influenced by factors within the national context, thereby making it more relevant and in alignment with social economic priorities and cultural practices.

Technical high schools figured prominently in TVET in Jamaica from the 1970s and strengthened throughout the 1980s, 1990s and 2000s through expansion in the number of schools and an increase in the programme offerings. Technical high schools have played significant roles in advancing technical and vocational education or workforce education in Jamaica and can be described as institutions facilitating workforce development and equipping students for work, (including entrepreneurship), and further education. This workforce development focus that is aligned to economic growth, is the major feature that defines technical and vocational training and is seen as equipping individuals to contribute to productivity and, hence, social and economic development. Marope et al., (2015) describe this as the economic rationale for TVET that emphasizes equipping individuals with skills, knowledge and technology to drive productivity in the 21st century economy.

Sangster (2004) describes significant government policies that have impacted and fuelled the growth of technical and vocational education in Jamaica during the period 1900–1960. He argued:

> Technical and vocational education, with the establishment of vocational schools, technical institutions, CAST and the renaming and relocation of the Jamaica School of Agriculture, were the earliest planned departure from educational provisions fashioned and adopted under colonial rule. Education was no longer provided as a social service but as an integral part of the programme, designed to provide the manpower requirements for the economic development of the population. (p.38)

He cited some major achievements and specific policy initiatives that have strengthened and created an impact on technical and vocational education between the period 1960–2002. These included the construction of 12 'new' secondary schools in addition to one technical high school and the expansion of five existing technical high schools during the period 1970 to 1982. Also, during this period, the Passley Gardens Teachers' College merged to form the College of Agriculture, and the Human Employment and Resource Training (HEART) Trust NTA (National Training Agency) was established in 1982.

These key improvements impacted TVET in the technical high schools in Jamaica. They took place between the period 1997 to 2002 and were catalysts for advancing TVET in Jamaica. It was during this period that the Government of Japan funded a project, with the aim of improving the quality of TVET. The Jose Marti Technical High School was established as a result of this project. The school was a gift from the Government of Cuba to the people of Jamaica and is named after a national hero of Cuba, Jose Marti. The school was upgraded to a high school in 1977 and the status changed to that of a technical high school in 1989.

SIGNIFICANCE OF TECHNICAL HIGH SCHOOLS IN JAMAICA

The Technical High Schools Development Project (THSDP) was launched in March 1995. It aimed to reposition technical high schools through leadership training, professional upgrading of teachers, and the upgrading of laboratories and equipment. Importantly, seven technical high schools were upgraded during this period to include Grades 10–13, and access to technical and vocational education increased as many of the traditional high schools began adding TVET programmes to their curriculum, thus increasing participation in technical vocational education at the secondary level in Jamaica.

In describing the significance of technical high schools to technical and vocational education in Jamaica, Sangster (2004) argues that they have helped to positively impact the perception of technical vocational education and training in Jamaica. The perception of TVET began to shift from the focus on offering skills at the lower level and an association with students who were not doing well academically, to the recognition that technical and vocational education could equip students with competencies for work at higher levels. These competencies would not be confined to technical competencies but would expand to include cognitive and attitudinal competencies such as problem solving, critical thinking, creativity, innovation, teamwork, empathy, respect, and resilience.

Technical high schools have been described as "pioneers in developing the legitimacy of technical and vocational education and as real alternatives to the traditional academic programmes in the high and grammar school . . . helping to advance the idea of specialised vocational training" (Sangster 2004, p. 38). According to J. L. Morrison, (personal communication, March 12, 2018), former Assistant Chief Education Officer in the Technical Vocational Unit in the Ministry of Education Youth and Information, technical high schools were defined by their strong focus on technical and vocational subjects. These technical vocational subjects are arranged in broad curriculum areas such as agricultural education, arts and craft education, business education, home economics education and industrial education. In the provision of technical and vocational education and training, the focus has been on practical subjects that are aligned to occupational standards.

THE ORIGIN OF TECHNICAL HIGH SCHOOLS IN JAMAICA

Figure 1 identifies the location of the technical high schools in Jamaica. There are five major technical high schools that can be described as contributing significantly to technical and vocational education and training. These are Dinthill Technical High School, St Andrew Technical High School, Holmwood Technical High School, St Elizabeth Technical High School and Vere Technical high school. Their establishment began in the 1950s and extended to the early 1960s. Their development has been characterized by expansion in programme offerings and the development of infrastructure.

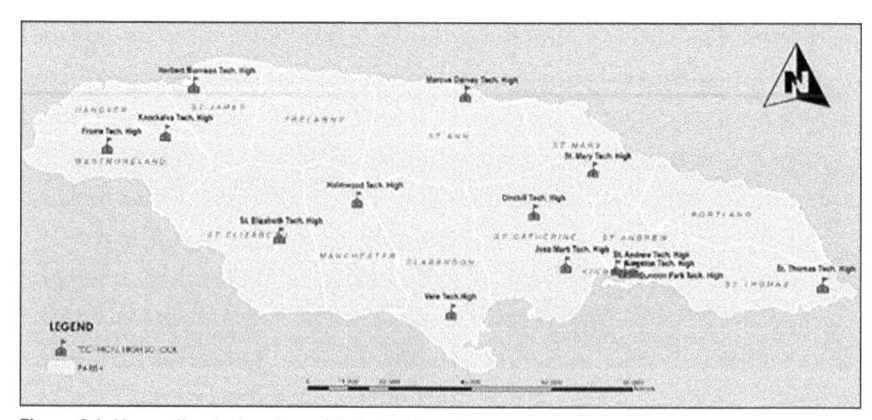

Figure 2.1: Map outlining the locations of Technical High Schools in Jamaica

Holmwood Technical High School

Holmwood Technical High School is one of the vocational high schools that evolved to become a technical high school. It originally started out as Holmwood Vocational School, a practical training centre for Boys in 1936. The school became a technical high school in 1961 and was co-educational in nature. When it was upgraded to a technical high, its curriculum offerings extended to include programmes such as Mechanical Engineering, Auto-Mechanics, Woodwork, Technical Drawing, Surveying, and Electrical Installation. There was the inclusion of a vocational department in the 80s and, in the 90s, the inclusion of a science laboratory. To provide higher-level programmes, a sixth form programme was introduced in 2003. The school welcomed its first set of Grade Six Achievement Test (GSAT) students in 2012. Under the Technical High Schools Development Project, improvements were made to the library, the science labs, the computer labs, and the automotive workshops, and a greater focus placed on strategic planning for school development.

Dinthill Technical High School

Dinthill Technical was one of the first technical high schools. It started out as a practical training centre in 1938 with a focus on Agriculture, catering to students 15–17 years old. In 1959, Sir Florizel Glasspole, the then Governor-General of Jamaica, announced that the school would become a technical high school. Its offerings were extended to include carpentry, welding, motor mechanics, shoemaking and mattress making. Over the years, the school has made significant progress in the following areas:

- Upgrading of the farm buildings, which were destroyed by Hurricane Gilbert in 1988;
- Upgrading of laboratories by the Human Employment and Resource Training, National Training Agency, through the Technical High Schools Development Project;
- Expansion of curricular offerings through the inclusion of subjects such as natural and social sciences, liberal arts, industrial technology, and information technology;
- Strengthening of extra-curricular activities with a focus on sports.

St Elizabeth Technical High School

St Elizabeth Technical High School (STETHS) was established in 1958 to further strengthen technical vocational education in Jamaica and, more specifically, in the parish of St Elizabeth. The community played an important role in its establishment as it was initiated by the Santa Cruz Citizens Association. As a technical high school, STETHS has recorded its achievement, not only in the academics and the technical vocational subjects but also in sports, cultural activities and community service. The school was involved in the Ministry of Education and Culture's rationalization pilot project in 2013/2014 and Centres of Excellence were established for other schools to use their laboratory facilities.

Vere Technical High School

As one of the first technical high schools in Jamaica, Vere Technical began as a free trade school in 1958. In 1960, the Ministry of Education carried out development work on the school and established it as an institution offering technical and vocational subjects. Vere Technical currently offers programmes in a wide range of skill areas. These include Agro-Processing, Greenhouse Technology, and Drivers Education. In 2015, it was designated a STEM Academy. The Caribbean Vocational

Qualification (CVQ), the National Vocational Qualification of Jamaica (NVQ-J) and the Caribbean Secondary Education Certificate (CSEC) are examinations currently pursued by the students. The institution is seeking accreditation from the National Council on Technical Vocational Education and Training (NCTVET) as an Approved Training Organisation (ATO). This status will allow the school to offer and assess various TVET programmes.

Over the years, the enrolment at the school has grown, and an adult education and apprenticeship division has been added. Information from an interview in 2017 with a former Principal, Mrs Rosemary Logan, indicated that the programme offerings have expanded to include Digital Animation, Drivers' Education, Agro-Processing and Barbering. There is continuous professional upgrading for teachers and the Sixth Form students are pursuing programmes in the Career Advance Programme (CAP) as one of the pathways for Sixth Form.

St Andrew Technical High School

St Andrew Technical High School has contributed significantly to the advancement of technical and vocational education in Jamaica. The school was established in 1961 with the aim of providing technical and vocational education. Its establishment was driven by the then Minister of Education, the Honourable Sir Florizel Glasspole. Sir Florizel undertook this mission at a time when he recognized that technical vocational education was perceived as inferior and, through the establishment of St Andrew Technical High School, he sought to address the negative perception. The school later strengthened its ability to focus on technical education by merging with the neighbouring Trade Training Centre in 1971. The merger led to an increase in enrolment and the extension of the duration of the training programmes. Building Construction, Plumbing, Electricity, Welding, Machine Shop, Mechanics and Technical Drawing were initially offered. The school, however, has increased its offerings since it was first established to include programmes such as Engineering, Agro-processing, and Metalwork.

Fourteen Established Technical High Schools

The foregoing are five of the 14 established technical high schools (Table 2.1). They characterize the growth and development that have taken place across technical high schools in Jamaica. There has been an expansion in programme offerings, an increase in the students doing the national vocational qualifications and the expansion of infrastructure.

Growth and Expansion of the Technical High Schools

The significance of technical vocational education and training has been further strengthened through the establishment of additional technical high schools during the period 1970 to 1990. According to an undated paper from the former Technical Vocational Unit in the Ministry of Education Youth and Information, during the period 1970 to 1982, existing secondary schools were upgraded to technical high schools. These schools included Frome Technical High School, Herbert Morrison Technical, Marcus Garvey Technical, St Thomas Technical, José Martí Technical,

Table 2.1: Technical High Schools in Jamaica – Year of Establishment

Schools	Year of Establishment
Kingston Technical	1896
St Andrew Technical	1961
St Mary Technical High School	1995
Herbert Morrison Technical High School	1976
Dunoon Park Technical High School	1979
St Elizabeth Technical	1958
Holmwood Technical	1961
Dinthill Technical	1960
St Thomas Technical	1970
Vere Technical	1960
Knockalva	1996
Marcus Garvey Technical	1971
José Martí Technical	1977
Frome Technical	1957

St Mary Technical, and Knockalva Technical. With the changing profile of students entering the schools, programme offerings were increased and there were significant infrastructural developments.

Many of the technical high schools started out as trade schools and evolved to become technical high schools. This was so in the case of Holmwood, Dinthill and Knockalva Technical High Schools. In the growth and evolution of these schools, supports were often provided by international donors such as the Cuban government, the International Development Bank, and the World Bank. A World Bank loan in the 1970s not only provided for the construction of an additional technical high school, but the expansion of five existing technical high schools (Undated paper from the Technical Vocational Unit, MoEYI).

Kingston Technical started out as an elementary school for boys and girls in 1896. It evolved through the years to offer advanced manual training – catering to disabled soldiers and technicians. By 1962, it began to offer radio servicing for technicians. In the early years of Kingston Technical High school, the emphasis was on the training of teachers, and the principal of the school had the responsibility to provide supervision for the manual training across the island (Whyte, 1977). Kingston Technical High remained the only technical high school until a grant of $520,000.00 was made available for it to be expanded along with the establishment of the Jamaica Institute of Technology in 1958 (Whyte, 1977). In 2008, under the Reform of Secondary Education (ROSE) Programme, Grade 7 was introduced.

St Mary Technical High School was established through a change of status. In an interview in October 2016 with the Principal, Mrs. Glascine Lazarus, she explained that St Mary Technical started out as a junior secondary school and was upgraded in 1995 to become a technical high school. This, she attributed to the local politician who saw the need for technical education in the parish of St Mary.

Another school which evolved to become a technical high school was the Marcus Garvey Technical High School. It started out as the St Ann's Bay Junior Secondary School in 1971 and was renamed the Marcus Garvey Secondary School in 1975. In 1987, there was a name change to Marcus Garvey Technical High School. With this change came greater emphasis on self-help projects to assist the school in funding additional activities. These projects assisted the school in constructing a playing field and netball court. The shift system was introduced in 1975, but there was a change in 2012 to one shift from 8:00 am to 3:00 pm.

The school operates a senior campus at its plant in St Ann's Bay and a Junior Campus at its Mansfield campus in Ocho Rios. New and emerging programmes have been introduced in the school's curriculum, including AutoCad and Theatre Arts. Additionally, it offers the Career Advancement Programme. The main qualifications have been the Secondary School Certificate, Caribbean Examinations Council and the National Vocational Qualifications of Jamaica. The school has been performing well in football and cricket competitions. Starting with 780 students from Grades 7–9 in 1971, Marcus Garvey Technical High School grew to an enrolment of 2,160 in 2001 and was then the largest technical high school.

Herbert Morrison Technical High School was initially called the Catherine Hall Secondary School when it was established in 1976. Its name was later changed to Herbert Morrison Comprehensive in 1977 and, in 1988, was renamed Herbert Morrison Technical High School. The school has a dynamic Music programme and has introduced a Sixth Form.

ENTRANCE TO TECHNICAL HIGH SCHOOLS

Initially, many of the technical high schools started out at the Grade 9 level. During the initial phase of their establishment, students entered through the Grade Nine Achievement Test. Those who were not successful in the Common Entrance Examination did the Grade Nine Achievement Test. Over time, Grades 7 and 8 were introduced and this was made possible with funding assistance from the World Bank in 1999. Students later gained entry to technical high schools at the Grade 7 level through the Common Entrance Examination, which was later replaced by the Grade Six Achievement Test. The GSAT was later replaced in 2019 by the Primary Exit Profile Examination. For many of these technical high schools, in the 2000s, the qualification for entry was from junior schools and students would enter at Grades 8 or 9. Other students entered Grade 7 from primary schools, and this was determined by the examination

Table 2.2: Enrolment for the 2014/2015 Academic Year

Schools	Number of Students
Dinthill Technical High School	1,412
Dunoon Technical High School	951
Frome Technical High School	1,256
Herbert Morrison Technical High School	1,504
Holmwood Technical High School	1,365
José Martí Technical High School	2,009
Kingston Technical High School	1,169
Knockalva Technical High School	1,003
Marcus Garvey Technical High School	1,840
St Andrew Technical High School	1,692
St Elizabeth Technical High school	1,776
St Mary Technical High School	1,307
St Thomas Technical High School	1,381
Vere Technical High School	2,010

Source: Education Statistics 2014–2015 – Planning Unit, MoEYI

results. With these changes came an alteration in the profile of students who attend technical high schools.

Enrolment has increased significantly since the technical high schools were first established. In addition to the day school, many of these schools offer part-time and evening classes. Table 2.2 displays the enrolment of students for the 2014/2015 academic year.

STRATEGIC FOCUS OF THE TECHNICAL HIGH SCHOOLS

The philosophy and focus of the technical high schools were captured in the strategic mandate of the former Technical Vocational Unit of the Ministry of Education, Youth and Information. The Unit describes the learning experience in the technical high schools as providing education and training so that students can attain a level of technical and vocational training which will satisfy the minimum entry requirements for tertiary institutions and the world of work. In addition to emphasizing the focus on work, the focus on further education is also highlighted. Additional key roles and responsibilities of the Unit that reflect the philosophy include:

- Offering technical and vocational programmes that will be geared to develop the types of skills, knowledge, attitudes, habits and values that are in demand in the society and which, consequently, will contribute to the nation's productive goals;
- Fostering the development of potential for self-expression, creativity, and inventiveness that can result from the pursuance of a course in technical and vocational education;
- Assuming a major role in the development and implementation of teacher-training programmes that will produce the calibre of teachers who are qualified to contribute to the achievement of the foregoing goals.

Since 2013, the Technical Vocational Unit has been merged with the Core Curriculum Unit in the Ministry of Education Youth and Information. In 2018, Dr Clover Hamilton Flowers, Assistant Chief Education Officer, Core Curriculum Services, described this as a strategic move driven by the recognition that technical vocational areas are a major dimension of the national curriculum and part of the programme of learning for all learners. This, she said, will allow for better integration through collaborative teams.

The Subject of Resource and Technology

A major introduction in the curriculum of technical high schools is the subject of Resource and Technology (R & T) that was introduced in 1998 under the Reform of Secondary Education programme. This was designed to be a pre-vocational programme to serve as a foundation for exposure to the technical vocational skills. The R & T curriculum focused on Home and Family Management, Industrial Technology, Resource Management, Agriculture, the Environment, and the Visual Arts.

Shifts in Curriculum and Infrastructure Development

To support the growth and expansion of technical high school, many schools have undergone shifts in their curriculum and infrastructure development. St Mary Technical High School introduced a Sixth Form in 2014 and added new TVET programmes. These programmes can be described as new and emerging areas leading to non-traditional careers. These include Geometric and Mechanical Drawing, Renewable Energy, Environmental Science, and Entrepreneurial Skills. Other newly introduced programmes in schools, such as Herbert Morrison Technical High School, include Web Page Design and Bartending.

Many schools, in an attempt to develop an entrepreneurial mindset among students and to hone their technical competencies, offer services aligned to various TVET programmes as an income-generating project. Entrepreneurship forms a critical part of the technical high schools' curriculum and is integrated as a core subject. Entrepreneurship provides opportunities for students to apply competencies learnt by making products or providing services. For example, at St Andrew Technical High School, students work on metal furnishings which generate income. This opportunity can raise the image of TVET and facilitate learning in authentic settings.

The programmes in the technical high schools are often focused on key skills areas and subjects are organized according to related specializations. Key areas include Business, Agriculture, Visual Arts, Engineering, and Family and Consumer Studies. An important addition to the technical high schools has been the introduction of Science, Technology, Engineering and Mathematics subjects and skills. This is an initiative that is being driven by the Ministry of Education Youth and Information. Currently there are nine STEM institutions in Jamaica. Eight of these institutions are technical high schools and one is a non-technical high school. The technical high schools engaged are Herbert Morrison Technical High, St Mary Technical High, Vere Technical High, Dinthill Technical High, Dunoon Park Technical High, St Andrew Technical High, and Kingston Technical High. In addition to teaching discrete STEM subjects, the STEM principles are emphasized. These are problem-solving, analysis and data interpretation, communicating information, and using mathematical and computational thinking as detailed in the National Standards Curriculum (NSC).

Previously, students sat the Associated Examination Board Examination. However, as the schools evolved, they are now exposed to a variety of examinations administered by various examining bodies. In addition to offering the Caribbean Secondary Examination in a variety of technical vocational areas, many technical high schools are pursuing Caribbean Vocational Qualifications examinations and National Vocational Qualifications of Jamaica examinations in a variety of technical and vocational areas. They also pursue the Caribbean Advanced Proficiency Examinations (CAPE), the City and Guilds examination, and the Secondary School Certificate. The CVQ and the NVQJ are promoted in the schools as national certifying examinations and allow for articulation with programmes offered at tertiary institutions, based on the National Qualifications Framework of Jamaica (NQFJ). Many of these schools, such as St Thomas Technical High, have established key targets for passes in TVET subjects as detailed in their School Improvement Plans.

To better prepare students for employment upon graduation, the CVQ was introduced in schools and students were assessed for the first time in June 2015. The CVQ is being administered in the schools by the Caribbean Examination Council body. However, many schools still grapple with the challenges of the technical vocational qualifications being prioritized as there is the perception that the Caribbean Secondary Examination has more status. From discussions with principals and teachers, there appears to be increased focus on doing well in the CSEC examinations as this affects the ranking and perception of the school among key stakeholders such as parents, students, and the general public. There is also the preference among parents who strongly influence the choice of subjects pursued by students. Many parents have a preference for students pursuing the CSEC as opposed to Caribbean Vocational Qualification and National Vocational Qualifications of Jamaica, as it is perceived to have more status. According to a former senior officer in the MoEYI, speaking in 2018, this can be viewed as schools taking on the features of the grammar school and also a departure from the philosophy they started out with.

The number of subjects being pursued by the technical high schools has increased significantly over the past few years. This is an important policy direction from the MoEYI in recognizing the importance of TVET as crucial to national development. In 2016, the then Minister of Education, the Honourable Ruel Reid, announced that all students should pursue at least one TVET subject. This policy direction is in alignment with what is happening regionally and internationally and is promoted by international organizations such as the United Nations Educational, Scientific and Cultural Organization (UNESCO), the International Labour Organization (ILO), the Organization for Economic Co-operation and Development (OECD) and the Caribbean Community and Common Market (CARICOM). The focus is on technical vocational education to prepare work-ready graduates who can contribute to productivity in the workforce. Over the years, infrastructure has improved in technical high schools. This is demonstrated in the upgrading of libraries, resource centres, and the strengthening of information and communication technology in the curriculum. In 2008, St Thomas Technical High School was upgraded with five additional classrooms.

In the history and evolution of the technical high schools in Jamaica, there are two interventions that have significantly impacted their development. These are the Basic Skills Project and the Technical High Schools Development Project.

THE BASIC SKILLS PROJECT

The Basic Skills Project was introduced in the 1984/1985 academic year and contributed significantly to the strengthening of the technical high schools. According to the 1984/1985 report from the Ministry of Education, the introduction of the Basic Skills Project sought to improve the quality of technical and vocational education and training in the existing technical high schools and to expand by adding four additional schools. The Project was characterized by a multi-sectoral approach and included organizations and agencies such as the United States Agency for International Development (USAID), the HEART Trust NTA and the Ministry of Youth and Community Development. The Project contributed to facilities upgrading, curriculum development, instructional training, and leadership training and development among technical high school staff.

THE TECHNICAL HIGH SCHOOLS DEVELOPMENT PROJECT

The contribution of the Technical High Schools Development Project to the upgrading of the technical high schools in Jamaica has been significant. The evolution of the schools has, in large part, been defined by the contribution of the project to the schools. According to Mrs Loveda Jones, who was the director of the Technical High School Development Project from 1992 to 2007, in an interview in September 2018, the THSDP sought to reposition the technical high schools in Jamaica. The Project was described as seeking to revise and reposition the focus and programmes of the Jamaican technical high school system. The Project was funded by the HEART Trust NTA and launched on March 9, 1995. Close collaboration was formed with the then Ministry of Education, Youth and Culture and the Reform of Secondary Education Programme.

The Technical High Schools Development Project has been responsible for institutional capacity building of the technical high schools. This has been guided by a three-year development plan, the upgrading of facilities and equipment, laboratories, science laboratories, classrooms and libraries, and the strengthening of the National Vocational Qualification of Jamaica through increased offerings and certification in the schools. Importantly, each school was required to have a three-year development plan that was tailored to the needs of the school.

At the mid-term evaluation of the THSDP, technical education in Jamaica was described as 'high tech', "thanks in main to the inputs of the project and very noticeably the contribution of the Ministry of Education and Culture (MOEC) and the Japanese agency, JICA, at Jose Marti" (2001, p.2). The evaluation spoke to the perceived major success of the Project and recommended that it should continue and eventually be institutionalized, in some form, as a permanent adjunct to the technical high school system in Jamaica. This will be necessary, the evaluation continued, as equipment that was upgraded will eventually need replacement; training for staff will have to be ongoing to have any lasting benefit; and the schools will require a central focal point of enthusiasm to draw them together into some semblance of a technical education system.

CHALLENGES FOR THE TECHNICAL HIGH SCHOOLS

Many technical high schools now struggle with challenges that often negatively impact their ability to offer quality learning experiences. The negative perception of technical and vocational education continues to be a challenge. There is still a significant percentage of parents and teachers who view TVET negatively and associate it with students who are not doing well academically. As a result, many students are not inclined to pursue the TVET qualifications such as the Caribbean Vocational Qualifications and the National Vocational Qualifications of Jamaica and prefer, instead, to do CSEC subjects. In an interview with one of the technical high schools principals in 2017, the principal bemoaned the fact that many parents and teachers still associate students who are less academically inclined with TVET. This view is aligned to the perspective described by Consultants, Murgatroyd and Hilsum (2001), of the Technical High School Mid-Term Evaluation. They stated that "at present, all technical high schools for different reasons are staggering under policies which select second- or third-rate students" (p. 2). It must be acknowledged that significant policy changes from the Ministry of Education have contributed to changes in this perception. However, there is still room for this perspective to be improved.

Additionally, because technical and vocational education and training is expensive, many schools find it a challenge to maintain the laboratories which have up-to-date and adequate equipment. To mitigate this challenge, some schools establish priorities in funding the laboratories. As a result, some curriculum areas are given priority. A further challenge is that of recruiting qualified teachers, which is often due to a lack of qualified personnel in key areas. Automotives and Plumbing are often two areas cited for which there is a shortage of qualified teachers. This is also often the case in new and emerging areas. Where possible, the Ministry of Education Youth and Information collaborates with the HEART Trust NTA to upgrade existing teachers to deliver new and emerging areas. This is done during the summer months, utilizing the laboratories and equipment in the HEART institutions. The focus goes beyond upgrading in the technical areas and includes pedagogical upgrading. As such, sessions are offered to equip teachers with the competency-based methodology - the methodology that emphasizes the importance of the hands-on practical approach in the pedagogy of TVET.

However, in spite of the challenges, many school administrators and policymakers are of the view that the perception of technical vocational programmes has undergone major positive changes since the increased focus on TVET from the MoEYI and the introduction of the TVET policy in 2014. This change is taking place among school administrators, teachers, parents, and students.

THE CAREER ADVANCEMENT PROGRAMME

Many of the technical high schools have now added the Career Advancement Programme (CAP) to their curricula. CAP was introduced in 2009 and the goal of the programme was to address the increasing number of graduates leaving high schools without qualifications. Students were kept in the secondary schools for an additional two years to pursue TVET programmes to equip them for the workforce and to pursue further education. The Programme targets unattached youths, and the Registered Apprenticeship Programme (RAP) is a key component. The Programme is being delivered in the secondary and high school system. It extends to Grades 12 and 13. In addition to the technical areas, the components include personal development and life-coping skills. The Programme was initially managed under the HEART Trust NTA from 2010 to 2014. However, it is now being led by the Ministry of Education, Youth and Information.

Work-based learning is a key component of the Programme. The HEART Trust NTA, the National Youth Service (NYS) and previously, the Jamaica Foundation for Lifelong Learning, are key partners in the execution of the Programme. Students can pursue programmes to acquire City and Guilds qualifications and NCTVET qualifications. In 2019, these institutions were merged to form the HEART Trust NTA. In 2014, the

Programme was rebranded to improve the leadership and the quality mechanisms to lead to improved certification rates. To strengthen the leadership and management of the programme, a Technical Working Committee (TWC) was established to provide oversight and schools were required to submit an expression of interest, indicating their willingness to participate in the Programme and to undergo a facility audit to determine the suitability of their resources to effectively deliver the identified programmes. Additionally, access was expanded to include Grades 12–13. The Programme is now offered through three modalities. Based on examination results, the Programme has seen major improvements in passes for the City and Guilds and the NCTVET examinations since it was rebranded in 2014. There are technical high schools that have offered CAP as a key strategic objective to have students in Grades 12 and 13 enrolled in at least one CAP programme.

MAINSTREAMING TVET IN SECONDARY SCHOOLS

In order for the curriculum to remain relevant and connected with the needs of the labour market, in 2013, the Ministry of Education Youth and Information introduced new and emerging skill areas in the technical high schools. These include Call Centre Operations, Crop Production, Apiculture, Hydroponics, Renewable Energy, Motor Vehicle Air Conditioning, Fashion Designing, Food and Drink, Floral Arrangement, and Digital Animation. Capacity-building workshops were conducted in 2015 to upgrade teachers with the necessary competencies to implement these programmes. From 2014 to 2019, more than 1,000 teachers from the MoEYI schools were upgraded by the HEART Trust in both technical and pedagogical areas.

While the introduction of these new programmes has not been confined to the technical high schools, these are among the schools in which the programmes have been introduced. In fact, the offering of TVET has extended beyond the technical high schools to include other secondary schools. A policy directive from the Ministry of Education Youth and Information, in 2016, sought to increase TVET offerings in schools by stating that all secondary schools should offer technical and vocational subjects.

TVET has also been strengthened through the integration of Science, Technology, Engineering and Mathematics. This initiative has been extended to TVET at the secondary school level, including technical high schools. A concept paper from the Ministry of Education, Youth and Information, in 2014, stated that technical high schools will be transformed to strengthen the alignment of STEM education. Key features will be the upgrading and equipping of technical high schools according to the specific STEM specializations and the professional upgrading of staff so they can effectively integrate STEM in their programmes.

The National TVET Policy 2014, referring to the need to strengthen TVET in the Jamaican education system stated:

> Throughout the education system, curriculum offerings and delivery modalities have focused on academic outcomes and not sufficiently on the attainment of competencies necessary for meeting the needs of the labour market. Despite the introduction of technical vocational education to Jamaica – with the establishment of Kingston Technical High School in 1896, and the subsequent establishment of thirteen other similar institutions – no serious consideration was given to the development of a national TVET policy for secondary schools, to drive its importance to generate education, and to promote the recognition of TVET as a key component in the development of skills and competencies needed in the workforce. (TVET Policy 2014, p. 9)

The policy seeks to drive access, relevance, quality and equity as key areas of focus in the delivery of technical vocational education and training. In addition, the Policy for Technical and Vocational Education and Training (2014) articulates the framework for the development and sustainability of TVET in the Jamaican education and training system by listing the following features:

- A comprehensive, integrated and outcomes-based TVET system.
- A coherent framework for TVET systems to encourage research and development, stimulate productivity, and guide career development and lifelong learning.
- Pathways to facilitate the progression of individuals through competency levels and career changes in keeping with current demands.
- Quality of TVET at all levels and responsiveness to the labour market and accessibility.

- A culture of entrepreneurship and the support of job creation in the economy, with focus on emerging industries.
- Establishment of a sustainable financing system for building and maintaining TVET structures.

The recognition that technical vocational education needs to be mainstreamed in the education system was strengthened with the merging of the Technical Vocational Unit with the Curriculum Unit in 2017. This was seen as part of a larger restructuring and transformation of the Ministry of Education, Youth and Information. It also strengthened the focus that TVET is a part of the learners' development and that it begins from the early years.

Strategic goals being pursued for technical vocational education in the secondary school system extends to expanding and strengthening TVET offerings; increasing access for all senior students at Grades 10–11 to be enrolled in a TVET programme; establishing partnerships; and increasing certification. Key emphasis in the strategic direction of technical high schools includes access through increased certification, the granting of centre approval status by the National Council for Technical Vocational Education and Training and seeking to ensure that all students graduating at Grade 11 are certified in a skill area. These initiatives have sought to get students ready for the future world of work and to strengthen the focus on technical and vocational education as an agent of workforce development and further learning.

CONCLUSION

The technical high schools in Jamaica have contributed significantly in advancing TVET across the Jamaican education system. They have evolved to offer new and emerging programmes that are in alignment with new and emerging occupational areas. Greater emphasis has been made in equipping students with relevant skills for the world of work. Significant infrastructural and capacity-building improvements have been made to these schools through the Basic Skills Programme, the Technical High Schools Project and the TVET Rationalisation Programme. These have extended to teacher capacity building and the upgrading of laboratories. Technical high schools have served as catalysts for increasing TVET offerings at the secondary level, thus leading to the mainstreaming of TVET in the secondary education system. These high schools continue to seek innovative and creative ways to address challenges such as teacher shortages in key technical areas, keeping their laboratories upgraded at current standards and meeting certification targets.

BIBLIOGRAPHY

Billett, S. (2018). Improving the image of TVET. https://unevoc.unesco.org/up/vc_synthesis_21.pdf

Facilitation and Consultancy Training Services. (2008). *Preliminary Implementation Plan for Mainstreaming TVET Rationalisation in Jamaican High Schools – 2009/2010 and 2013/2014*. Wilbert Tomlinson.

Frome Technical High School. (2018). *School Improvement Plan for the Academic Year 2018/2019*. Author.

HEART Trust NTA. (1982). Human Employment and Resource Training Act. https://laws.moj.gov.jm/library/statute/the-human-employment-and-resource-training-act

Herbert Morrison Technical High School. (n.d.). *School Development Plan 2016–2020*. Author.

Holmwood Technical High School. (n.d.). *Holmwood Technical High School Improvement Plan 2018–2021*. http://holmwoodtechnicalhigh.org.jm/main/index.php/about-our-school/

Jamaica Information Service. (2015). *Education ministry to cover exam fees under CVQ programme*. https://jis.gov.jm/education-ministry-cover-exam-fees-cvq-programme

Jose Marti Technical High School. (n.d.). *TVET Strategic Focus and School Improvement Plan 2015–2018*. Author.

Knockalva Technical High School. (n.d.). *School Improvement Plan 2018–2021*. Author.

Marope, P., Chakroun, B., Holmes, K. (2015). *Unleashing the potential: Transforming TVET and vocational education*. UNESCO.

Ministry of Education, Youth and Information. (n.d.). *Concept Paper – The Stem Academy: Transforming Technical High Schools into STEM Academies*. MoE.

Ministry of Education, Youth and Information. (2014). *Career Advancement Programme (CAP) Rebranding Strategic Plan*. Technical Working Committee. Author.

Ministry of Education, Youth and Information. (1998). *Government of Jamaica World Bank Reform of Secondary Education, Curriculum Guide. Grades 7–9*. Author.

Resource Applications Limited. (2001). *HEART Trust NTA, Technical High School Development Project, Mid-Term Evaluation Report*. Murgatroyd and Hilsum.

Sangster, A. W. (2004). *The Kingston Technical High School story with short histories of Dinthill, Dunoon, Holmwood, St Andrew, St Elizabeth and Vere Technical High Schools*. Author.

St Andrew Technical High School (n.d.). *History of St Andrew Technical High School*. History Department.

St Andrew Technical High School. (2001). *Student handbook*. Author.

St Elizabeth Technical High School. (n.d.). *Student handbook* (version 1.1). Author.

St Mary Technical High School. (n.d.). *St Mary Technical High School Improvement Plan*. Author.

St Thomas Technical High School. (n.d.). *History of St Thomas Technical High School*. Author.

Technical High School Development Project. (n.d.). *Proposal for a Sustainability Plan*. Ministry of Education, Youth and Information.

Technical High School Development Project. (2005). *Annual Report Summary 2004/2005*. Ministry of Education, Youth and Information.

Tingling, M. (2016, March 8). "Herbert Morrison carving out its own space". Jamaica Information Service. https://jis.gov.jm/herbert-morrison-carving-space.

Whyte, M. (1983). *A Short History of Education in Jamaica*. Hodder and Stoughton Ltd.

CHAPTER 3

TVET Rationalization in Secondary Schools

CAROLE POWELL

THE SECONDARY SCHOOL SYSTEM IN POST-MODERN SOCIETY is seen as a key agent of growth and development because it accommodates and caters to that critical mass of human energies known as youth, holistically. Powell (2008) stated, "To await a time beyond early school life to learn to apply knowledge gained, is postponing the inevitable. It becomes increasingly difficult to retrace unpractised steps" (p. 4), thus the application of knowledge beginning at the level of the school is regarded as paramount. Technical and vocational education and training (TVET) has been characterized as the application of knowledge and is recommended for inclusion in schools' curricula. Whiteman (1992) described TVET as "experiences and opportunities which provide the individual with the competencies (knowledge, skills and attitudes) required for entry into and advancement in a job or occupation of his or her choice" (p. 1). He further emphasized that TVET is not 'reclamation' education for those who fail to achieve academic excellence. TVET thus requires a knowledge base as it is, in itself, the application of knowledge. Since school inculcates the imbibing of knowledge, the secondary school system must be supported in realizing its true potential as an engine of growth and national development, by enabling positive human capacity development (HCD) through the incorporation of TVET in curricula.

BACKGROUND

Since the restructuring of Jamaica's Human Employment and Resource Training (HEART)Trust National Training Agency (NTA) as a full-blown training agency in 1991, that body has been recommending TVET as the vehicle through which the human resource (HR) stock of the country should be enriched to attain a competitive edge in the global economy. In spite of this acknowledgement of the potential of TVET as a national developmental agent, the momentum towards its integration into the system for human resource development (HRD) seemed slow. The agency further claimed that one of the main issues of the day was the near exclusion of the school system from the system for HRD to satisfy the workforce. This was due to the traditional view that the aim of successful schooling resided solely in the academics.

In 1993, a United Nations Educational, Scientific and Cultural Organization (UNESCO) research on the Jamaican education system revealed that the school system did not prepare its leavers for the world of work. During the same period, the Ministry of Education (MoE) launched research that concurred with the UNESCO finding, and the discussion began as to how best to address the obvious gap and engage the school system as a vital agent in that regard. One of the staunch discussants at the time was an emerging professional organization, Jamaica Association for Technical Vocational Education and Training (JATVET). The executive body of that association had several meetings with the Minister of Education and helped to spur the action that was brewing in the Ministry itself. In addition, scholars like Morris (1998) encouraged that "technical and vocational education at the secondary level should be promoted nationally . . . ." (p. 125). By 1998, the HEART Trust NTA supported the Ministry in launching a pilot project that would, by way of Action Research discover the best way to integrate TVET into the curriculum of the secondary school system. The project was named "TVET Rationalization in Secondary Schools" and, from planning to implementation through to expansion/replication, it lasted 12 years. A mainstreaming road map that was developed by the pilot staff and consultants was said to have been pursued by the Ministry, albeit there had been necessary adjustments to suit the passage of time.

Indeed, there were financial challenges in pursuing such a project. As a regional misgiving, funding had always been identified as a great challenge. Addressing TVET in the Caribbean, Eastmond (as cited in Morris and Powell, 2013) stated, "One of the challenges facing TVET is the high cost and sustainability of its Programming." Further, Hutton (2012) reviewed the Caribbean Common Market (CARICOM) regional strategy for TVET and found that, among other things, areas of least accomplishment centred on inadequate or obsolete infrastructure, which resulted from inadequate funding mechanisms. Establishing informed and viable TVET systems in an affordable manner thus became the daunting task to accomplish.

GLOBAL OUTLOOK

Developed countries, such as Australia, South Korea and the USA, had gone ahead and implemented models for the expansion of TVET (Career and Technical Education in the USA) into their respective education systems. Australia, for example, saw the need for an "Education Revolution." Boston (2005) zeroed in on the significant progress made in New South Wales. He shared that, in 1997, schools and the technical and further education colleges were sustained by the Department of Education and Training. This made it possible to share the facilities of the entities as they could be managed as a single resource. Integrated timetables were developed to facilitate the movement of students between school and college. In terms of the curriculum, students from Grades 10 to 13 spent three weekdays in school – one day in college, and one day in the workplace as paid employees. In Grades 12 and 13, students were prepared for the National Vocational Qualification and all five days contributed to completion of their high school certificate. According to Boston, implementing this plan successfully relied on the supportive response of industry.

South Korea saw TVET as a part of an "outward looking economic strategy" (Taeck-Duck, 1994, p. 4). For individuals preparing to enter the labour force, (although vocational competencies were usually developed solely by way of school curriculum and training), the new thrust was to shrink the gap between school education and market demands. This was implemented in order to promote relevance and sustainability as well as to make learning substantial within the school system. The route taken, as described by Hong, (as cited in Chang, 2009) was "active vocational education." The development of cooperation between schools, colleges and businesses would lead to the expansion of learning exposure and experiences for the nation's youth. The establishment of comprehensive schools also supported this thrust, especially in terms of access.

In the USA, the Carl D. Perkins Act (1984) renewed the Federal commitment to improve and expand quality vocational education programmes in response to the demands of globalization. An example of a response to the thrust was seen in the operations of a school district in Georgia, USA which bussed academically gifted students to neighbouring vocational institutions for training activities. This led to the growing trend of career development in schools' curricula, whereby students were placed in career tracks and assigned academic courses to complement their vocational programme. Keen attention was also paid to ensuring the requisite resources for the variety of learners in developing and presenting that which became known as 'out-based' curricula for TVET. The out-based curriculum was key among the requirements of the learner-centred methodology employed: Competency Based Education and Training (CBET). There was also the Vo/Tech, now Career and Technical Education system in Oklahoma, which offered its programmes and services throughout nearly 400 public school districts, 29 technology centres with 58 campus sites, and 17 skills centres located in correctional facilities. Here again, students travel to technology centres that work closely with advisers from the local industry to ensure that they learn the skills needed to become valued members of the workforce.

UNESCO (2013) recounted that several developing countries in Asia-Pacific had also sought ways to expand TVET in respective education systems at the secondary level. Thailand, for example, strengthened their work-based learning and students were required to complete work placement every other semester and spend alternate semesters in regular school. The approach in Malaysia was to create vocational colleges by way of transforming vocational and technical schools. The establishment of comprehensive schools enabled joint delivery of general and vocational education and saw to the increase in registration figures as experienced in China and Thailand.

The TVET Rationalization approach engaged in Jamaica has been said to be "one-of-a-kind", especially since it employed a unique mode by which resources for TVET were shared. This chapter examines the TVET Rationalization Pilot Project, giving highlights from the selected regions: Westmoreland, St Elizabeth, and the Corporate Area. It will examine:

- The period of preparation and early outputs such as a TVET Rationalization Plan;
- The segmented implementation – 1998–2010;
- The Corporate Area expansion – 2004;
- Challenges and lessons learned, including important outcomes such as A Policy for TVET;
- Returns on investment as seen by stakeholders and participants;
- General recommendations in support of sustainability.

THE TVET RATIONALIZATION PILOT

Preparation and Early Outputs

The Ministry of Education, in conjunction with the HEART Trust/NTA, launched the Pilot Project in Westmoreland and St Elizabeth in November 1997, and operations began in earnest January 1998. Whereas the Ministry officially offered neither pre-set instruments nor pre-conceived ideas in respect of the pilot process, two preconditions were issued. One of the preconditions related to the four indices undergirding its philosophy – to ensure access, equity, quality and relevance throughout the process. The other concerned itself with the full recognition of the paucity of Government funds. The notion of sharing resources found its anchor in this latter precondition and proved to be the linchpin for the TVET Rationalization endeavour. The boundaries of a case study on the pilot done by Powell (2014) were said to be identified by "definition and context" as advised by Miles and Huberman (1994). The discussions around the preconditions issued morphed into the following definition:

> TVET Rationalization in Secondary Schools refers to the integration of TVET in secondary schools' curricula, emphasizing: the ensuring of access and equity, the assurance of quality and relevance, while creating greater efficiencies in a comprehensive education framework. (MoE, Charnwood, 2010)

Contextually, the project was designed to address Grades 10–11 as a sequel to Resource & Technology (R&T) which was fielded at Grades 7–9, in keeping with the ministry's Reform of Secondary Education (ROSE). The primary objective of the pilot was to provide access to quality TVET facilities equitably for those students in 17 secondary-level schools in two adjoining rural parishes, and later 15 such schools in the Corporate Area.

Early consultations engaged groups in schools, communities, and government ministries as well as NTA officials. This provided a backdrop of rich information that served to inform in-depth planning and implementation of the pilot. Each of the 17 schools within the rural domain was visited to conduct preliminary interface with principals, students, and staff, and to enable first-hand view of physical plants, programme laboratories, and available equipment. This phase was known as "Fact-finding" and began as early as February 1998. The revelations from these visits were stark. For example, in the non-traditional and non-technical schools, there were great material and equipment demands in the face of meagre resources. In addition, up to 50% of the students in the TVET area were not reading at proficiency levels. The prospect of accommodating any demanding intervention at that time proved intimidating for school administrators and staff. Fortunately, students were receptive; they were completely relaxed from the first day of interface and showed a willingness to listen and to share. In a very general way, the notion of 'TVET for all' by way of sharing resources was introduced. At each school, pilot personnel interfaced with mixed student-groups of 15 or 18, three from each grade cohort. From Powell's expose (2014), three early responses from students readily came to mind: "All you have to do is to bus us to where we can find our programme."; "I am dying to go and link with those other stars in other schools."; "I am sorry this thing is coming as I am leaving, because I aim to become a dermatologist and doing cosmetology would let me hit the ground running."

Fact-finding, in respect of physical facilities and programmes, revealed a mismatch in that most non-technical schools reported to host more TVET programmes than they had laboratory spaces to accommodate. There were instances of classrooms alternating as TVET laboratories. With general studies such as English Language, for example, there were cases of two different TVET programmes sharing the same small space, and cases of laboratory spaces that were sheds. Significantly, it was said that scant regard was given to these programmes by school administrators, since TVET was set aside largely for the non-academic performers and non-readers in those schools.

This first phase was completed May 1998, after a five-month series of meetings, briefings, consultations, school tours, and planning. The first major report was to become the guiding light of the entire TVET Rationalization project process as it chronicled all team activities since inception and laid out the sought-after TVET Rationalization plan and principles. The content of the report spelt out the findings as they related to staff, students, infrastructure, TVET programmes, enrolment patterns and, apart from community interface, some feedback on stakeholders' reactions, perceptions, and concerns. There were many findings of note, but what was most significant was the difference in approach and outlook of students as against those of responsible adults. It was reported that during students' interface sessions with implementers of the pilot, students focused on benefits and possibilities, while making useful recommendations. In contrast, adult stakeholder population tended to focus on obstacles and impending woes. However, all feedback from stakeholders, along with implementers' observations, combined to enable the production of the TVET Rationalization plan and principles.

THE TVET RATIONALIZATION PLAN

The plan was derived largely based on stakeholders' feedback and the Ministry of Education's preconditions to ensure access, equity, relevance and quality in the most cost-effective manner. The following recommendations were far-reaching:

1. The sharing of scarce resources.
2. The formation of school clusters and derivation of integrated time-tables.
3. The derivation of an optimal mix of TVET programmes.
4. The physical upgrading of existing school plants to accommodate 68 work laboratories or centres of excellence.
5. The installation of modern equipment, tools, and furnishing.
6. The instituting of strong Career Guidance programmes.
7. The upgrading/sensitization of school and Ministry staff, and the general community.

Proposed Model for Sharing Resources

School Clusters. Geographic proximity of schools dictated the formation of clusters to a great extent. At least three schools were constituents of an ideal cluster, and this facilitated access to TVET for students at Grades 10 and 11. The cluster also ensured equity by promoting the sharing of resources (plant, materials, and human) among cluster schools. A basic cluster model complete with economic justification was designed (Figure 3.1)

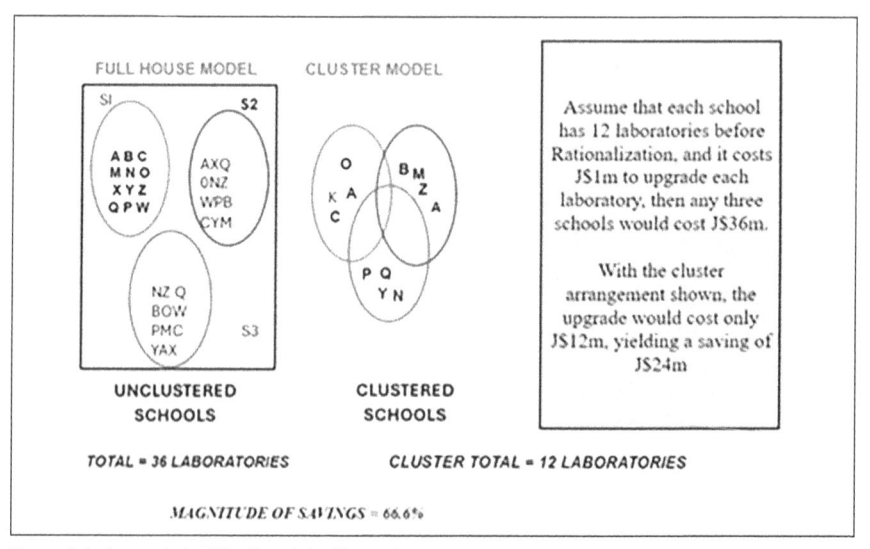

Figure 3.1: Economic Justification of the Cluster System

In the example, there are three schools, S1, S2 and S3. The left hand side of the diagram assumes that each school received 12 laboratories before rationalization and it costs J$1m to upgrade each laboratory. The cost to furnish the three schools with upgraded laboratories would then be J$36m. With the cluster arrangement shown on the right of the diagram where resources are shared, although the same programmes are offered, only nine different programme laboratories and three constants would be necessary (12 laboratories in all). The upgrade would thus cost only J$12m, yielding a 66.6% saving of J$24m. The example shown was based on the notion that if resources were to be shared among a total of three or four schools, as opposed to concentrating the lot in individual schools to serve unitary student bodies, then savings would be impressive and real.

Five clusters were identified in the domain: two in Westmoreland (see Figure 3.2) which included all of the seven secondary-level schools in the parish at that time, and three in St Elizabeth (see Figure 3.3) which included all of the 10 secondary level schools in the parish at that time.

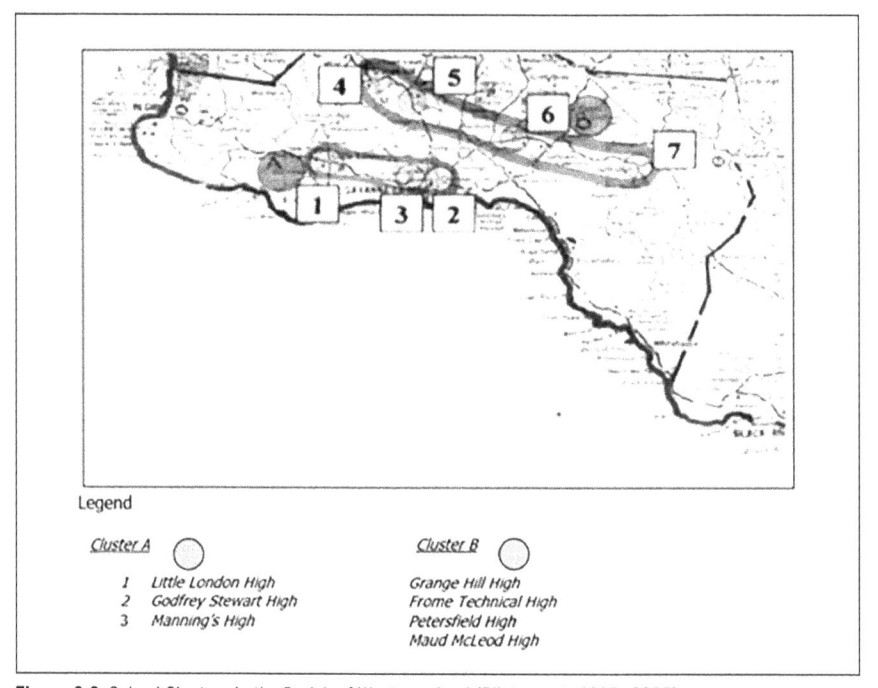

Figure 3.2: School Clusters in the Parish of Westmoreland (Pilot report, 1995–2005)

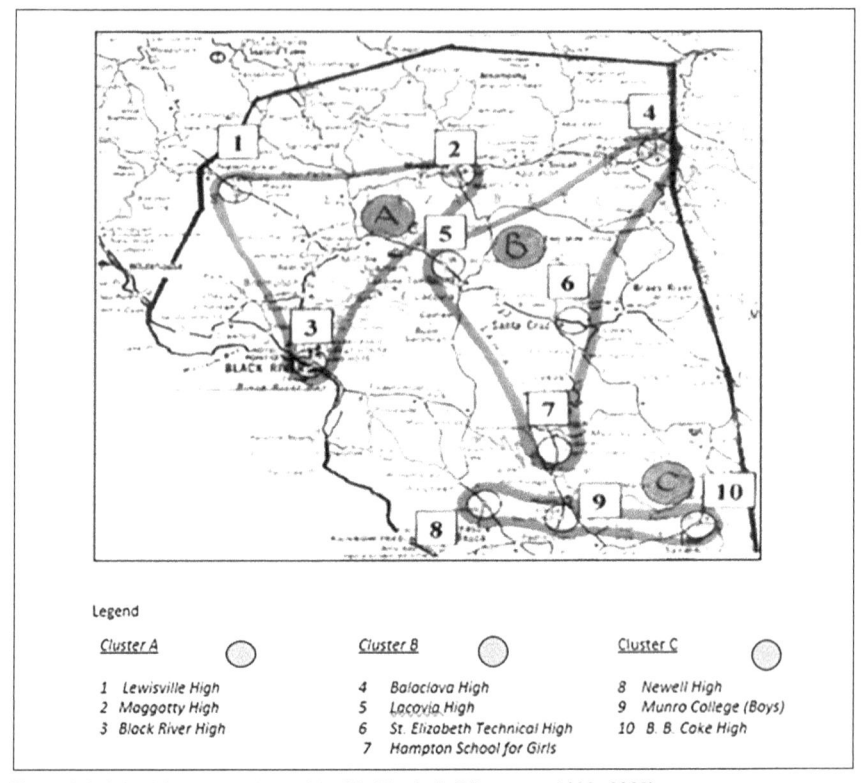

Figure 3.3: School Clusters in the Parish of St Elizabeth (Pilot report, 1998–2005)

Legend

Cluster A
1 Lewisville High
2 Maggotty High
3 Black River High

Cluster B
4 Balaclava High
5 Lacovia High
6 St. Elizabeth Technical High
7 Hampton School for Girls

Cluster C
8 Newell High
9 Munro College (Boys)
10 B. B. Coke High

Each cluster school was suited out with at least two physically upgraded and highly equipped programme laboratories termed 'centres of excellence'. There was no duplication of pilot programmes within a cluster and the total number of programmes to be offered from the laboratories in a cluster equated the number and nature presented in the 'Optimal Mix' of programmes as identified by the Ministry and the NTA. Students from Grades 10–11, after being groomed by specially developed Career Guidance programmes, opted for their suited TVET area from the 'Optimal Mix' and commuted (if necessary) twice per week to access the programme at what was termed their lab-school. Thus, the operating arrangement was termed 'home-school to lab-school cluster model'.

Optimal Mix of TVET programmes. An array of 10 TVET programmes was identified by stakeholders, including the National Council on TVET (NCTVET), as being relevant to the communities' and the country's needs.

The programmes were also deemed practicable for delivery in schools and, indeed, would be offered in every cluster to ensure equity. The list could not be exhaustive for reasons of practicability and funding, but it provided the best possible base for introduction to work-based education in mixed areas of TVET skills, hence the mix of programmes was deemed to be optimal. Within each cluster, schools were assigned to host specific programmes based on the concept of 'lower hanging fruit' by which the projected least financial cost and effort for development, based on plant and equipment, would be ascertained. Some schools were already hosting comparatively successful programmes because of infrastructure and set-up; these laboratories were seen as 'lower hanging fruits' and were upgraded to suit the new requirements and to accommodate the expanded numbers. Importantly, selection of host schools never relied on the human factor, mainly because people may separate or naturally expire.

Staff Development. The section of the plan that spoke to staff development indicated reliance on the Ministry's Tech/Voc Unit to recommend and follow through with the upgrading of existing TVET teachers in the skill areas and in pedagogy. Also, the section indicated reliance on HEART Trust NTA's Professional Guidance Information Services (PROGIS), now Career Development Services Unit (CDSU), in the area of Career Development & Counselling. This body took responsibility for upgrading Guidance Counsellors and Work Experience Coordinators in career awareness, planning, and the development of career programmes for their respective schools.

The plan also included targeted upgrading and awareness sessions aimed at principals and other school administrators, board members and Parent Teachers' Associations (PTAs), education officers, senior directors, managers, and directors of both the Ministry of Education and the National Training Agency. All of this were done and, in most cases, were ongoing.

The TVET Rationalization Principles

A set of principles that would act as a pointed guide was drafted based on the plan and became an imperative in shepherding the process. They were:

1. All secondary-level schools will be organized into geographic clusters to facilitate sharing resources.
2. Each school will be examined for its potential to host Tech/Voc Centres of Excellence.
3. The work area(s) identified in each school will be physically upgraded and equipped.
4. Tech/Voc instructors, guidance counsellors and work experience coordinators will be upgraded to ensure quality guidance and instruction.
5. Adequate staffing including Laboratory Assistants will be engaged.
6. Each student will opt to pursue a Tech/Voc progrmme, as advised by career guidance and counselling.
7. Students must have achieved a Grade 9 academic qualification in order to pursue any TVET Programme offered at a Centre of Excellence.
8. Students will attend classes at the programme laboratory twice per week, for a total of at least four hours of hands-on and two hours of related theory.
9. If the opted programme is not offered at his/her home-school, the student will be scheduled to commute to the specified lab-school within the cluster.
10. Special means of transportation will be arranged for commuting students at minimal cost.
11. Parents will be required to give written permission for students to commute, as a means of indemnity. In this regard, special forms will be made available at each school.
12. Each cluster will host similar programmes as far as is practicable. In the case of impracticability, students will be enabled to gain access across clusters.
13. Where necessary, qualified staff may commute to instruct at the relevant Centre of Excellence.
14. Classrooms will be recovered by refurbishing and furnishing redundant laboratory spaces.
15. Notwithstanding the foregoing, special circumstances and needs will be dealt with on merit.

PILOT IMPLEMENTATION

The pilot took the form of action research following the spiral model: planning, action, monitoring and reflection. Thus, it was best executed in phases and segments, specifically to facilitate learning from previous steps and phases, then acting accordingly.

Phase I: Pilot-in-Pilot, 1998–2000

This earliest phase of implementation was dubbed 'pilot-in-pilot' mainly because only a subset of the domain (17 schools from which five clusters were formed) was to be addressed. The subset included two clusters, one in each parish, which involved three schools in Westmoreland and four schools in St Elizabeth. The inclusion of both parishes and the involvement of a three-school and a four-school cluster provided ample cases for purposes of comparison and discovery. Pilot-in-pilot also meant that operations were limited to one laboratory or centre of excellence per cluster school.

Having completed preliminary recommendations of TVET programme assignments to schools, and receiving acceptance, the process flowed as follows:

1. Site selection on school plan (for laboratory) as advised by Principal, School Consultative Committee (SCC) and Board.
2. Site visits with technical persons (draftsmen and contractors).
3. Examination of physical upgrade plans and quantities.
4. Submissions for approval of Pilot Management Committee.
5. Physical upgrade of sites.
6. Submissions for acquisition of relevant tools, equipment, and furniture.
7. All parties sign-off for completion of physical upgrade works.
8. Installation of furnishing and equipment.
9. Procurement and purchasing of two shuttle buses (one per cluster).
10. Drafting of a generic timetable.
11. Derivation of integrated cluster timetables.
12. Derivation of shuttle schedules.

13. Engagement and training of bus drivers/shuttle monitors.
14. Operationalization of upgraded TVET programmes.

Simultaneously with these activities were the sensitization and upgrading of school leaders, staff and the general community. The activities included a travel tour, involving some of the Principals, to the rationalized system in Oklahoma, USA, as well as a retreat for the Principals and Vice Principals of the seven schools involved at this point of the operations. Based on these sessions with school administrators, general centre of excellence operational principles were also derived.

The first set of pilot students (521 in number) was from the Grade 10 cohort and pursued respective TVET programmes over the two-year period. At the end of the first year, students progressed to Grade 11 and a new set from Grade 9 joined the pilot as Grade 10 in September 1999. By July 2000, this phase was at its closing when the project's first Grade 11 cohort sat external TVET examinations as set by the NCTVET and the Caribbean Examinations Council (CXC). Students were examined in all seven programme areas as hosted by the seven schools in two clusters. Good intra-cluster communication experienced in one cluster benefitted the pilot-in-pilot process in such a way that relevant staff such as Guidance Counsellors, Work Experience Coordinators, Programme Instructors and Timetable Constructors from each of the schools within that cluster formed an action group to rationalize student intake to programmes, in terms of prerequisites, numbers and orientation. The action group sought to sensitize related students, teachers and parents to the new demands that would better prepare students for effective participation in TVET programmes. Subsequent clusters benefitted from this example shown. This justifies the action research approach.

Phase II: Pilot Roll-Out, 2001–2005

The initial segment of this phase addressed the operationalization of the remaining three clusters within the pilot domain, one in Westmoreland and two in St Elizabeth. The main activities for resource development and management were informed by those in Phase I, and saw to human resource development as well as physical plant upgrade and the equipping of centres of excellence at the rate of one per each of the remaining ten schools. In like manner, as in pilot-in-pilot albeit with recommended adjustments, 10 centres of excellence were established and operationalized.

The second segment of the phase addressed the development and operationalization of 33 centres of excellence throughout all five clusters, as reckoned by the optimal mix of TVET programmes. The assignment of programmes to schools was advised by analyses of schools consultative committees' (SCCs) feedback. This work was ongoing and lasted even beyond the official life of the pilot due to several debilitating circumstances, chiefly:

1. Negative public attitudes towards TVET, which led to prolonged resistance to the process;
2. Absence of a policy to give authority to pilot proceedings for expeditious execution;
3. Uncertainty in the flow of funding, accompanied by attendant bureaucratic delays;
4. Identifying and refurbishing existing plant, which seemed more tedious for contractors than establishing new buildings for work laboratories;
5. The emergence of new procurement measures, which required bidding exercises for all levels of expertise in construction and for all suppliers of goods and equipment.

Replication I: The Corporate Area, 2004

The Replication 1 involved 15 high schools in West-Central Kingston and Western St Andrew. By then, the established operating model of the pilot became known as "Home-School to Lab-School Cluster Model", thus the 15 Corporate Area schools were grouped into three geographic clusters of five schools each, and the optimal mix was kept at 10 TVET programmes to be developed and hosted within each of the three clusters for intra-cluster sharing. Conferences, seminars, retreats and meetings similar to those held during pilot-in-pilot were held with key stakeholders, for purposes of sensitization and upgrading. Importantly, whereas the study tours for pilot-in-pilot involved a sample of school principals travelling to the rationalized system in Oklahoma, USA, at this stage, the study tour involved a sample of principals travelling to the rationalized pilot domain in Westmoreland and St Elizabeth, Jamaica.

Embarking on this phase of the pilot project proved most valuable to the introduction of a policy, as it revealed challenges in addition to those already encountered. Significant challenges were stakeholders' misgivings concerning:

1. Legality of commuting students.
2. Special insurance for students.
3. Safety of commuting students, especially in vicinities of social tension.
4. The necessity to consult with political representatives in some cases.
5. The necessity to consult with the Mayor of the Kingston and St Andrew Corporation (KSAC).
6. Weakening the autonomy of church/trust-schools.
7. Fears regarding the erosion of single-sex schools.

In respect of these and other issues, resistance was so strong in five schools that the Ministry relented and directed that those be omitted from practical participation. The issues were addressed in some measure; however, their occurrence pointed not only to the need for a national TVET policy, but also to the need for administrators of schools and officers of the MoE to be upgraded in Change Management and Transformational Leadership skills. The extent of differences seen in this regard was said to have prompted Ministry officials to deem this segment 'the urban pilot'. While conferences, seminars, retreats and meetings were being held with urban stakeholders for purposes of sensitization and leadership upgrading, the first draft of a policy position paper was presented in 2005, leading to a draft policy concept in 2007 and, finally, the National Policy on TVET in 2014.

OTHER IMPORTANT DEVELOPMENTS

1. **Implementation Plan for Mainstreaming TVET in Schools.** During the continuation of capital works, and procurement and operationalization within the project overall, the directive for the development of a Strategic Plan towards refinement of and mainstreaming the process was made by the Ministry of Education. A special focus group was formed by inviting persons from the Education Transformation Team (ETT), the Ministry of Labour and Social Security (MLSS), the Private Sector of Jamaica (PSOJ), the Trade Union alliance, the Tourism sector and the Jamaica Employers' Federation (JEF). Based on the strategy, a subsequent assignment for the project staff and consulting team to furnish an implementation plan that would advance and stabilize the process was fulfilled and culminated in the drafting of the Roadmap for Mainstreaming TVET in Jamaican Public High Schools 2010–2014. Implementers worked on the derivation of this plan, which was finally prepared and submitted by the Facilitation and Consultancy Training Services (FACTS) Limited in 2009. The Roadmap detailed the major tasks for mainstreaming TVET in the secondary school system and gave a full breakdown of activities and costs, while pointing to social benefits and elements for avoidance. The Log Frame methodology employed was very useful as it facilitated the production of an iterative model for operations (Table 3.1).

2. **Merger With Related Projects.** Subsequent strategies for the merger of this and related projects, such as the Technical High Schools Development Project (THSDP) and the Career Advancement Programme (CAP), were approached as all bore in mind the complementarities between TVET and General Education subjects.

3. **Connecting With the Region.** The pilot project was said to have fostered regional appeal when the Organization of American States (OAS), enthused by an Inter-American Development Bank (IDB) evaluation of the pilot, launched a special hemispheric project for the CARICOM sub-region. The project (2006–2009), was slated to introduce TVET in schools within the region. The Director of the TVET Rationalization in Secondary Schools pilot was named Country Representative and, over the period, was invited to share strategies and progress reports with the

Table 3.1: Iterative Operation Model for 10 Parishes (Roadmap for Mainstreaming 2009)

Mainstreaming – PART A	Mainstreaming – PART B
Planning & Implementation	*Planning & Implementation*
Indirect Activities (Mostly Ongoing)	*Indirect Activities (Mostly Ongoing)*
1. TVET Mainstreaming Policy approved	1. TVET Mainstreaming Policy approved
2. TVET Mainstreaming Policy promulgated	2. TVET Mainstreaming Policy promulgated
3. Sourcing of funds	3. Sourcing of funds
4. TVET Mainstreaming Organization Structure established	4. TVET Mainstreaming Organization Structure established
5. Effective Marketing & Promotion Programmes implemented	5. Effective Marketing & Promotion Programmes implemented
6. Consensus Building and Team Development Seminars in all clusters	6. Consensus Building and Team Development Seminars in all clusters.
7. Institutional capacity building. Direct Activities (Mostly scheduled) Parishes: Clarendon (7), St James (11), Portland (7), St Ann (8), St Mary (9)	7. Institutional capacity building. Direct Activities (Mostly scheduled) Parishes: Manchester (11), Clarendon (12), St Catherine (22), Portland (5), St Thomas (6).
8. Mobilization for TVET mainstreaming	8. Mobilization for TVET mainstreaming
9. Fact finding visits for data analysis	9. Fact finding visits for data analysis
10. Physical upgrade, tooling & equipping	10. Physical upgrade, tooling & equipping
11. Laboratory equipment maintenance	11. Laboratory equipment maintenance
12. Staffing for laboratories	12. Staffing for laboratories
13. Establish cluster operations	13. Establish cluster operations

rest of the 14 countries within the sub-region. The Pilot Director was also invited to make a presentation focussing on the pilot to the Caribbean Association of Principals of Secondary Schools (CAPSS), at the 21st Biennial Conference in Barbados in 2007. The principals' resolution was moved to embark on the path to introduce TVET as a viable option in their schools' curricula. An early presentation to the International Vocational Education and Training Association (IVETA) Conference, in 2001, introduced the pilot, its aim, objectives and principles. This was also regarded as being germane, since it was held in the region (Montego Bay) and, beside heavy international presence, regional representation was significant.

4. **Portfolio Analysis Outcome.** In a subsequent case study of the pilot, the status of the intervention was demonstrated by way of portfolio analysis as advised by Heitmann (1996). According to Powell (2014):

> For this study, portfolio analysis was carried out on a sub-set of the Jamaican formal subsystem which was the rural/urban pilot domain.... the sample represented 17% of the population; the entire range of school types was found within the sample; and the sample spanned the rural-urban mix.... The analysis proved to be an interesting and creative method... to advance recommendations in respect of policy development and expenditure. (p. 125)

The portfolio analysis served to summarize much of the findings as it addressed the major themes identified by way of stakeholders' feedback: internal efficiency and external productivity of the pilot project. After identification of themes, variables and indicators, careful analysis of weightings resulted in findings which showed that the internal efficiency or the pilot condition received a high rating of 86%, while the external productivity or labour market orientation received a low rating of 39% (Table 3.2). In other words, the Ministry's and implementers' inputs and resources were adequate and bore fruit to a great extent. However, little time, resources and effort were afforded in gaining recognition and buy-in from the wider Jamaican society. Owing to the fact that TVET bears much of the ingredients to promote national economic development, the government should garner advice from the analysis in regard to future effort and expenditure.

5. **External Examinations.** Each year, Grade 11 students sat external examinations in TVET. These were fielded by the NCTVET and CXC whose exams were the National Vocational Qualifications of Jamaica (NVQJ) and Caribbean Secondary Examination Certificate (CSEC), respectively. In comparing exam data over a six-year period (Table 3.3), Powell concluded, "Interestingly, according to the documents, CSEC though not showing significant differences in entries and successes throughout those years retained more than three times the number of entries and successes of the NVQJ" (p. 236).

Table 3.2: Rating the Pilot Condition and labour Market Orientation Variables According to Indicator Scores

Variable	Indicator	Score	Variable	Indicator	Score
Sub-System Condition	Quality and condition of TVET		Labour Market Orientation	Government TVET policy and objectives	0.15
	Training programmes	2		Qualification needs and manpower distribution	1
	Curricula	2		Attitudes of firms/organizations towards TVET	0.25
	Textbooks	1.5		Employment of graduates in posts corresponding to their training	0.17
	Education principles	1			
	Equipment	2			
	Physical plant	1			
	Training of teachers and instructors Diplomas/degrees	0.71			
	Career guidance	1			
		11.21/13			1.57/4
	Rating	86% High		Rating	39% Low

Table 3.3: Comparative Exam Data: CSEC & NVQ, 2000–2007

Year	CSEC		NVQJ		Totals		Pass
	Entries	Passes	Entries	Passes	Entries	Passes	%
2001	572	423	37	30	609	453	74.4
2002	772	455	123	96	895	551	61.6
2004	432	255	153	109	585	364	62.2
2005	372	282	165	124	537	406	75.6
2006	539	434	122	85	661	519	78.5
2007	482	406	444	146	926	552	59.6

CONCLUSION

Powell (2014) opined that, contrary to popular belief that returns on investment (RIOs) can only be measured in dollars and cents, measurement is also effected by way of the enduring non-monetary valuables brought to bear on a society's cultural, socio-political and ethical status. The TVET Rationalization Project brought a new look at the way in which curriculum could be designed in order to advance the nation's Human Resources standards; it also pointed the way to greater efficiencies in successfully addressing the HR status, and should be lauded for these returns. In listing some other considerations for recognition, Powell averred: "The investment in such a project had been far-reaching and should never be regretted" (p, 175). The Researchers' list of significant returns included:

1. Initiation of the formulation of a policy for TVET – seen in the policy concept paper Towards a Policy for TVET in Jamaican High Schools (November 2010).
2. Initiation of the effective synergizing of action within the National TVET system, chiefly the Ministry of Education, HEART Trust/NTA and secondary schools.
3. Unearthing the benefits of enhanced social interchange among individuals and institutions (staff, students, schools and community groups).
4. Fostering regional appeal: The OAS, enthused by the IDB evaluation of the pilot project, launched a special hemispheric project to introduce TVET in schools within the region (2006–2009).
5. Promoting the establishment of complementarities between the academics and TVET: Munro College, Manning's, and Hampton Traditional High Schools' successful experiences.
6. Instilling cost effectiveness and efficiencies in the secondary system: sharing human and material resources among schools in a cluster.
7. Providing a sample of good practices in TVET for the formal system: obviating the need to travel abroad for examples, as done through a study tour to Oklahoma during the early days of piloting.
8. Formulation of Strategic and Implementation Plans for national roll-out [2010–2015], (pp. 175–176).

Based on recommendations emanating from the TVET Rationalization pilot experience, there is still much more to be pursued by the Government of Jamaica in advancing human resource development, certainly by strengthening work-based learning from the level of the school. Fortunately, the pilot-initiated National Policy for TVET is now a reality and, from this lead, much can be facilitated, since it is argued that, in the absence of a policy for TVET, any action to foster enhancement of external productivity would be futile. It is hoped that further research, consistent with the times, will be pursued in order to ratify measures to be employed in integrating TVET into schools' curricula and, by extension, into the national and regional psyche.

BIBLIOGRAPHY

Boston, K. (2005). *How to draw vocational qualifications into secondary education. Shaping TVET to meet labor market needs.* http://www.tvetcouncil.com.bb/events_secondary.html

Chang, H. G. (2009). "The Reform of the TVET System in the Republic of Korea for an Ageing Society". In R. Maclean, D. Wilson, (Eds.), *International Handbook of Education for the Changing World of Work* (pp. 2,431–2,444). Springer. https://doi.org/10.1007/978-1-4020-5281-1_160

Heitmann, W. (1996, December). "Development of a Portfolio Concept in Sstrategic Technical Education and Vocational Training Planning". Paper presented at Cincinnati Convention Centre.

Miles, M. & Huberman, A. (1994). *Qualitative Data Analysis: An Expanded Sourcebook* (2nd ed.) Sage.

Morris, H. (1998). Technical and vocational education at the secondary level in Jamaica. *Institute of Education Annual, 1,* 110–127. https://www.mona.uwi.edu/soe/publications/institute-education-annual/article/1440

Morris, H. & Powell, C. (2013). Delivering TVET at the secondary level: A practical approach. *Caribbean Curriculum, 21,* 1–18. https://journals.sta.uwi.edu/ojs/index.php/cc/article/view/542/474

Powell, C. (2008). *Establishing Complementarities at Grades 10–11.* Unpublished manuscript, Ministry of Education.

Powell, C. (2014). *Towards a Model for Engaging the Jamaican Secondary Schools in Efficient Delivery of TVET* [Unpublished doctoral dissertation]. University of the West Indies, Mona.

Taeck-Duck, K. (1994). *The role and function of vocational education and training in the new economic plan in Korea. Case studies on Technical and Vocational Education in Asia and the Pacific.* UNESCO, UNEVOC.

UNESCO (1993). *Country report: Jamaica.*

UNESCO (2013). *Expanding TVET at the Secondary Education Level.* Asia-Pacific Education System Review Series No. 7. https://unesdoc.unesco.org/ark:/48223/pf0000226220

Whiteman, B. (1992). *Development in Jamaica's TVET system.* Ministry of Education and Culture.

CHAPTER 4

The Toolmaker's Institute, Supporting the Jamaican Industrial Manufacturing Sector
Achievements, Impacts and Challenges

CHRISTOPHER O'COY BRYAN

THIS CHAPTER AIMS TO ASSESS THE ACHIEVEMENTS, impacts and challenges of the Toolmaker's Institute, (now the National Tool and Engineering Institute (NTEI), since its establishment in regard to its objectives in the Jamaican industrial sector and with specific emphasis on the period from 1969 to 1984. Of primary focus is the juxtaposition of the rivalry between the distributive trade and the manufacturing sector, taking into account the transformation of the global economy and the performance of the Jamaican economy over the period.

The chapter reveals that Jamaica's industrial development was a credible model. This model, however, was not sustainable due primarily to national issues such as the lack of a skilled labour force, the high national debt burden, and the rapid decline in foreign exchange reserves, among other things. These factors also exacerbated the dilemma of low productivity in the manufacturing sector, which stifled or overshadowed the contribution of the Toolmaker's Institute to the manufacturing sector. The most stunning of all the findings was the fast pace of the implementation of policies and decision-making. This occurred without a proper management framework for the cohesion and control of the interaction of technical, economic, and social issues. These are complex when they stand alone and moreso when interrelated and have impacted many stakeholders of the Government, such as the opposing political party, academia, importers, manufacturers, lenders, international agencies and foreign states.

The result of those complexities provided challenges to the overall success of the Toolmaker's Institute in meeting its mandate of providing competency training for toolmakers and maintainers of the manufacturing sector, and to improve and maintain the productivity levels desired for world-class productivity and competitiveness. Government spending was limited or scarce; therefore, funding the Institute was rationed, resulting in a scaling down of direct and indirect programmes. Social tension also detracted focus and buried the gains of the Toolmaker's Institute to the economy. But, despite the issues and challenges, significant achievements were made in technology transfer, development of sustainable infrastructure, and the training and development of some of Jamaica's finest craftsmen toolmakers – some of whom became manufacturers in today's economy. Unfortunately, no economic data was available to quantify the contribution of the Toolmaker's Institute to the Gross Domestic Product (GDP) throughout the 15-year period, although it is certain that it contributed to the growth of many small, medium and large manufacturers, present and past.

BACKGROUND

Jamaica aspired to be one of the world's most respected and attractive economies through the creation of value from its physical and human resources. As a result, following the 1943 population census, the Central Planning Unit (CPU, 1955) was formed and, by January 1958, the National Plan for the years 1957 to 1967 was published and operationalized, starting in April 1957. This was primarily to transform the economy from an agricultural-based economy into an increasingly industrial society, which would include some diversified manufacturing of goods such as sugar, condensed milk, rum, edible oils, cloth carpet, cigarettes, and shoes. Adding to the GDP was the production of heavier industrial goods, such as sulfuric acid, detergents, fertilizers, gasoline, petroleum, batteries,

Portland cement, light bulbs and steel. This initiative gave birth to the Industrial Development Corporation Law, Cap 160 and the policy which subsequently piloted the manufacturing sector under the office of the Jamaica Industrial Development Corporation (JIDC).

In parallel, Jamaica has a long tradition of providing training in Technical Vocational Education and Training (TVET) to the local workforce and, in the last 60 to 70 years, the demand for a technical workforce showed significant changes due to developments in various sectors of the Jamaican economy, including manufacturing. The maturing manufacturing-based economy justified the need for a mature and progressive TVET training system that was based on a clear and specific strategy to provide resource support in labour productivity, skilled craftsmen, and maintenance to the manufacturing sector to fulfil the mandate of the policy which was intended to reduce Jamaica's import bill through the model import substitution, which was the focus of the Industrial Development Corporation Law, Cap 160. Consequently, the Jamaica Industrial Development Corporation was formed and projects were established to aid in the delivery of the mandate. The Government of Jamaica made its request official in March 1966 to the United Nations Development Programme (UNDP) for assistance to establish the Productivity Centre within the JIDC. This project was declared operational for a period of five years between December 27, 1966, and December 31, 1971. According to Black (1976), the JIDC was organized to perform a variety of functions through principal divisions and departments namely, the Planning and Research Division, and The Productivity Centre and Industrial Service Division, which was further subdivided into smaller units like the Toolmaker's Institute and the Training Department. The move demonstrated positive support to the industrial sector, which was rapidly increasing in a variety of industries in the manufacturing sector. This was corroborated up to the 1980's and, according to Ayub (1981), the most striking feature of the manufacturing sector of Jamaica was that it was relatively varied for a country of just over two million inhabitants.

UNDP/ JIDC PRODUCTIVITY CENTRE PARTNERSHIP PROJECT

The manufacturing sector grew rapidly in relation to the rest of the economy and, by 1950, the sector was accounting for 11.3 per cent of GDP, a share which increased steadily to 18.2 per cent by 1977 (Ayub, 1981). Based on the response to the import substitution strategy of industrializing by invitation, the JIDC provided consultancy, technical training and support for the manufacturing sector. One primary project was the establishment of the Productivity Centre and Industrial Services Division to include the Toolmakers Institute as the premier training facility for technical skills, with support from UNDP and the United Nations Industrial Development Organization (UNIDO) in 1972 (Ministry Paper No. 25, 1976, p. 4).

According to the report on the Productivity Centre, Phase 2 (International Labour Organization [ILO], 1976), in March 1966, the Government of Jamaica made an official request to the UNDP for assistance in establishing a Productivity Centre within the JIDC as an expansion of its Industrial Services Division. The plan of operation was signed on October 28, 1966, and phase 1 of the project was declared operational on December 27, 1966 with a cut-off date of December 31, 1971. The objective of the project was to achieve effectiveness in the five years of operation. The project was intended to concentrate on a selected number of growth-potential industries with the capability to make a significant contribution to the national economy and, simultaneously, provide increased employment opportunities. The plan of operation provided for a partnership between the Government of Jamaica with a contribution of US$1,949,684, and a UNDP contribution of US$968,200. At the end of the phase 1, April to May 1971, the government sought an extension of the project through supplementary assistance from the UNDP and the ILO to improve the performance of the National Productivity Centre. Phase 2 was approved in January 1972. The project revision for the supplementary assistance project was signed by the Government on April 11, 1974, by the ILO on July 3, 1974, and by the UNDP on September 24, 1974 with the specific objectives:

1. To initiate a capability for training and developing management consultants;
2. To ensure that this capability can be maintained by national counterpart staff after completion of the supplementary assistance;
3. To raise the operating skills of the Centre's staff by additional guidance, both in-depth and in a variety of techniques;
4. To publicize and promote industrial productivity in Jamaica with a view to increasing the level of productivity in industry.

Phase 2 of the project commenced in January 1972 with a cut-off date of December 31, 1975. The total combined project cost from December 1966 to December 1975 for phase 1 and 2 was approximately US$5.2 million, with the Government of Jamaica funding approximately 70% of the cost. Government's contribution was drawn from duties and taxes from manufacturers and their employees.

The garment industry was the main focus of phase 2. While the ILO report (1976) reported the closing date for the project as December 1975, Ministry Paper no. 25 (1976) which reported on the work of the JIDC for the year 1975 to 1976, stated that "the operation of this project has ably assisted with equipment and expert personnel by the UNDP. Their involvement came to an end in October 1975". The ILO report also indicated that there was doubt in its findings about the national staff operating the Productivity Centre onwards from 1975 and stated:

> The interim report of the first phase of the project concluded, inter alia, that "the Productivity Centre and Things Jamaican Ltd., have been set up as viable institutions, in terms of organisation, physical facilities and numbers and competence of staff, although some further assistance is still required in certain areas. (ILO, 1976)

After phase 1, doubts were ascribed to the success of phase 2. The report stated that developments during the period 1972–75 required further consideration in regard to the actual viability of the Productivity Centre, particularly regarding its ability to operate efficiently on its own at the end of phase 2 in 1975. The Productivity Centre was the parent of the Toolmaker's Institute and problems associated with the second phase of the project would automatically affect the viability of operations at the

Toolmaker's Institute. While the mandate of the Productivity Centre was to concentrate on formal training programmes and consultancy assignments, it did not exist solely for the purpose of developing its staff, but also to discharge its responsibilities to assist Jamaican industry and commerce. This mandate was not fully achieved due to problems such as reduction in staff, high staff turnover, low recruitment of qualified counterpart staff, and unattractive wages resulting from the wage restriction imposed by the Government. The reduction in the number of counterpart staff seriously affected the full achievement of the goals of the project and, in January 1975, the situation was very serious. Fortunately, during the first months of 1975, for the first time in the past two years, three new counterparts of a high level were engaged and the policy of making frequent transfers seemed to have been modified (ILO, 1976). Problems arising from a shortfall of staff were also due to a considerable delay in the selection and appointment of experts during 1972. Another major problem was the inability to agree on a project manager, a problem which remained unsolved until nearly mid-1973. During the first half of 1973, several senior counterparts were transferred to line management positions in subsidiary companies of the JIDC which were experiencing development and managerial problems. Moreover, new recruits could not be attracted to the Productivity Centre because of salary restrictions imposed by the Government. Clearly, there were significant economic challenges in the economy.

A summary account from the report concluded that although the Productivity Centre was not yet fully viable, it had the potential to become viable if the Government took the appropriate actions to correct shortcomings, particularly in regard to the extension of trained counterpart staff and the recruitment of additional staff. While there were merits to the programme and the Productivity Centre, there were scepticism and drawback echoed in some parts of society about the operations. According to the ILO's (1976) findings, the structure wherein the Productivity Centre was a part of the JIDC inhibits the recruitment of additional well-qualified personnel; does not readily provide suitable career opportunities for staff; does not encourage the Centre to be self-financing; and confused clients as to the true purpose of the Centre, which was sometimes regarded as a governmental investigative agency.

Economic Challenges

Coupled with the internal issues of the Productivity Centre were difficulties stemming from severe economic problems due to loss of foreign exchange, security and social issues. As early as 1972 and 10 months after the General Elections, according to the Minister of Finance (Core,1972), the Government presented detailed analyses of the structural weaknesses of the Jamaican economy and a corrective plan of action to the Legislature and the country. The analyses briefly showed that, while the main outward manifestation was the continued loss of foreign reserves, the basic problem had been the inability or failure of the economy to produce the goods and services which were demanded by the private sector (including personal consumption), and the Government. Over the five years to December 1971, this excess demand on the economy amounted to J$504 million and, for 1972, the excess was between J$150 million and J$170 million. Up to December 1971, the excess was fully met by foreign capital inflows. For 1972, the excess was accommodated by running down reserves by approximately J$50 million.

The Government implemented policies to address the economic growth and establish new par value for the Jamaican dollar. The action plan included stemming the drain on reserves. Failure to halt the fall would have resulted in defaults on the payment of foreign liabilities, both in the private and public sectors. The inability to borrow from abroad and the drying up of further foreign private investment and restrictions on consumption were so severe (simply because of the inability to pay for imports) that serious hardship would have been caused at all levels of the society (Ministry Paper No.1, 1973). One precondition of success, however, was increasing local production so that a competitive edge can be given to local producing entities over imports, and providing incentives to exports. It was felt by the Government that the uncompetitive position of locally produced goods *vis-a-vis* imports, can be demonstrated whenever incomes were increased either by bank credit or through the budget. The increased incomes were spent largely on imported goods rather than on locally produced goods. In other words, efforts to stimulate the economy by budgetary action or by credit merely exacerbated external payment problems. Local production was not effectively stimulated. Whether this disparity in competitiveness was caused by low productivity, poor technology or tastes and attitudes of the Jamaican consumers, the simple fact was that it existed and meant that local costs were out of line with foreign costs, as was reflected in the exchange rate. The most effective way to adjust this relationship between local costs and foreign prices was to adjust the exchange rate. On the other hand, the protection provided by the quantitative restrictions and other trade policies was heavily biased towards import-substitution and discouraged exports of manufactured goods (Ayub, 1981). The new par value implied a devaluation of the Jamaican dollar in 1973 of about 13 per cent. At the same time, after 1973, the inflation rate in Jamaica increased rapidly, compared with its main trading partners, fuelled mainly by oil price increases and large wage demands.

According to Ayub (1981), the payrolls of firms as a proportion of wages and salaries paid in the manufacturing sector under the incentive schemes, grew from 1.3 per cent in 1965 to 23.5 per cent in 1973. If this increase had been reflected in the relation of the tax liability of these incentives companies to the taxes actually paid by all companies, the figure would have risen to at least J$5 million. He noted that the figure was almost certainly underestimated. The total number of firms approved and operating declined from 246 in 1974 to 73 in 1978. On this basis, the total revenues forgone under the incentives schemes is estimated at J$6 million to J$7 million. It could be concluded that the Government was losing income from tax-evading companies. This, in turn, affected the operations of the Productivity Centre directly and caused some manufacturers and importers to speculate that the Centre acted as a tax administration investigative agency, and were therefore not willing to open up to the services offered. The investigation also revealed that the Government lost revenue due to uncoordinated approach between government agencies or a lack of monitoring of firms operating under the incentive laws. Consequently, there was recommendation for coordination between the various government agencies (eg., the Ministry of Industry and Commerce, the JIDC, and the Income Tax and Collector General's Departments) to ensure that the costs and benefits of these schemes were evaluated on a continuous basis.

Security and Social Challenges

Social tension throughout the society was increasing during the period when importation was being restricted while, at the same time, the Government was appealing for cooperation from the nationals. In order to control the escalating tension and national security threat, a State of Emergency was implemented. On Saturday, June 19, 1976, the Governor-General, acting on the advice of the Government, declared a State of Public Emergency for a period of one month. This was, however, extended by the House of Representatives three times to last up to June 30, 1977, a total of 377 days. The General Election was held in December of 1976, and this further derailed the operations of the JIDC and its subsidiaries, including the Toolmaker's Institute. Participants in the programme could not attend training nor work in the normal way. Most companies could only operate in the daylight hours or provide security and transportation for staff at an added cost to the operations and at a lower rate of production. Progressive training, recruitment and selection were hampered at the training facilities located in the volatile community of Kingston 11, the industrial 'belt'. Ayub (1981), reported that a few garment, textile, and electrical appliance firms operated two shifts. There were some food-processing industries that operated three shifts, which produced perishables. Three-shift work was also carried out in some subsectors such as cement, where the high costs of shutting down and starting up appeared to dominate other considerations. The premium for overtime work was typically 50 per cent for weekdays and Saturdays and 100 per cent for Sundays and public holidays, although there was some variation between and within the subsectors. The premium for night shift varied between J$0.15 and J$0.25 an hour, determined generally by union agreements and management. As already mentioned, other factors such as problems of security for nightshift workers annulled some of the incentives for the shift, even when demand existed. Many firms employing three shifts said that recruiting workers for the third shift (11:00 p.m.–7:00 a.m.) was extremely difficult and absenteeism on that shift was very high. Ayub (1981) concluded that long-term factors leading to the existence of excess manufacturing capacity were related to the pattern of incentives provided to the firms in the past as well as to more specific factors such as crime, improper lighting, inadequate transport, and so forth, all making the use of second and third shifts impractical or unprofitable or both. Ayub (1981) further stated that, over the preceding years, the shortage of imported raw materials and insufficient domestic demand were the predominant factors. One of the specific reasons for the excess capacity in certain subsectors had been the restrictive nature of some of the licensing agreements of the franchised firms.

The State of Emergency was enforced, and two national elections were called, the General Elections held in December 1976 and the Local Government Elections held in March 1977. Simultaneously, political tension was high and significant escalation in the incidence of crimes and violence involving the use of firearms was occurring. Those incidences were believed to have been mainly politically motivated. Statistics from the review of the State of Emergency revealed that, during the period, some 3,039 violent crimes had been reported, of which 1,968 involved the use of firearms; 130 were gun-related murders; over 1,000 armed robberies were committed; and there were over 540 incidents of shooting (Munn, 1977). Criminal activities assumed new and critical dimensions – they included urban terrorist activities like fire-bombing of properties. These activities were previously unknown to Jamaica. Several citizens, including prominent businessmen, politicians, workers, trade unionists and even trainees who were alleged to be threats to the national security, were detained at "Wire Fence" and "Red Fence" at Up Park Camp. The Honourable Pearnel Charles, then Speaker of the House of Representatives, spent 283 days in detention during the State of Emergency. This event led many Jamaicans to oppose any effort by the Government to recover the economy and to avoid any association with government programmes due to fear of being labelled. The Government reiterated that its main focus was to recover the confidence of the people and improve the economy (Munn, 1977).

PLAN FOR ECONOMIC RECOVERY

By 1977, after four and a half years of the operation of the Toolmaker's Institute in supporting the manufacturing sector, the chronic decline in the sector was evident amidst the social tension and major economic downturn. According to Ayub (1981), the distributive trade regained first place in the economy by a small margin. However, the data showed that the manufacturing sector was always trailing the distributive sector, though the gap between both sectors for a margin of contribution to national productivity was constantly narrowing from 1950 to 1978. In 1950, manufacturing accounted for 11.3 per cent of GDP, a share which increased steadily to 15.7 per cent in 1970 and to 18.2 per cent by 1977. By the latter years, manufacturing had become the largest sector in terms of its contribution to GDP but, in 1978, distributive trade once again regained its status with 17.1 per cent in comparison to the manufacturing sector's 16.9 per cent contribution to GDP (Ayub, 1981), and manufacturing has not regained first place since.

During April of 1979, the Michael Manley Government announced an economic recovery plan designed in consultation with stakeholders from the private sector, public sector, trade unions, employers and the labour force. The presentation reviewed the state of the economy, referencing the foreign exchange crisis of 1977 and 1978 and the expected outcomes of economic policies. The overall plan was supported by the International Monetary Fund (IMF), signalled by the agreement of April 1977 between the Government and the IMF for the sum of US$74.6 million to cover the areas of income policy, fiscal policy, balance of payments, exchange control and exchange rate policy. Although there was an agreement, there were outstanding issues. The policies of the Government included the reduction of the level of consumption, which could be supported by the available local and imported resources; restrictions on importation; a rapid but controlled increase in prices; and a change in the exchange rate to achieve a reduction in consumption as well as to restore the competitiveness and profitability of local industry. The economic package policies were presented as being successful in achieving its objectives and showed that the country survived the turmoil of 1977 and 1978 without destruction of the social fabric and without sacrifice of the fundamental rights and freedoms of the people. In admitting that there was social tension caused by the decision, Manley stated:

> The nation, particularly the poor, has had to make tremendous sacrifices in terms of living standards, and the pressure of these sacrifices has, not surprisingly, led to a sense of national discouragement and a heightening of social tensions. (Manley, 1979)

By June of the same year and while the economic recovery plan was still in its infancy, the nation was hit by a massive flood bill. The natural disaster hit the western end of the island affecting approximately 16,000 persons in the parishes of St James, Hanover, Westmoreland and St Elizabeth. This also affected production in JIDC facilities in those regions and indirectly affected the service of the Toolmaker's Institute.

During the same period, and arising from the UNDP/ILO recommendations, the role and function of the JIDC was significantly modified. JIDC's role was now to achieve a more effective and streamlined research, planning, implementation and promotion of industrial development, as well as re-definition and rationalization of the functions between the JIDC and the Ministry of Industry and Commerce. This required the Corporation to concentrate on essentially technical areas of industrial development. It was stated that training of Toolmakers and Repair and Maintenance Technicians continued to be a key function of the JIDC, but the report to Parliament did not discuss the performance or projected future of the Toolmaker's Institute. The report, however, mentioned activities surrounding management, consultancy and training. While the JIDC continued to operate in the new form, and companies tried to expand production in the manufacturing sector, one of the largest hindrances identified was the shortage of skilled manpower and this was placed squarely at the feet of the Toolmaker's Institute. The claim of shortage of skilled manpower was supported by Ayub (1981), who indicated that in the tobacco subsector, both the sample firms produced only for markets outside CARICOM. Production was efficient, with zero or negative protection. The largest bottleneck to expansion, however, is the shortage of skilled cigar makers and other skilled manpower.

The economy continued in the downward spiral, while declining social conditions prevailed, even in the face of the government's economic recovery plan. The situation was deemed so bad that the credit worthiness of the state was threatened during 1978 through to early 1980. By this time, conditions were combustible and a spate of violence popped up like land mines all over the country. The link between external debt, economic growth, and a decline in social conditions was now real. In another response to counter the worsening situation, the Government sought to use the budgetary solution, (which it resisted in the preceding years), and restructure the cabinet. For the second time, Jamaica went to the IMF for support of the finance of the 1980 to 1981 budget, even though default on debt repayment in the first programme was looming. The second work plan was based on a programme of improving financial responsibility and, in the address to the nation on February 5, 1980, Prime Minister Manley announced the work plan:

> We have worked out new systems of financial control and these are being put in place as a part of a general restructuring exercise aimed at more efficient government and better management of resources. We have looked at production plans and worked out strategies which are aimed at improving performance in agriculture, industry, tourism and other areas of production. We have to face the reality that the Budget cannot be used to subsidize industries and enterprises, and in some cases, the consuming public.

Cuts in subsidies were made to utility companies, transportation, and the Special Employment Programme as a sacrifice to keep adequate financing for areas such as health, education and security. The government disagreed with the IMF Team regarding their view that developing the 1980/81 budget as a continuation of the 1979/80 recurrent budget, (using inflation), would reduce the budget by J$150 million. The Government made adjustments within J$100 million, but the balance of J$50 million was achieved by the layoff of up to 11,000 employees or further removing subsidies from food, the Jamaica Omnibus Service (JOS), fertilizers, and closing the Jamaica Movement for the Advancement of Adult Literacy (JAMAL). Requiring students at all tertiary educational institutions to pay full tuition fees was a sticking point. To combat the issue, the Government requested a waiver, but the IMF refused. All of this occurred in the midst of a General Election which was eventually held on October 30, 1980, and which the Manley Government lost.

The Edward Seaga Government came into power and in less than six months and Jamaica was granted the Special Drawdown Rights (SDR) of more than J$500 million to support the 1981/82 budget (Seaga, 1981). According to Seaga, the new IMF agreement was formed on the basis of a "desperate state", resulting from the macroeconomic data for the preceding eight years. Gross Domestic Product declined year over year to an absolute of 18 per cent and inflation reached a peak in 1978 when the domestic price reached a 50 per cent high, even though prices still rose to about 30 per cent and unemployment increased to above 30 per cent in 1980. There was substantial decline in investment activities in both the public and private sectors with gross capital formation falling to 13 per cent of GDP by 1979, compared to 25 per cent in 1973. The data indicated that manufacturing was down below 40 per cent; hotel occupancy was 45 per cent of capacity, while utilities and other government services deteriorated to very low levels of efficiency. There was a significant shortage of foreign exchange, which hampered the availability of adequate levels of imports of raw material, spare parts, and equipment required for reasonable economic activity. The priority of the Government then was to promote economic activity, reduce unemployment, restore efficiency in sectors of utility services, improve social and economic infrastructure to support the economic growth strategy (Seaga, 1981). The economy of the world was changing and therefore state governance principles changed to restore the economy, and expansion demanded that management policies were accompanied by activities geared at deregulation and the diversification of the economy (Robinson, 1990). Jamaica encountered a difficult cycle of debt and limited ability to repay, hence investment was discouraged. Uncertainty associated with high debt and the probability of debt relief and/or default reduces investors' incentives and economic growth. Further, high debt service crowded out private investment (Blavy,

2006). It was argued that Jamaica was caught between the ideologies of the USA and the USSR, and Jamaica became a flash point in the Cold War between both superpowers.

There were hopes of an early recovery in the manufacturing sector, and the restoration of programmes such as those provided by the Toolmaker's Institute, with the restoration of confidence in the economy and funding provided by the IMF. In fact, there were optimistic projections of GDP growth of 3 per cent in the financial year 1981/82, 4 per cent in 1982/83, and 5 per cent in 1983/84. According to Robinson (1990), the policy initiatives were taken to deregulate the economy so as to release private initiatives, rebuild confidence, and support the operation of an efficient market economy. The announcement by Seaga (1981) stated, "The activities of the public sector in industrial and commercial operations will be reduced; and the financial operations of the Central Government will ensure that an appropriate share of national resources is retained by the productive sectors". Those activities were met with less than desired success over the period 1981–1983. Inflation moderated to an annual average rate of increase of 7 per cent in this period compared to an annual average of 30 per cent in the latter half of the 1970s, while real GDP grew on average by 1.5 to 2.0 per cent during this period (Robinson, 1990). The recovery, however, proved short-lived and, since then, the umbilical cord between the local manufacturing sector and skills training, with the specific aim of increasing national productivity through the Toolmaker's Institute, was injured and productivity growth in the Jamaican economy was further threatened. The injury never healed, and the manufacturing sector has not recovered. This may explain the case of the Toolmaker's Institute not fulfilling the mandate.

THE JAMAICAN ECONOMY AND LABOUR FORCE TODAY

The Jamaican economy today is heavily dependent on services and the distributive trade, which accounts for more than 70 per cent of the GDP. The country continues to derive most of its foreign exchange from tourism, remittances, and bauxite/alumina. Remittances and tourism each account for 30 per cent of GDP, while bauxite/alumina exports make up roughly 5 per cent of GDP (CIA Fact Book, 2014). Overall, manufacturing contributes approximately 8.3 per cent of GDP (*The Economjc & Social Survey Jamaica [ESSJ]*, 2014).

Before getting into the further discussion about trained labour in manufacturing, it is imperative to set the context of the evolution of the Jamaican economy relative to the evolution of the global economy, which is interrelated. It must be noted that the growth of the Jamaican economy has been predicated on numerous foreign policies since the 1960s, including the Lomé Agreement, the Caribbean Basin Initiative, and the Caribbean Common Market (CARICOM), to name a few. These are highly linked to the external world and therefore any growth policies must factor into the external environment heavily. The Capri Report (2007) captured the essence of the issue when it indicated that, in general, small states' interactions with the external world is conditioned primarily by external variables; therefore, small states are price takers, not price makers, and small states are reactive, not proactive, for example. Therefore, the Jamaica economy is not driven from within, hence is susceptible to the effects of deliberate, direct or indirect action and conditions of trading partners and territories. The truth, though, may lie in the answers to this question: Has Jamaica's foreign policy history taken true account of income-producing properties such as the human resource? It is an established fact that Jamaica is earning from its natural resources, but one can argue that the GDP growth rate could be significantly higher and sustainable if manufacturers were converting more local raw material into final products, intermediate raw material or consumer goods, balanced by the understanding of the correlation of continuing skills training, evolving technology, productivity and trends in global economic shifts and counter measures.

PERFORMANCE OF TOOLMAKER'S INSTITUTE, 1975–1980

In August 1975, 18 Toolmaker graduates were all employed in the industry with accolades from the National Tooling and Machining Association, the governing body in the training of Toolmakers in the USA. The cohort, at the time, stood at 19 second-year students and nine first-year students, while 10 were being recruited for September 1976. The institution earned $19,000.00 by providing services to the industry through the design and manufacture of equipment. The institution also provided advice in the selection of machinery and tools. Knox College introduced a course in Sheet Metal Works as a satellite training institution to Citrad Limited to improve their tooling and productivity. Additionally, 14 trained toolmakers were placed in industry and some operating tool rooms.

National Tool and Die, as the name implies, was established to produce tools, dies, and other specialized equipment for industry. Invoiced sales during the year 1978/79 amounted to $237,000, compared with $150,000 during the previous 11 months of 1977/78. Existing economic conditions adversely affected the operations of this company, but its existence was justified by the assistance which it afforded and what it was capable of doing for industry.

During middle of the 1980's, under the direction of the Jamaica Promotions Corporation (JAMPRO), the Toolmaker's Institute, National Tool and Die, and the Repair and Maintenance Unit were rationalized as part of the general public sector reorganization. This rationalization activity produced two entities of the National Tool and Engineering Institute (NTEI) – a merger of the Toolmaker's Institute and the Repair and Maintenance Unit and the National Tool and Engineering Company (NTEC), the rebranded National Tool and Die. The evolution continued in 1995 when both entities began operating under the management of the HEART Trust/National Training Agency (NTA).

Verbal Account of the Achievements, Impact and Challenges

During the decade of the 70s, there were several factors in the Jamaican economy that stagnated the trend of growth and industrial development seen in the 60s. The introduction of the bauxite levy in 1974, with the intention to collect revenue from the different bauxite companies to develop other manufacturing companies, was an example of this. Smallman (1977) indicated that the bauxite levy resulted in prohibitive growth of the sector as, in Jamaica, the comparative cost of producing bauxite was also the highest internationally. Smallman cited political turmoil and uncertainty as a contributor to a decrease in Jamaica's bauxite shares internationally.

According to Chin-Young (1972), not only did this political uncertainty affect bauxite, but also it affected the development of the manufacturing sector. These manufacturers used the political system to their own benefit through lobbying for tax incentives. The incentives, however, did not prove to be of any advantage to the development of manufacturing, and there was also lobbying for its restructuring to promote true growth in the industrial sector.

A comprehensive insight from Robert Gregory provides a perspective of what led to the demise of the manufacturing industry and, subsequently, the Toolmaker's Institute. He stated:

> . . . around that time the country developed notions of self-reliance and import substitution, therefore, imported finished goods attracted high importation duties in order to protect the local manufacturers. This was an attempt to create a fledgling 'manufacturing industry' which was in essence still an assembling industry. These local manufacturers because of these duties enjoyed a more favourable price for their products locally than their imported counterparts.

He went on to share that because of this protection, local industries became very complacent:

> The initial idea was to give the local manufacturer protection for a time until they reached a level of global competitiveness, after which this protection would be lifted as they are now able to compete. This, however, was not the case – instead the converse took place, as their complacency led to them producing sub-standard goods. This can be attributed to companies not retooling and training their workers as they were satisfied with the 'eating a food' mentality. There was no need to develop beyond the local market as there was no real competition and the owners were making 'ends meet'. When cost of production went up the government would increase the import tariffs on the foreign goods, providing further protection and complacency for the local manufacturers. It is believed that the government did not insist on communicating to companies that the protection was a temporary one thus encouraging them to retool and produce goods at a high quality. They did not insist that companies should benchmark their product with the best in the world. It is the view that most of the government ministers then were insular in their view, thinking 'Jamaica is the world, and the world is Jamaica'. It was the notion then that global

competition was not an issue. This is now the reality where the world is a global market and goods move freely through countries. (R. Gregory, personal communication, April 24, 2014)

Winston Mahfood, who was vying for the presidency of the Jamaica Manufacturers Association (JMA), stated that manufacturers were experiencing problems of high interest rates and financing which cause stagnation in the industry. So the argument that protectionism that manufacturers enjoyed did not give the local manufacturers an edge over their imported counterparts, as their product was of an inferior quality, advanced. Local consumers developed the notion that locally produced goods were inferior, resulting in a greater appetite for foreign goods.

Noel Gray, owner of Graymill Engineering, supported the claim that the Second World War was a factor in Jamaica's move towards the development of a manufacturing sector. He said this was so because the war inhibited exports and imports among a number of countries because of the threat of military attacks. Out of the thrust to manufacture various products, the Jamaica Industrial Development Corporation was formed to create a clear vision for the way forward. During this time, manufacturing was poised for growth (N. Gray, personal communication, May 14, 2014).

CONCLUSION

There has been a decline in the country's productivity since the 1960s and, in the 1970s, the low growth cycle became more pronounced. This was corroborated by the Jamaica Productivity Summary Report 1972 to 2007 which showed that real GDP for the period 1972 to 2007 grew by 0.5 per cent, while labour productivity or output per worker declined by an average rate of 1.3 per cent per annum over 30 years. While the decade of the 70s was terrible, some economic focus groups attributed the underperformance to poor financial management, high debt, high inflation, increase in the exchange rate, and exogenous factors such as the oil crisis; world political instability; a decrease in the demand for alumina on the world market; and the local political climate. While Total Factor Productivity (TFP) in Jamaica was growing above the world and regional averages in the 1960s, since the 1970s, performance collapsed despite investments. This has been attributed to the spread of low productivity across the economy. Estimations for 1992–2008 show that labour productivity was negative in eight of 10 sectors, and it was positive but negligible in the sectors for communication services, manufacturing and transport. Jamaica's TFP per worker also lagged behind significantly in most other countries in the Latin America and the Caribbean (LAC) region (World Bank, 2011, p.5).

The main issues that affected the performance of the Toolmaker's Institute stemmed from macroeconomic issues and, in general, the poor social and economic conditions of the country and, more specifically, the lack of funding throughout the period of review. These issues were multi-dimensional, and the most prominent was the cynicism of the manufacturers towards the Productivity Centre acting as a tax investigative agency, which was the parent of the Institute. The reduced funding stream caused premature termination, high staff turnover, and low recruitment of qualified staff. Reducing foreign currency reserves and increasing the debt burden forced the Government to rationalize funding and therefore staffing was not optimal. Other significant debilitating factors included the rising tension in the society due to the State of Emergency which resulted from efforts to control crime and violence during the 1976/77 period. The heightened and out-of-control violence of the period crippled economic activity to the extent that the programme of the Toolmaker's Institute was stalled. The change in administration and policy objectives in a deregulated economy facilitated greater importation of finished goods and reduced the importance of training skilled labour. Thus the Toolmaker's Institute lost its prominence and momentum in the manufacturing industry during the first period of the 1980s.

One of the main challenges observed was the lack of synergy in government institutions to protect the revenue as doubts were raised about the earnings from companies operating under the incentives law, due to the inability to track sources. Tax administration and governance significantly improved over the years, therefore the viability of the institution was not an immediate threat.

By all accounts, the Toolmaker's Institute can boast several achievements. Chief among them is achieving its primary mandate of providing technically trained labour resources for the manufacturing sector. It has a robust and sustainable infrastructure and attracted bipartisan support because of its growth inducement potential. Though the skills-training opportunities offered today at the now National Tools and Engineering Institute are more varied with less focus on tool and die making, it has remained an iconic skills-training facility which produced noteworthy toolmakers and manufactures in the 1970s and 80s.

BIBLIOGRAPHY

Ayub, A. M. (1981). *Made in Jamaica: The development of the manufacturing sector OCP31*. Johns Hopkins University.

Black, V. (1976). *Ministry of Industry and Commerce: Ministry Paper No. 25, 1976.* http://www.nlj.gov.jm/MinistryPapers/1976/25.pdf

Blavy (2006). *Public debt and productivity: The difficult quest for growth in Jamaica. IMF Working Paper. WP/06/235*.

Caribbean Policy Research Institute. (2007). *Jamaica's foreign policy: Making the economic development link*. https://www.capricaribbean.org/archive/200706

Canadian International Development Agency. (2012). *National Tool & Engineering Institute Jamaica – Renewable energy. August 2012. Ref CAR-02*. https://docplayer.net/51048629-National-tool-engineering-institute-jamaica-renewable-energy.html

Charles, P. (1977). *Detained: 283 days in Jamaica's detention camp, struggling for freedom, justice, and human rights!* https://original-ufdc.uflib.ufl.edu/AA00030299/00001/1j

Core D. H. (1973). *Ministry of Finance. Ministry Paper No. 1, 1973.*

Core D. H. (1977). *IMF agreement. Ministry of Finance. Ministry Paper No. 28, 1977.* File No. 406/02.

International Labour Organization. (1976). *Productivity centre (Phase 11) JAM/66/507. Jamaica, project findings and recommendations*.

Lightbourne, R. C. (1962). *Ministry of Trade and Investment. Ministry Paper No. 62, 962.*

Lightbourne R. C. (1970). *Ministry of Trade and Investment: Ministry Paper No. 31, 1970*, file no. 66/1/03.

Manley, M. (1979). *Programme for economic recovery. Prime Minister. Ministry Paper No. 18*, May 3, 1979.

Munn, K. (1977). *Minister of National Security. Ministry Paper No. 22.*, June 7, 1977.

Planning Institute of Jamaica. (2014). *Economic and social survey Jamaica, 2014.*

Robinson, M. (1990). *Debt management in Jamaica.* http://www.worldbank.org/en/country/jamaica/overview

Seaga, E. (1981). *Extended fund facility arrangement with International Monetary Fund. Ministry Paper No. 9, 1981.*

The World Bank. (2011). *Jamaica - Country economic memorandum: Unlocking growth* Author. http://documents.worldbank.org/curated/en/920121468042544307/Jamaica-Country-economic-memorandum-unlocking-growthFindlay J. & Straus A, 2013. The Wisdom Economy: Opportunity in the Chaos

The World Fact Book. (n.d). https://www.cia.gov/library/publications/the-world-factbook/geos/jm.html

CHAPTER 5

Non-Traditional Skills Training for Career Development

DISRAELI M. HUTTON

HISTORICALLY, TECHNICAL VOCATIONAL EDUCATION AND TRAINING (TVET) has focussed on traditional industries related to areas such as manufacturing, construction, agriculture, and transportation, among others. However, a broader focus on career education would naturally include other areas of skills development. Hughes et al. (2016) define career education as training which enables "students to acquire the knowledge, skills, and attitudes that will allow them to understand and succeed within and beyond their schooling and so underpin individual as well as national economic performance" (p. 5). Within the broader ambit of effective work performance preparation, skills development is about the capacity to be a productive person through the acquisition of competencies that will make a difference for the individual and the economy. King and Palmer (2007) define skills development in terms of job performance:

> Skills development is not equated with formal technical, vocational and agricultural education and training alone, but is used more generally to refer also to the productive capacities acquired through all levels of education and training, occurring in formal, non-formal and on-the-job settings, which enable individuals in all areas of the economy to become fully and productively engaged in livelihoods and to have the opportunity to adapt these capacities to meet the changing demands and opportunities of the economy and labour market. (p. 8)

Both definitions seek to take a more all-encompassing view of training, thus clearly recognizing skills areas that are not treated as strictly technical or even vocational in nature. The uneven development of the occupations areas has resulted in the fragmented nature of training in the workplace today, that is, training is emphasized more readily for some occupations than for others. For example, the hotel industry, and particularly the accommodation subsector, has benefitted significantly from the major forms of training including formal, non-formal and informal training. In the case of the 'popular' music industry in Jamaica, training is mainly informal and non-formal.

The introduction of Science, Technology, Engineering and Mathematics (STEM), which has now been modified to Science, Technology, Engineering, Arts and Mathematics (STEAM), is a clear recognition that the arts must be included in any rethinking of skills training and development. To be adequately prepared for the workplace, the learner must take full advantage of the integration of the sciences and arts because, in the real world of the production of goods and services, they are never separated. According to the University of Central Florida Online (2023), "by integrating the arts into STEM, STEAM-focused curricula incorporate the study of the humanities, language arts, dance, drama, music arts, visual arts, design, new media and more" (p. 2). So, associating the arts with TVET is in keeping with the decision to modify STEM by incorporating the arts. It is within this context that it has become necessary to highlight several areas where job creation and work performance are evident, but they have not been brought into the traditional TVET paradigm. Based on the Jamaican experience, three areas of skills development that are excluded from TVET include arts, sports, and maritime-related occupations. These areas are represented by (a) Edna Manley College of the Visual and Performing Arts (EMCVPA), (b) G. C. Foster College and (c) Caribbean Maritime University (CMU). Thus, the fragmentation that was evident with formal and non-formal training, real or imagined, must be addressed so that the full integration of skills development can be realized.

EDNA MANLEY COLLEGE OF THE VISUAL AND PERFORMING ARTS (EMCVPA)

The Edna Manley College of Visual and Performing Arts currently located in Kingston, Jamaica, is the primary tertiary-training institution for the arts. The College represents a merger of two schools, namely, the School of Art and the School of Music, which were established in 1950 and 1961, respectively. According to Patterson (2015), "It was in 1950 that the first formal art school opened its doors at the DaCosta Institute at 1 Central Avenue, Kingston Gardens, with a number of leading Jamaican artists collaborating on the initiative, including Albert Huie who was one of the tutors" (p. 1). The school later relocated to North Street, with Barrington Watson establishing a four-year Art Diploma in 1962, the same year that Jamaica obtained independence from the British Empire. In 1967, the school was renamed the Jamaica School of Art and, in 1976, nine years later, it was incorporated into the Cultural Training Centre and moved to the current facilities. In fact, three other schools offering programmes of the arts, including the Schools of Drama, Music, and Dance started at different locations in Kingston but were incorporated into one unit (*College Handbook*, 2016).

With administrative responsibilities assigned to the Institute of Jamaica, an agency of the Ministry of Culture, the institution expanded its offerings to include Art, Music, Dance, and Drama. The Edna Manley College of the Visual and Performing Arts "is the first institution of its kind within the English-speaking Caribbean to provide professional and technical training in the Arts, offering qualification at the Bachelor, Associate Degree and Certificate level" (Jamaica Information Service [JIS], 2017). According to *Edna Manley College Handbook* (2015), the United Nations Educational, Scientific and Cultural Organization (UNESCO) identified the four institutions as not only important to the development of Jamaica culturally, but also to the development of the Caribbean region. This recognition was concretized even further when, in 1983, the Organization of American States (OAS) designated the institution the Inter-American Centre for Caribbean Cultural Development, thus recognizing it as a regional cultural resource institution (*Edna Manley College Handbook*, 2015).

The EMCVPA received its name in February 1987 in honour of its founder, the late Hon. Edna Manley, OM, who died in February 1987 (Edna Manley College of the Visual and Performing Arts, 2017). Although the institution was established in 1976, it was not until 1995 that the institution was formally renamed the Edna Manley College of the Visual and Performing Arts in honour of the Hon. Edna Manley, OM (Edna Manley College for the Visual and Performing Arts, 2017).

The mission, vision and core values of the institution are used as guiding principles for development. The mission of the EMCVPA is to enrich the aesthetic sensibilities and promote the cultural diversity of the Caribbean through the highest quality of education and training in the visual and performing arts (Edna Manley College of the Visual and Performing Arts, 2015). The core values that have guided the college have led to its development and impact within the society. These values include diversity, service, innovation, transparency, commitment, partnership, lifelong learning, integrity and ethics, truth and respect (Edna Manley College of the Visual and Performing Arts, 2017). Further, past principal Burchell Duhaney outlined the purpose as "primarily to enrich the artistic sensibility of Jamaica and the wider Caribbean nation and to highlight all the areas of the arts, not just as entertainment but also a scholarly area for study" (Cooke, 2010).

The four areas of emphasis by the EMCVPA – Visual Arts, Music, Dance and Drama – are highlighted in order to show the level of skills and related job opportunities provided in the arts. It would not be far-fetched to assert that the potential for job creation is as viable as the tourist industry, which is currently on a growth path. Moreover, a mainstreaming of the training in the arts could lead to a better integration of both industries.

Visual or Fine Arts

The areas of specialties associated with the fine arts include painting, sculpting, sketching and digital art. Persons who offer these competencies will be self-employed and/or they will be employed by organizations that make use of these skills. Those who are self-employed will offer these products for sale or produce fine art based on commission from organizations and individuals (Indeed Editorial Team, 2023). Indeed Editorial

Team (2023) identified a variety of jobs ranging from cake decorator to architect, and pointed out that "a degree in fine arts allows people to develop technical skills while expressing their creativity" (p. 1). From among the 40 professions identified, some of the familiar jobs include animator, graphic designer, web designer, filmmaker, fashion designer, sculptor, jeweller, photojournalist, illustrator, photographer, social media specialist, and art teacher (Indeed Editorial Team, 2023). As noted earlier, while the basic skills of those trained in the fine arts are consistent with training in any other profession, the creative portion is unique to the individual, thus the name 'art'.

Music Industry

Fiero (2005) places the music industry into four broad categories: creative, performance, business and professional support. Like the fine arts, the industry is also characterized as creative. According to Fiero, the music business is considered high risk and music artists who are the foundation of the industry seem to have limited influence on the business. Music Industry (2023) describes the industry as comprising both organizations and individuals who write "songs and musical compositions, creating and selling recorded music and sheet music, presenting concerts, as well as the organizations that aid, train, represent and supply music creators" (p. 1). For the four categories identified by Fiero (2005) for the music industry, there were 32 occupations. The following are selected occupations for each category:

- Creative category – Includes recording artists, songwriters, record producers, production companies, performing artists and musicians;
- Performance category – Includes radio, film, television, cable, concerts and Internet;
- Professional support category – Includes entertainment attorneys, personal managers, talent/booking agents, business managers and accountants;
- Business category – Includes record companies, independent record labels, publishing companies, music libraries, music licensing, distributors, retailers (record stores), marketing and promotions.

Dance Industry

The dance industry comprises two major sectors, namely, professional and amateur sectors. In the case of the professional dance sector, the "industry is made up of dancers, choreographers, rehearsal or master dancers, costume and set designers, make-up artists, publicists, and others behind the scenes" (Vault, 2023, p. 1). Professional dance companies are made up of numerous sectors, but the most prominent and widespread are the traditional ballet and the more modern dance companies. There are also individual dancers who perform at special concerts as guest dancers. Dance companies perform on a seasonal basis and for Jamaica the National Dance Theatre Company (NDTC), which was founded by the late Rex Nettleford, is the most established local dance company. As pointed out by Vault, "During the off-season, performers and others find work at resorts, cruise ships, and similar places. Dance companies are usually not self-supporting" (p. 1).

Drama Industry

StudySmarter (2023) represents drama as a form of play based on fictional or non-fictional narrative in which a written script is presented before a live audience in a theatre setting. In addition, "a drama could also refer to any other performance that may be either live or recorded, such as mime theatre, ballets, musicals, operas, films, television shows, or even radio programmes" (p. 5). StudySmarter emphasized that the plot of a drama is meant to be performed before an audience; "therefore, no aspect of the character's thoughts should be presented in a way that is not performable or meant for private reading, such as a book or a poem" (p. 7).

Australian Curriculum (2023) indicated that the learning process is extensive, and the learner is expected to "develop their understanding of the processes of dramatic playing, role-playing, improvising, process drama, play building, interpreting scripts, rehearsing and directing, and responding to drama as the audience" (p. 2). As learners master the basic skills identified, especially at the secondary level of the school system, "they add specific skills and processes of drama practice . . .

[which include] acting, directing, scriptwriting, dramaturgy, designing, producing, managing and critical analysis (p. 2). York University (2023) identified careers associated with studies in drama and creative arts which include actor, critic, director, drama editor, drama teacher, theatre journalist, magazine contributor, media correspondent, playwright, and producer. This means that dramas should not contain elaborate imagery but, instead, include stage directions and stage setup.

THE GROWTH AND DEVELOPMENT OF EMCPVA

There has been significant growth and transformation within the Edna Manley College since the merger of the four schools. The College has since collaborated on a number of programmes with The University of the West Indies and other academic institutions and cultural agencies. In 2015, the institution celebrated the 115th anniversary of the birth of Edna Manley. During that period, the institution highlighted a large volume of work produced by Edna Manley herself, as well as other artists that have emerged out of the institution (Edna Manley College of the Visual and Performing Arts, 2015). The historical roots of the College can be traced back to 1941 when, under the voluntary leadership and instruction of Edna Manley, adult artists met regularly, two to three evenings weekly at the Junior Centre of the Institute of Jamaica. It is widely acknowledged that the establishment of the Jamaica School of Arts and Craft in 1950 was born out of the weekly classes which were eventually upgraded to regular workshops. As Aldred (2021) pointed out, Manley's desire 'to pass [on] her knowledge' of the arts was a major factor supporting the establishing the Jamaica School of Arts and Craft, which was renamed the Edna Manley School of the Visual and Performing Arts in 1995.

As the institution developed, the four schools (art, dance, drama, and music) operated under one administrative structure with a Board of Directors, a principal, and two vice principals. The first school was the School of Arts, Management and Humanities which focusses on the arts in arts management; second, was the School of Drama which emphasises drama in education and theatre; and third, the School of Music, which focusses on music in performance – the playing of instruments such as the violin, wind instruments, steel pan and percussion, and contemporary music studies. In addition, the School of Music offers a Bachelor of Music Education degree which prepares students in areas of specialization such as choral and instrumental music. The School of Dance, the forth school, offers a four-year Bachelor of Fine Arts (BFA) degree in performance and choreography and traditional and folk-dance studies, also dance in education and performance. Today, the Edna Manley College emphasizes different aspects of the Arts. Edna Manley herself was an expressive individual, and she was often referred to as the 'Mother of Jamaican Art' ("A Success Story," 2001).

The Edna Manley College of the Visual and Performing Arts focusses on the creative aspect of skills training for career development. These skills are outside of the traditional technical and educational training that is usually found in the education system. Skills training is an asset that can be used for job security and employment, which this institution focusses on. The focus on these skills has led to the development of the position of Education Officer for theatre arts within the Ministry of Education. These non-traditional skills for career development have contributed to the wider culture of the country, leading to the Jamaica Cultural Development Commission's (JCDC) Speech and Drama Competitions. According to the Edna Manley College for the Visual and Performing Arts (2017), the College is invested in promoting the cultural diversity of the Caribbean and enriching the aesthetic sensibilities of its students through quality education and training in the visual and performing arts. With the School of Arts Management, the College further taps into the unlimited potential of the cultural and creative industries to bolster economies and create meaningful careers for its graduates.

Non-Traditional Skills in Society and Career Development

According to Cooke (2010), The Edna Manley College of the Visual and Performing Arts has been through several stages in its evolution into a comprehensive professional and technical training institution for the arts. He quoted Principal Burchell Duhaney who said that "a significant [number] of persons in the Caribbean have been trained and have gone on to establish their own cultural divisions, teach extensively in all areas of the arts, establish art as an important part of the development of culture and open new career paths" (Cooke, 2010). Based on the nature of the skills training provided by the institution, one would be able to see the impact of the college on society as it uses its diversified values to add to the culture and career path of the Caribbean.

In addition to career development, the Edna Manley School has contributed greatly to the field of academics. In 2013, the Edna Manley College of the Visual and Performing Arts launched a Jonkonnu Arts Journal (Cooke, 2013). Cooke (2013) noted that the initial Jonkonnu Arts Journal published seven research articles: "The Impact of Dance on Middle School Outcomes and General Society" (Vickie Casanova); "Music and the Rise of Caribbean Nationalism: The Jamaican Case" (Gregory Freeland); "Doris Campbell: A Forerunner in Jamaican Textile Art" (Margaret Stanley); 'Clothes That Wear Us: Caribbean Identity and the Apparel Art of Robert Young' (Marsha Pearce); 'Caribbean Intransit': Museology in the Caribbean, a Different Approach' (Marielle Barrow); 'We are not Minstrels': Nettelfordian Political Aesthetics and the Discourse of Caribbean Development' (Wigmoore Francis); and 'Literary Black Power in the Caribbean' (Rita Keresztesi). He also noted that former Minister of Education, the Hon. Rev. Ronald Thwaites, said that the Edna Manley College of the Visual and Performing Arts plays an important role in honing the creative talents of Jamaican youth and will continue to be the cradle of cultural studies in the island (Cooke, 2013).

In addition to the skills training that the Edna Manley College is offering, the institution is also focussed on Animation. Jamaica's strategic location within the global marketplace has made it an ideal hub for outsourced Animation from the North and South Americas. The EMCVPA, the premier institution in the region for training in the arts, with its rich heritage and expertise, is the institution most equipped to educate students in all the facets of the Animation pipeline (Edna Manley College of the Visual and Performing Arts, 2017). Moreover, the training and practice in the world of animation will ensure that the students have the opportunity to gain some practical knowledge of animation. Internships and interaction with industry professionals will build on the knowledge base and skills developed at this level, offering students the opportunity to apply their creativity in an industry context.

Future Development

Currently, the College operates six schools – Visual Arts, Music, Dance, Drama, Arts Management and Humanities, and Continuing Education and Allied Programmes (EMCVPA, 2022). The College is also the first of its kind within the Caribbean to provide technical training in the arts, offering qualification at the Bachelor, Associate Degree and Certificate levels, accredited by the University (Caribbean Jobs.com, 2024). The long-term goal of the College is to continue "to create opportunities that will ultimately lead to the development of the region and the wider global community through the arts, urging students to persevere through adversities, towards the achievement of their goals" (Caribbean Jobs.com, 2024, p. 1). Its vision is Caribbean-focused, and it speaks to the promotion of the cultural diversity of the Caribbean through the highest quality education and training in the visual and performing arts. The other targetted areas of the mission/vision of the College to be accomplished include (a) developing the College "as a centre in arts and culture, by creating a physical and an academic environment which will engender the highest quality study, research, scholarship and the pursuit of academic excellence"; (b) strengthening and broadening "the relationships between the EMCVPA and its stakeholders"; (c) sustaining the "social and academic environment that develops graduates who are devoted to sound moral, social, spiritual and ethical principles in their professional lives and leaders in the practice of the arts"; (d) creating "opportunities for economic enterprises that will support the development of the institution and the interest of the College Community"; (e) providing "quality staff who will support the mission of the College, be devoted to lifelong learning and professional growth in their area of expertise" (pp. 2–3).

G. C. FOSTER COLLEGE OF PHYSICAL EDUCATION AND SPORTS

G. C. Foster College is the premier tertiary sports institution in Jamaica and the English-speaking Caribbean. The formation of the College has seen the dramatic improvement in Jamaican students' performance in all areas of sport offered at the institution. Overall, the international status created in athletics, particularly in track and field events, is directly related to the programme instituted by the College.

Skills in athletics are about the training of the human mind and body. So training is central to the building and development of these skills. Sport is divided into four types or categories – individual, partner, team, and extreme (Leadership and Sport, 2023). The individual sports include athletic track and field, badminton (singles), bodybuilding, bowling, boxing, chess, cycling, diving (singles), draughts, golf, gymnastics, judo, powerlifting, tennis, sport climbing, and swimming. Partner sports include badminton, diving, figure skating, golf, table tennis and volleyball. The team sports include athletics, baseball, basketball, bobsleigh, cricket, hockey, netball, polo, rowing, softball, swimming, volleyball, and water polo. Extreme sports include bobsleigh, climbing, freestyle skiing, gliding, ice diving, luge, mountain climbing, rock climbing, scuba diving, ski jumping, trail running, skateboarding, and skydiving (Leadership and Sport, 2023).

Central to effective performance in sports is sports training and the aim is to "achieve maximum individual or team efficiency in a selected sports discipline limited by rules" (Zahradnik & Korvas, 2012, p. 1). Zahradnik and Korvas (2012) outlined that sports training consists of four individual key areas:

1. Physical components – Physical components are primarily concerned with the development of the person's motor skills which are related to sports skills. The significant and most relevant to sports which are related to motor abilities include the following: force abilities, endurance abilities, speed abilities, coordinative abilities, and flexibility.
2. Technical component – Technical training focuses on acquiring, keeping and transferring motor skills. The motor skills are placed into two groups: (a) Fundamental Skills and (b) Movement Skills.

Fundamental skills reside with the athlete for the duration of his/her sporting career, and they include gait, running, jumping, climbing, basic overarm throwing, etc. With these skills, the athlete will display an automatic response in performance. The second type of motor skills is the movement skills which are classified in accordance with three basic motor behaviour criteria. These include (a) general versus special skills, (b) closed versus open skills, and (c) continuous versus discrete versus serial skills.

3. Tactical component – The tactical component focuses on acquiring and further developing different ways to conduct sports contests on a purposeful basis to become successful. The two critical elements of the tactical component are strategy and tactics. Strategy means that preplanning precedes the execution of the sports. It is based on experience and knowledge of what kind of engagement is likely to bring success. Tactics are about the actual implementation of the strategy contemplated before the sports. This practical execution is determined by the options which were contemplated before the commencement of the sport or race.

4. Psychological component – The psychological component is focused on improving the athlete's personality which is underpinned by the quality of fair play. The fact is that the length of sports training will determine the level of efficiency that will be achieved with time and maturity. It is an accepted fact that each person is different, so there can be no expectation of having any two persons with the same personality. But generally, the personality of each individual is evident by a number of factors. First, there is temperament which is manifested on the outside through emotions. Second, there is motivation which is the driver of the behaviour displayed to achieve the desired results in the person performing. Third, personal qualities which are innate and fall into two categories – positive which emphasizes devotion and persistence or negative which signals dependence and selfishness. Fourth, attitudes which are not innate but are based on environment and experience. These can be positive or negative, but they can be changed with deliberate external assistance or personal rethinking and behaviour modification.

So effective performance in any sport will depend on the level and quality of preparation which is a precondition for achieving maximum efficiency (Zahradnik & Korvas, 2012).

Growth and Development of G. C. Foster College

The G. C. Foster College of Physical Education and Sports institution resulted from a donation made by the Government of Cuba to the people of Jamaica. In 1978, Prime Minister Michael Manley announced a grant provided to construct learning institutions by the Fidel Castro regime in Cuba. Among the schools that were built by the Cubans were the Garvey Maceo, which is situated in Clarendon, and both Jose Marti Secondary and G. C. Foster College located in the vicinity of Spanish Town, St Catherine (G. C. Foster College, 2007A).

The G. C. Foster College was constructed in 1980, and named after Gerald Claude Wugene Foster who was hailed as a dedicated and versatile sportsman. Foster was born in Spanish Town, St Catherine, in 1885 (G. C. Foster College, 2007A). The primary purpose of the College was to "train teachers and coaches for the important task of physical education in Jamaica, with special emphasis on serving the Ministry of Sports in those areas" (G. C. Foster College, 2007A, p. 1). The institution is guided by a vision, a mission, and core values. The vision for the College is to be "a world class training institution producing excellent teachers, sports and recreational professionals to meet local, regional and international demands" (G. C. Foster College, 2020, p. 1). The mission of the G. C. Foster College is to "contribute to social and economic development through the optimal preparation of Physical Education teachers; athletes; recreation and sports specialists, utilizing qualified personnel and contemporary resources" (G. C. Foster College, 2020, p. 1).

Programmes

The College is governed by Board Members including the School Chairman, the Principal, as well as the Student Council Representative. This is important to the management of the school and its daily operations. The G. C. Foster College has transformed over the years, and the institution has grown in capacity and programmes. According to G. C. Foster (2014C), the College has, over the last four years, introduced training programmes in response to the needs of the market and to further contribute to the growth and development of sport in Jamaica. These programmes include offerings in sport/recreation, sports massage therapy, sports fitness, coaching techniques, and sport officiating (umpiring and refereeing). The College also offers a variety of degrees and certification. These include Teacher Training Degrees; Diploma in Coaching; Pre-Degree (designed for students who have done single-option Physical Education [P. E.] courses); Diploma in Sports Fitness Instruction; Diploma in Sports Massage Therapy; Master's in Physical Education and Sports; Continuing Education; the Community Inclusion Programme (CIP); Occupational Studies and Short Courses (G. C. Foster College, 2014C).

Institutional Collaboration – Internal and External

The Community Inclusion Programme offered by the institution benefits the broader community. The CIP is the outreach arm of the G. C. Foster College of Physical Education and Sport. The programme was first organized in 2012, and the main purpose was to foster a healthy and productive partnership between the College and the surrounding communities (G. C. Foster College, 2014B). The College collaborated with the Social Development Commission (SDC), the Human Employment and Resource Training (HEART) Trust National Training Agency (NTA), and surrounding communities to execute this programme. The initiative assisted individuals in developing employable skills, getting into the habit of living a healthy lifestyle, and unearthing sporting talents among unattached youths in their communities. The programme also offers training in housekeeping and food preparation. The G. C. Foster College has had over 79 graduates from this programme up to 2013 (G. C. Foster, 2014C). The College also offers a Master's degree in Sport which is in collaboration with the University of Technology. The College has also extended its offering to an international audience. For example, in 2014, six Chinese coaches benefitted from an Advanced Coaching training at the College (G. C. Foster, 2014C).

Impact of the College on Sports and the Broader Society

In 2013, the Office of the Prime Minister, in assessing the National Sports Policy that examines sports development and enhancement, highlighted the G. C. Foster College as an institution that provides a high standard of training for physical education teachers and coaches. Moreover, the policy also stated that the staff and facilities at the G. C. Foster College are prepared and can support national teams in various sporting events (Office of the Prime Minister, 2013). According to Franklyn (2010), the G. C. Foster College of Physical Education and Sport has produced some coaches who are plying their knowledge throughout the country and the region, thus helping to guide sportsmen and women and those they serve to realize their potential. Additionally, Palmer (2015) noted that the G. C. Foster College of Physical Education and Sport is impacting the lives of residents of nearby communities through several specially designed short courses.

FUTURE PERSPECTIVES OF THE INSTITUTION

According to Palmer (2014), the Principal, Dr Joyce Graham-Roya, stated that she is aiming to transform the institution into a university college. To make this a success, she indicated that the institution is revamping the academics programmes as well as adding new programmes such as a sports management and sports journalism. Additionally, she intends that the school offers online programmes to prospective students from as far as Indonesia and China. Further, the principal stated that there will be a Sports Research and Data Analysis Centre. Dr Graham-Roya sees the need for the development of the Sports Research and Data Analysis Centre as "a lot of people know a lot, but it is not documented" (Palmer, 2014, p. 1). The institution also plans to establish an Emergency Medical Technician (EMT) programme, an initiative that is already underway. The EMT Programme will run in collaboration with the Spanish Town Hospital to address the need for "adequately trained (EMTs) working on ambulances and in the hospitals" (Palmer, 2015, p. 1).

CARIBBEAN MARITIME UNIVERSITY

The training of seafarers and services in the maritime industry started in Jamaica only 43 years ago. Nevertheless, the shipping industry has been a part of the economic life of the country since slavery and before. Kuhlase (2020), describing the nature of the industry in South Africa, said: "This is a global industry that has a rich history. As global as it is, it is equally a much closed industry. However, through education, change can occur in the way the country relates . . . [to] the industry" (p. 58). As it is in South Africa, the industry in Jamaica was never afforded the status of other income-generating industries such as bauxite and tourism and remained on the periphery in terms of formal training locally for many decades.

With the arrival of COVID-19 in 2020, the maritime industry was forced to adjust in order to respond to the worldwide needs created by the pandemic. Additionally, the industry is being forced to respond to rapidly changing economic needs that are influenced by climate change; conflicts among nations which interfere with shipping; and the growing transformation in technology which could change how the industry functions. As The Nautical Institute (2022) indicated, "The maritime industry is experiencing a paradigm shift, operating in an ever-changing environment influenced by digitalisation and decarbonisation. Technological developments, particularly the new digital technologies . . . are rapidly reshaping the maritime industry" (p. 1). Thus, the need for training at the highest level is required if any institution preparing the workforce for this industry is to meet international standards. The Secretary-General of the International Maritime Organization (IMO), Koji Sekimizu, celebrating World Maritime Day, remarked that "without a quality labour force, motivated, trained and skilled to the appropriate international standards, shipping cannot thrive . . ." (p. 3). She further emphasized that ". . . all the many advances that have been made, in terms of safety and environmental impact, are at risk if personnel within the industry are unable to implement them properly" (p. 3). Making reference to the maritime needs in the United States, the Maritime Administration (2023) outlined that "to fill the array of maritime-related specialties and career paths, the Maritime Administration vigorously supports maritime training and education programs designed to prepare a new generation of mariners to take the helm" (p. 1). So training is central for an industry that is evolving rapidly, and the skills needs are themselves evolving. Presenting the importance of the shipping industry, Maritime Education and Training (2023) said:

> Despite the current global economic downturn, demand for shipping services over time will continue to rise. Today, international trade has evolved, to the point where almost most nations can be self-sufficient. Every country is involved at one level or another in the process of selling what it produces and acquiring what it lacks: none can be dependent on its own domestic resources. Shipping has always provided the only real cost-effective method of bulk transport over any great distance, and the development of shipping and the establishment of global system of trade are inextricably linked. (p. 1)

Highlighting the effects of challenges facing the industry, The Nautical Institute (2022) pointed to the fact that the working relationship and quality of interactions among producers, manufacturers, and consumers are uncertain and lack the required confidence during these critical times. But more importantly, "the traditional structured and measured approach of implementing technologies is no longer able to keep pace with the rate of change. This change creates a need for new skills and competencies for maritime professionals – both afloat and ashore" (p. 3).

There is a wide range of jobs which can be obtained in the maritime industry. These span from food services, which are deck jobs, to engineers who operate and maintain the operations of the ship. While most of the jobs for the industry are performed on ships, critical shipping jobs are located on land (ZipRecruiter, 2024). Summarizing the job types, "the most in-demand jobs include naval architecture, marine and ocean engineering, ship and boat building, electricians and pipefitters, welders, and mechanical engineers" (ZipRecruiter, 2024, p.1). Other in-demand jobs identified by ZipRecruiter include boat pilot, ship pilot, first officer, port engineer, ferry pilot, ship engineer, tugboat captain, port captain, naval architect, cruise director, marine engineer, waterfront director, marine service manager, first mate, able seaman, marine surveyor, ship superintendent, ordinary seaman, marine diesel mechanic, mate, ship captain, marine technician, marine mechanic, radio technician, and third mate. Other jobs identified include shipping agent, skipper, barge engineer, cargo engineer, motorman, and shipping broker (Maritime Insights, 2019).

The Jamaica Maritime Training Institute (JMTI) started 33 years ago in 1980. The visionary behind this training institution was Vance Lannaman who saw the Caribbean benefitting from a training programme "to produce personnel of international calibre to man the Jamaica Merchant Marine (JMM) fleet of five ships and to help to fill the worldwide shortage of seafarers" ("Shipping Industry Remembers," 2017). The institution was born out of an agreement between the Norwegian and Jamaican governments. The JMTI commenced its operation with the training of 30 students as Deck Engineering Officers at Class III at the Merchant Certificate level. All five lecturers in the programme were from Norway. With its increased regional and international status underpinned by the quality of its graduates and rapid enrolment, the basis was created for the full ascendency of the institution to tertiary-level education.

As indicated in "A Success Story" (2001), the main aim of this programme was to equip senior and middle-level managers of the shipping and allied industries with the skills needed to function effectively in the global market. The institute soon established itself as a significant component in the development of the maritime sector, not only in Jamaica, but increasingly in the wider Caribbean (Rattray, 2001). Established as a tertiary Institution, the Caribbean Maritime Institute (CMI) provided training in Maritime Education and the professionals who function in the field. From the outset, the Institute provided training to students from a number of Caribbean countries including St Lucia, Dominica, St Kitts, the Grenadines, Barbados, and Trinidad and Tobago. In building its credentials and recognition, the Institute received support from "the International Maritime Organisation (IMO), the Caribbean Development Bank, Caribbean Shipping Association, the European Union and the Government of Japan" (Rattray, 2001). At the local level, both the University of the West Indies (UWI) and the University of Technology (UTech), Jamaica, and the University Council of Jamaica (UCJ) were moving from a 'Jamaica-only' focus.

The elevation of CMI to University status was enabled by a bill in the Jamaican Parliament which "establishes the CMU as a degree granting institution and defines it as a specialized university providing education, training and consultancy in maritime, logistics, engineering, customs, immigration and related fields" (Caribbean Maritime Institute, 2017, p. 1). The then Minister of Education, the Hon. Ruel Reid, indicated: "The university, which was established [as the JMTI] in 1980 with 30 students, has grown significantly over the years. Enrolment increased from 300 students in 2007 to just under 5,000 in 2017" (p. 1). Embarking on a scheme to admit over 4000 students with its new status, the University is geared to provide "services such as dry docking; ship building and construction; naval architecture; underwater welding; marine electronics repair; aviation and ground transportation repair; marine equipment repair and maintenance; plumbing; and carpentry" (Caribbean Maritime Institute, 2017, p. 1).

Describing the University's philosophy of doing business, the then President of the CMU, Fritz Pinnock, indicated that the institution is led by the requirements of the marketplace: ". . . We go to the industry first, find out what their needs are, and work backwards and create the training programmes" ("Caribbean Maritime Institute – Smooth Sailing," 2016). So the approach used in recruiting students for the programme, coupled with the fact the graduates are prepared for the 'global marketplace', explains the reason for them having "the highest placement of graduates among all the tertiary institutions throughout Jamaica, despite the recession . . ." ("Caribbean Maritime Institute – Smooth Sailing," 2016). Addressing the employability status of its graduates, it was noted in 2017 that over 85 per cent of the graduates "gain employment (locally and abroad), start their own businesses or matriculate into higher studies within six months of graduating. The student population now stands at over 3000 with 24 core programmes, along with numerous customised courses" ("Shipping Industry Remembers," 2017).

FUTURE PERSPECTIVE OF THE INSTITUTION

As the University anticipates its future goals, it is prepared to exploit the opportunities that are presented while pursuing its institutional goals. Jamaica is strategically located in the pathway of a major international trading route involving both sea and air. In fact, the country is 1033 Kilometres (642 miles) from the Panama Canal (it should be noted that thousands of Jamaicans participated in the building of the Panama Canal which lasted for over 15 years). Thus, the country is well positioned, and it is recognized that it can become "an ideal trans-shipment hub for global trade" (*Student Handbook*, 2021).

With the global supply chain now replacing the traditional shipping arrangement which is made up of a network of trading partners, logistics is the primary cog that holds them together. Recognizing this opportunity to develop into a major enterprise sector, the Jamaican Government has embraced both shipping and logistics as two areas with great potential for major income-earning activities for the country and the Jamaican people. This shift in focus has provided the Caribbean Maritime University with a grand opportunity to focus its training, education, and overall skills development in the "areas of maritime, engineering, logistics, and allied industries. Further, the University is now extending its reach into Science, Technology, Engineering and Mathematics (STEM) education and applied research" (*Student Handbook*, 2021, p. 21).

CONCLUSION

There is no doubt that the Edna Manley College of the Visual and Performing Arts, the G. C. Foster College, and the Caribbean Maritime University are playing a prominent role in preparing the Jamaican workforce. So they should be brought under the ambit of skills development and their importance highlighted in the same way as the accommodation subsector of the tourist industry. While there are obvious differences in these institutions based on the nature of the skills they provide, mainstreaming them under the national TVET banner is more likely to bring an accumulative effect on the economic outcomes of the country because the focus will be on both traditional and non-traditional areas of skills development. Currently, there is a clear separation and a focus on the traditional areas of job preparation. One important area of concern is the allocation of funds to non-traditional institutions. Funding by the State through the HEART Trust NTA would have to be considered for these non-traditional areas.

BIBLIOGRAPHY

A success story. (2001, September 19). *The Gleaner*. https://newspaperarchive.com/kingston-gleaner-sep-19-2001-p-46/

Aldred, L. (2021, February 28). Remembering the mother of Jamaican art–Edna Manley. *The Gleaner*. https://jamaica-gleaner.com/article/esponsored/20210228/remembering-mother-jamaican-art-edna-manley

Australian Curriculum. (2023). *Structure-Learning drama*. https://www.australian-curriculum.edu.au/f-10-curriculum/the-arts/drama/structure/

Caribbean Jobs.com. (2024). *Profile of Edna Manley College of the Visual and Performing Arts*. https://www.caribbeanjobs.com/education/Profiles/Edna-Manley-College-of-the-15.aspx

Caribbean Maritime Institute–Smooth sailing to success. (2016, January 14). *The Gleaner*. https://jamaica-gleaner.com/article/news/20160115/caribbean-maritime-institute-smooth-sailing-success

Caribbean Maritime Institute: "The institution of choice" (2017, March 2). *The Gleaner*. https://www.pressreader.com/jamaica/jamaica-gleaner/20170302/283197263117652

Caribbean Maritime Institute to officially become university September 28. (2017, September 20). *The Gleaner*. https://jamaica-gleaner.com/article/news/20170921/caribbean-maritime-institute-officially-become-university-september-28

Caribbean Maritime Institute. (2018). *We've come a long way*. https://www.caribbean-maritime.com/index.php/latest22/issue-33-jan-march-2018/471-caribbean-maritime-university.html

Caribbean Maritime University. (2024). *What is known today as the Caribbean Maritime University*. https://www.caribbeanjobs.com/Caribbean-Maritime-University-CMU-Jobs-1243.aspx

Cooke, M. (2010, October 25). Arts and culture: Edna Manley College of the Visual and Performing Arts, speaking from the 'art'. *The Gleaner*. https://jamaica-gleaner.com/gleaner/20101025/news/news4.html

Cooke, M. (2013, October, 27). EMCVPA launches Jonkonnu Arts Journal. *The Gleaner.* http://jamaica-gleaner.com/gleaner/20131027/arts/arts5.html
Edna Manley College of the Visual and Performing Arts. (n.d). *Edna Manley School for the Visual Arts Handbook 1991-1994.*
Edna Manley College of the Visual and Performing Arts. (2014). *2014–2015 Student Handbook.*
Edna Manley College of the Visual and Performing Arts. (2015). *Edna Manley into the sun.* Author
Edna Manley College of the Visual and Performing Arts. (2015). *Animate your world.* http://emc.edu.jm/blog/2015/06/24/animation/
EMCVPA. (2022). *College handbook.* https://emc.edu.jm/wp-content/uploads/2021/09/EMCVPA_General_Handbook_2021-2022-min.pdf
Fiero, G. (2005). The entrepreneur's guide to doing business in the music industry. https://www.musesmuse.com/TheGuide.pdf
Franklyn, D. (2010). Sport in Jamaica: A local and international perspective. http://www.gracekennedy.com/images/lecture/GRACE-Lecture-2010.pdf
G. C. Foster College of Physical Education and Sports. (2014A). *History.* https://gcfostergroup.angelfire.com/history.html
G. C. Foster College of Physical Education and Sports. (2014B). *Strategic plan for the period 2014 – 2017.* Author.
G. C. Foster College of Physical Education and Sports. (2014C). *Student profile.* Author.
G. C. Foster College of Physical Education and Sports. (2020). *Vision and mission.* https://case.edu.jm/visionandmission/
G. C. Foster College of Physical Education and Sports. (2023). *College history.* https://janselgcf.tripod.com/id5.html
Hodges, P. G. (2017). Maritime Institute to officially become university on September 28. https://jis.gov.jm/maritime-institute-officially-become-university-september-28-2/
Hughes, D., Mann, A., Barnes, S., Baldauf, B., & McKeown, R. (2016). *Careers education: International literature review.* Institute for Employment Research/Education and Employers Research. https://educationendowmentfoundation.org.uk/public/files/Publications/Careers_review.pdf
Indeed Editorial Team. (2023A). *40 jobs you can do with a degree in fine arts.* Author. https://www.indeed.com/career-advice/finding-a-job/what-can-you-do-with-a-degree-in-fine-arts
Indeed Editorial Team. (2023B). *13 skills for fine artists.* https://www.indeed.com/career-advice/career-development/fine-artist-skills
International Maritime Organization. (2015). *Maritime education and training.* https://www.imo.org/en/MediaCentre/PressBriefings/Pages/39-WMD-2015-.aspx
Jamaica Information Service. (2017). *Edna Manley College of the Visual and Perform-*

ing Arts. https://jis.gov.jm/government/agencies/edna-manley-college-of-the-visual-and-performing-arts/

King, K., & Palmer, R. (2007). *Skills development and poverty reduction: A state of the art review.* European Training Foundation. http://www.etf.europa.eu/pubmgmt.nsf/(getAttachment)/B055AACF8E9CC19DC12573AF00520109/$File/NOTE79TKHJ.pdf

Kuhlase, P. M. (2020). *The importance of maritime education and training within the secondary education system in South Africa.* https://commons.wmu.se/cgi/viewcontent.cgi?article=2449&context=all_dissertations

Leadership and Sports. (2023). *What are the different types of sports?* https://www.leadershipandsport.com/types-of-sports/

Marine Insight. (2019). *50 marine careers essential guide.* https://www.marineinsight.com/careers-2/50-marine-careers-essential-guide/

Muni Sports. (2023). *Basis of sports training.* https://www.fsps.muni.cz/emuni/data/reader/book-6/02.html

Music Industry. (2023, November 15). *Wikipedia.* https://en.wikipedia.org/wiki/Music_industry

National Council on Educational Research and Training. (2023). *Sports training.* https://ncert.nic.in/textbook/pdf/iehp105.pdf

Office of the Prime Minister. (2013). *White paper on national sports policy.* http://jis.gov.jm/media/National-Sports-Policy-March-25-2013-FINAL-6.pdf

Palmer, S. (2014). *GC Foster eye university college status.* http://jis.gov.jm/g-c-foster-eyes-university-college-status/

Palmer, S. (2015). *GC Fosters offers short courses for community members.* https://jis.gov.jm/gc-foster-offers-short-courses-community-members/

Patterson, C. (2015). *Edna Manley College, the cradle of cultural studies.* http://jis.gov.jm/edna-manley-college-cradle-cultural-studies-thwaites/

Rattray, L. M. (2001, September 19). Significance of the maritime sector on the wider Caribbean. https://newspaperarchive.com/kingston-gleaner-sep-19-2001-p-46/

Shipping industry remembers Vance Lannaman as advocate, entrepreneur and mentor. (2017, March 13). *The Gleaner.* https://jamaica-gleaner.com/article/shipping/20170314/shipping-industry-remembers-vance-lannaman-advocate-entrepreneur-and

Student Handbook—2021-2022 (2021). *Structure of the university.* https://srs.cmu.edu.jm/web_student_information/static/src/pdf/CMU_Students_Handbook_2021-2022.pdf

StudySmarter. (2023). *Drama meaning.* https://www.studysmarter.co.uk/explanations/english-literature/literary-devices/drama/

The Nautical Institute. (2022). *Maritime education and training – Are we on* *track?*https://www.nautinstorg/resources-page/maritime-education-and-training-are-we-on-track.html

The Vault. (2023). *Overview.* https://vault.com/industries/dance

University of Central Florida Online (2023). *Comparing STEM vs. STEAM: Why the arts make a difference.* https://www.ucf.edu/online/engineering/news/comparing-stem-vs-steam-why-the-arts-make-a-difference/

US Department of Transportation—Maritime Administration. (2023). *Educating the maritime workforce.* https://www.maritime.dot.gov/education

York University (2023). *Drama and creative arts.* https://careers.yorku.ca/my-degree/drama-studies

Zahradnik, D., & Korvas, P. (2012). *Introduction into sports training.* Masaryk University. https://www.fsps.muni.cz/emuni/data/reader/book-6/02.html

Zip Recruiter (2024). *25 of the highest paying maritime jobs in 2024.* https://www.ziprecruiter.com/g/Highest-Paying-Maritime-Jobs

CHAPTER 6

TVET Policy Development and Implementation

GRACE A. McLEAN

THIS CHAPTER FOCUSES ON THE DEVELOPMENT AND implementation of policies in Technical Vocational Education and Training (TVET) over the last 60 years in Jamaica. An analysis of the policies and governance arrangements that currently exist in selected countries, Finland and Singapore, will be discussed and the policy framework for these countries will help us determine how Jamaica measures up when compared with these countries and the development of their TVET systems. An analysis of the impact of policy development on the performance of the education system in Jamaica will be presented and recommendations made regarding further improvements. This will serve to highlight the progression of Jamaica on a solid path as TVET mainstreaming and integration are used to revolutionize the education system and position Jamaica at the forefront of economic development and improvement in the quality of life of her people.

BACKGROUND

TVET, according to the International Labour Office (2008), has emerged in developing countries as the main vehicle for the development of economies and the improvement of the quality of lives for its people. This statement is supported by the UNESCO pillars of learning, the post 2015 millennium development goals and the ILO's Decent Work Agenda. It is evident, according to UNESCO (2013) that developed countries have utilized a seamless system of twinning TVET and academics which has resulted in these countries producing competent and skilled workers who become productive citizens contributing significantly to the sustainability of their economies. The 2010 PISA report alluded to the fact that developed and industrialized countries have built and improved on their historical practices and have been able to develop a culture where every work is seen as decent and as contribution towards nation building, hence no need for any negative perception and or discrimination of those who pursue traditional TVET occupations. In some countries, TVET is seen as the gateway for the development of a prosperous nation, hence occupational certification at all levels is driven from the Central Government to create a fully coordinated system of production and services, as well as internal and external trading, to give competitive advantage. Having come to this realization, Jamaica has seen the need to further document the formulation and development of TVET policies over the years and to make this information available.

The Jamaican TVET system has significantly evolved and can be considered to be one that is maturing incrementally. The major areas of a TVET system that must be focused on include: 1) existing policy and regulatory framework that inform TVET system development, 2) the quality of design and development, and 3) operating sub-systems and training infrastructure as well as the existing support and collaboration that allow for the appreciation of such role by key stakeholders and partners in the education system. A review of the governance structure and development of TVET systems in countries such as Singapore, Jamaica, Australia, United Kingdom, European and Asian States suggest that there are indeed variations, but what is critical is these countries all see the need to ensure that a proper structure is in place to guide and spearhead the development of TVET in their countries (Kuruvilla, Erickson & Hwang, 2002).

Jamaica has placed a lot of emphasis on the development of a TVET through programmes supported by policy and regulatory frameworks. This focus has been on different elements, including apprenticeship, traineeship, in-plant training, and the development of assessment pathways with a goal to certify the Jamaican workforce. This is in addition to students' pursuit of certification in 14 technical high schools and over 150 secondary schools (Ministry of Education, 2003). The Ministry of Education, Youth and Information has been driving the policy development to guide TVET mainstreaming and integration into the education system. This policy development started as far back as in the 1950s when a concerted effort was made to establish the apprenticeship programme, supported by the Apprenticeship Act to guide the placement of youngsters for skills training and development. Since then, significant efforts have been made towards the establishment of TVET policies and policy guidelines, as well as the development of strategies and implementation of various initiatives. TVET policies in Jamaica are guided by the Education for All Movement, 2000 Millennium Development Goals, ILO Decent Work Agenda and UNESCO's Pillars of Learning. Also, international, regional and local initiatives such as the Shanghai's TVET Declaration, 2012; the CARICOM Strategy for TVET, 2012; the principles of the Caribbean Association of National Training Authorities (CANTA); the Vision 2030 National Development Plan; and the Jamaica's TVET Declaration, 2012 guided decisions taken on TVET. As globalization creates more opportunities for collaboration and trade, the TVET system in Jamaica is also being guided by market forces and the need for trained and competent workers in new and emerging skill areas to meet the needs of the labour market. The Jamaican education system, therefore, has gradually become more customized to remain relevant and applicable to the needs of the country.

TVET POLICY DEVELOPMENT AND IMPLEMENTATION IN JAMAICA

TVET policy development and implementation in Jamaica is marked by significant milestones over the last 60 years. Some of these milestones are incorporated into general education policy development while others have been quite impactful and pronounced. These can be summarized as follows.

The 1960s

The New Deal for Education in Jamaica, referred to as the "New Deal" was the first major physical expansion of Jamaica's education system. The plan represented a change in philosophy, change of policy and change of objectives (Morris, 2011). This plan marked the establishment of Comprehensive High Schools within the education system. These institutions represented the introduction of TVET at the secondary level in various areas. The schools were also supported with the necessary equipment and trained teachers to support the areas selected. The foresight of the then Minister of Education, the Honourable Edwin Leopold Allen, was to ensure that students at the secondary level are fully rounded with a mix of both the practical and theory of education, along with the correct attitude as they exit the secondary system.

The 1970s

To support the establishment of the comprehensive high schools under the New Deal in Education and to broaden TVET, the Technical and Vocational Unit within the Ministry of Education was established as an administrative unit in 1975 and brought agriculture, art and craft, business education, home economics, and industrial education together as the five key areas that were driving all aspects of TVET development in the education system. The Unit was responsible for the development and implementation of all technical and vocational curricula at all levels of the formal education system – including primary, secondary, special and tertiary. It was expected at the time that schools would introduce aspects of technical and vocational skills in their programmes and the education officers would monitor and provide support accordingly. During this period the College of Arts, Science and Technology (CAST), now the University of Technology, was created. This institution was developed as a Polytechnic to support the training of skilled professionals for the world of work, as well as teachers for the education system.

The 1980s

In 1982, the Human Employment and Resource Training Act was passed to provide the statutory arrangements for financing and training of persons with a view to employment. Further to the Act, a corporate body was established known as the Human Employment and Resource Training Trust (HEART Trust). The body was empowered to establish a fund for the purposes of the HEART Act to carry out its established functions. Training commenced with the School Leavers Training Opportunities Programme (SLTOP). The HEART Trust's purpose was to provide skills training for the many young people who were leaving the secondary level with little or no form of qualification. This body was expected to assess students' skills needs and provide training so they can access job opportunities or move on to higher level training. The HEART Trust/NTA was established at a time when several companies had production operations in Jamaica, including the 807 garment manufacturing operations, and hence was timely to meet the needs of the workforce.

The 1990s

In 1991, the HEART Trust was re-branded the HEART Trust/National Training Agency (NTA), with a new mandate to consolidate, coordinate and effectively develop the Technical and Vocational Education and Training (TVET) system in Jamaica. In 1994, amendments to the HEART Act enabled the establishment of the National Council on Technical Vocational Education and Training (NCTVET) with responsibility for the development of a robust quality assurance system to include standards development based on labour market needs, curriculum development, supporting subject guides as well as for the auditing, administration and certifying of qualified persons for the NVQJ certification. In 1994, the HEART Act was further amended to establish a body to be named the National Council on Technical and Vocational Education and Training (NCTVET) to allow for the necessary funding through the HEART Trust/NTA. This was a significant move, as it supported the creation and development of a TVET quality system to support internationally recognized training and certification. Towards the end of the 1990s, significant funding was provided through the HEART Trust/NTA for the upgrading of Technical High Schools under the Technical High School Development Project (THSDP), as well as support for other secondary level institutions under the TVET Rationalization Programme. Employers become eligible to pay HEART contributions when their total gross emoluments (wage bill) exceed $14,444. Each month, eligible employers contribute to the Heart Trust Fund 3% of the total amount of monthly emoluments paid to employees. Significant investments were made in schools during this period by way of equipment upgrades, creating centres of excellence, and capacity building of teachers and administrators.

2000 and beyond

This period has seen the consolidation and advancement of TVET as greater effort was made to develop a TVET system that is on par with those internationally. The approval of the Jamaican TVET Policy for implementation in 2013 was significant. The TVET Policy has set the base for the full integration of TVET within the education system and for the inclusion/involvement of industry and is being used for the full mainstreaming and integration of TVET into the Education system. The main goal of the policy is to provide a national framework for the development, implementation and sustainability of TVET in Jamaica, contributing to productivity and economic development.

The main elements of the policy include:

1. Development of a comprehensive, integrated, outcome-based TVET system that is integrated fully in the general education system at all levels.
2. Strengthening institutions with a view to making them TVET Centres for Excellence.
3. Establishing and providing the necessary institutional set-up to manage and implement TVET quality management system (QMS).
4. Implementing Career Education in all schools.
5. Improving the quality of TVET (formal and non-formal) at all levels and making it responsive to the needs of the labour market.

6. Facilitating the expansion of relevant TVET offerings which are crucial to Vision 2030 Jamaica and in accordance with international trends and demands.
7. Strengthening the culture of entrepreneurship employment and support job creation in the economy, especially in the emerging industries.
8. Establishment of national partnerships to ensure alignment and coordination to meet national priorities.
9. Collaboration with industry to ensure that TVET education is customized to meet their needs.
10. Develop a sustainable financing system for sustainable TVET structures (TVET policy, 2013).

The Ministry of Education, Youth and Information embarked on steps to have TVET mainstreamed and fully integrated into the formal education system (Ministry of Education National Strategic Plan, 2012). The plan was to introduce TVET as a core area within the education system starting with the lower primary level. This would result in all students pursuing at least one area of TVET along with other core subjects at the secondary level. At the primary level greater emphasis is placed on induction, orientation and creating awareness of TVET. As students move into the secondary programmes, emphasis is placed on TVET development, career focus and advancement, followed by mastery at the tertiary level and further skills development aimed at retooling, continuing education and lifelong learning. This is encapsulated in a manual entitled, The TVET Integration Model – A Practical Guide Towards the Integration of TVET in the Education System, which was distributed to all schools. This text also supports the implementation of the National Standards Curriculum which commenced implementation in September 2016 with a strong TVET focus from the primary level. This introduction of TVET in the curriculum, especially at the primary level, was the first of its kind in the history of the Country. TVET components were fully embedded within the primary curriculum and teaching units were also developed to support its delivery. This allowed for a greater understanding of TVET at this level, and better adaptability and subject selection at lower and upper secondary levels respectively in regard to career pathways, which were also being introduced in a formal way in the system.

In 2012, the Caribbean Examination Council (CXC) developed and implemented its TVET assessment policy. The body reviewed its TVET offerings and branded these with the Caribbean Vocational Qualification (CVQ) to provide certification for candidates (Whiteman, 2012). This allows students who pursue selected CXC subjects to also receive certification in the CVQ. Since 2013, the Caribbean Examination Council has been the body offering the CVQ within the secondary level institutions.

To support the significant investment being placed in the system to integrate TVET, in 2013 the Ministry of Education announced as a policy that by 2017 all high school students should exit the system with at least five subjects which should include mathematics, English Language, a TVET subject and two others. Since then, steps have been taken to support this policy through the training of teachers, the introduction of over 13 new subject areas in the system and the subsidizing of examination fees for students. This represented a very significant step in the right direction as greater effort is being made to produce a trained and competent workforce to support the Jamaican economy and to attract investments.

The focus of the Ministry of Education, Youth and Information is to ensure that students pursuing TVET programmes generally, as well as under the Career Advancement Programme, also pursue Occupational Degrees. Consequently, in 2016 the Occupational associate degree was developed and launched. The programme commenced with 200 students and was expected to drive the tertiary pathway for occupational certification up to the applied doctorate level. This associate degree will be supported by the National Qualification Framework for Jamaica which was launched on February 22, 2017. This framework allows for matriculation and articulation of students at all levels of the education system, hence legitimizing multiple pathways for certification.

The Government of Jamaica now views TVET programmes as a critical component of its road map Vision 2030 Jamaica National Development Plan. This plan has been conceptualized to put the country on a path of growth and sustainability (Vision 2030 National Plan, 2010). Once the Education System continues on this trajectory then it is expected that

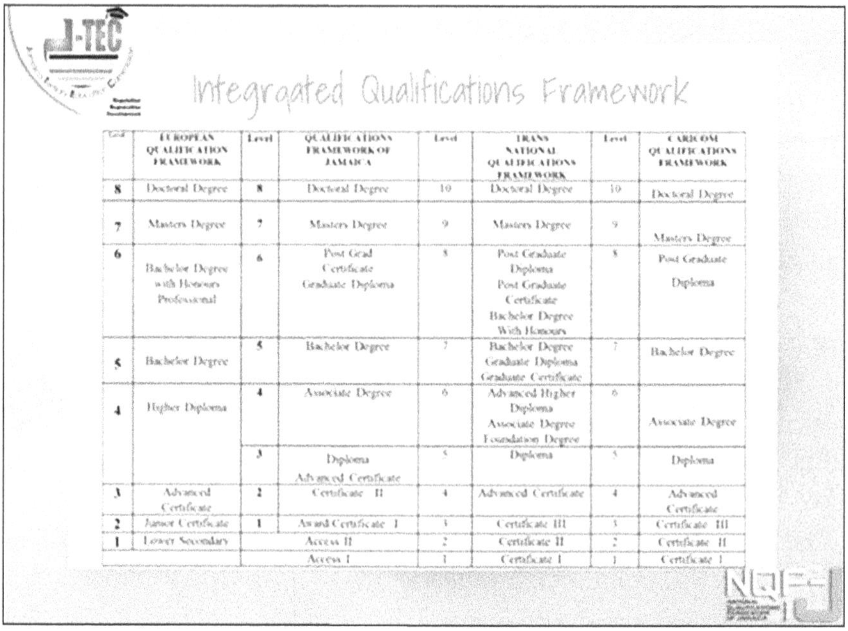
Integrated Qualifications Framework

Level	EUROPEAN QUALIFICATION FRAMEWORK	Level	QUALIFICATIONS FRAMEWORK OF JAMAICA	Level	TRANS NATIONAL QUALIFICATIONS FRAMEWORK	Level	CARICOM QUALIFICATIONS FRAMEWORK
8	Doctoral Degree	8	Doctoral Degree	10	Doctoral Degree	10	Doctoral Degree
7	Masters Degree	7	Masters Degree	9	Masters Degree	9	Masters Degree
6	Bachelor Degree with Honours Professional	6	Post Grad Certificate Graduate Diploma	8	Post Graduate Diploma Post Graduate Certificate Bachelor Degree With Honours	8	Post Graduate Diploma
5	Bachelor Degree	5	Bachelor Degree	7	Bachelor Degree Graduate Diploma Graduate Certificate	7	Bachelor Degree
4	Higher Diploma	4	Associate Degree	6	Advanced Higher Diploma Associate Degree Foundation Degree	6	Associate Degree
		3	Diploma Advanced Certificate	5	Diploma	5	Diploma
3	Advanced Certificate	2	Certificate II	4	Advanced Certificate	4	Advanced Certificate
2	Junior Certificate	1	Award Certificate I	3	Certificate III	3	Certificate III
1	Lower Secondary		Access II	2	Certificate II	2	Certificate II
			Access I	1	Certificate I	1	Certificate I

Figure 6.1: Integrated qualification framework displaying Jamaica's Framework

Jamaica will eventually boast one of the best TVET systems in the world. Having examined generally the development of TVET policies over time and their implementation, a comparison will now be made with two other countries' TVET systems.

THE SINGAPOREAN MODEL FOR TVET EDUCATION

According to Goh and Gopinathan (2006), Singapore became a sovereign state in 1965 after breaking off from Malaysia. The strategy of the Government then was to find the fastest way of developing an industrialized society. The Singaporean TVET system has developed significantly over the years from the more than 200 village schools to a system that caters to all levels and abilities of its citizens (Goh & Gopinathan, 2006). Lots of emphasis was placed on the development of the TVET system by ensuring that students are exposed to and placed on a vocational path based on their abilities and aptitudes.

The emphasis was also on the development of pre-employment training programmes to assist citizens in developing various skills or becoming technicians. The Institute of Technical Education through its vocational centres was responsible for the re-training and upgrading of workers on a sustained basis. The teaching factory initiative as well as the technology learning methodology all assisted in providing high quality TVET training. The Singaporean government therefore invested heavily in TVET as it saw this as a key strategy to drive the economy (Green, Ashton, James & Sung, 1999).

Singapore's main ministry for economic development is the Ministry of Trade and Industry. Within this industry there is the Economic Development Board and the Council for Professional and Technical Education. Although these two arms of the Ministry are charged with separate areas of focus, they interrelate. The Economic Development Board is responsible for analyzing the investment needs, determining and assessing skills requirements as well as skills gaps which may arise from these assessments. The role of the Economic Development Board is also to recommend to the Council for Professional and Technical Education the skills requirements for the country and determine whose role it is to ensure that the human capital is developed to meet the industry demands (Green, Ashton, James, & Sung, 1999; Kuruvilla, Erickson, & Hwang, 2002). In addition, the Productivity and Standards Board which also falls under the Ministry of Trade and Industry determines the on-the-job skills requirements and upgrading needed to ensure that there is a constant flow of skilled personnel to keep the industry functioning. The Productivity and Standards Board's mission, according to Wee (1997), is to raise productivity so as to improve Singapore's competitiveness and economic growth.

According to Kuruvilla, Erickson, and Hwang (2002), Singapore enacted legislation for employers to pay one percent of gross salary for employees earning less than SG$1,500 per month through a special arrangement called the Skills Development Fund. Employers are entitled to up to 80% of this amount paid to assist in the training of employees. This they indicated is a means of encouraging firms to support skills development. The kind of coordination that exists between the different entities would not have been effective if the Government did not coordinate the streamlining of the various roles and activities that allow structure and linkages between these bodies that can result in the growth and productivity of the country. It can be deduced therefore, and further reinforced by Bennell and Segerstrom (1998), that the Government of Singapore has invested heavily in the development of the TVET systems. This investment includes the creation of a centralized system that shows various Government agencies having responsibility for trade and commerce, manpower needs, training boards responsible for programme development, as well as training institutes responsible for delivery.

Both Jamaica and Singapore have taken steps to develop a TVET system that supports the economic strategies of their countries. The education and training culture in Singapore is one that sees a strong orientation to the development of skills for driving the economy. The government is involved in a well-coordinated agenda that develops the systems; defines the strategies and ensures that there is collaboration between government, private sector and foreign investors in meeting the skill needs of the country. Singapore has a vision of becoming the leader in research and development in the Asian region.

This goal has assisted in driving the country to pursue a path crafted to lead to the realization of this vision. In the recorded education statistics for Singapore, UNICEF (2008) listed the country as having an entrance and transition rate of over 92% for all its programmes. In line with its government strategies, programmes are offered for varying age groups and there is a high level of acceptance as each citizen sees and understands the need to support the country's strategy for economic development. Jamaica also has a robust TVET system that is coordinated by the government with varying opportunities being available for all citizens to access programmes. Jamaica enjoys universal education at the primary level but at the secondary level this is about 97% (Ministry of Education, 2015).

Both countries, therefore, see the urgency and importance of being involved in workforce development, hence the construction and regulation of TVET to ensure that their TVET policies are enacted to support their strategies (Bennell & Segerstrom, 1998). They have established policies and the necessary supporting regulatory framework to guide the implementation of these policies. Jamaica established an Education Act of 1965 and the supporting code of regulations which guide all aspects of the education system including vocational training. In addition to the Education Act, the country also has the Apprenticeship Act of 1954 (sections updated in 1973) and the HEART Act of 1982 which specifically guide apprenticeship and vocational training. Arising from the development of these Acts there are more than 5,000 educational and training institutions that cater to the needs of more than 650,000 students. Inclusive in this number are the private/independent institutions which are also guided by the Education Act.

Singapore is guided by the Education Act of 1957, the Institute of Education Act of 1992, the Singapore's Vocational and Training Policy and the Institute of Education Traineeship Scheme. Additionally, it is guided by the ten-year education programmes policy which was published in 1947 following the break from Straits Settlements, which resulted in Singapore becoming a separate colony. The policy focuses on Universal Primary Education for all and presents a broad framework which would assist the country in moving towards becoming a self-governing country. A number of other policies have been developed including the Bilingual policy which focuses on having all students develop the language skills common to both eastern and western cultures thereby assisting them to cope in a globalized economy. Policies have also been developed for private institutions, special needs students, as well as their school to work programme. Singapore has more than 350 schools from the primary to the post-secondary levels which cater to more than 532,000 students (Goh & Gopinathan, 2006).

It is clear that policies and a structured framework exist for the regulation and construction of TVET. The Singaporean system seems to have an excellent coordinated mechanism where there is involvement at all levels and the strategy for training is in line with the vision of the country. All systems from various levels of Government, along with the private sector, parents, and other interests within the country, seem to be effectively coordinated. This coordinated approach is led by the government and has assisted the country in its economic development and the preparation of a skilled workforce to meet the skill demands.

Kuruvilla, Erickson and Hwang (2002), pointed out that the Government provided incentives to foreign investors as a means of ensuring that citizens of Singapore are employed when these foreign firms are established. The Jamaican system is also effectively coordinated as the Government constantly seeks new ways of improving its systems making them more flexible and adaptable to the demands of the labour market. The push, however, by the Government to improve the quality of education through its transformation programme currently being undertaken is another indication of its commitment to the construction and regulation of TVET. The creation of a Ministry with focus on economic growth and development as well as the establishment of an Economic Growth Council, are two other indications of the seriousness of the Government to align education to industry needs and hence the need for the education system to respond with adequate TVET programmes to meet the training needs. The Government's plan as well to create a National Policy on Work also assist in further advancing TVET contribution towards economic development.

LESSONS LEARNT FROM THESE TWO COUNTRIES INVESTMENT IN TVET

There are many lessons to be learnt from these interventions. The present structure and focus of the Government of Jamaica indicates that a country needs to have a high-level structured approach to allow for order in the construction and regulation of TVET. So far Jamaica has been successful in the development of a structured body to coordinate all aspects of vocational training through the Ministry of Education, Youth, and Information. Through this organization, the HEART Trust/NTA (now HEART/NSTA Trust) was directly conceived, developed, and implemented by the Government and has been effectively and successfully providing quality vocational education to Jamaicans to meet the labour market needs. Both countries have shown a certain level of independence for their TVET system but reliance on Government for sustainability.

The Finnish Model for TVET Education

Finland is noted to have one of the best education systems in the world. The Finnish has a seamless education system with Vocational Education and Training (VET) fully aligned and integrated. As a result, their policies on education generally impact those on Vocational Education and Training. General comprehensive education is offered in the Finnish system from ages seven to sixteen. The system is so designed that after exiting basic education, students then move into areas of specialization. There are, however, specific legislations according to the Finnish National Board of Education (2010). Vocational Education and Training falls within the administrative sector of the Ministry of Education and Culture. Provisions on vocational education and training are defined in Acts of Parliament and include key legislation such as the Vocational Education and Training Act (630/1998), the Vocational Adult Education Act (631/1998), and the Act on the Financing of the Provision of Education and Culture (1705/2009). These pieces of legislation make provisions for the offering of VET in the three areas that fall under vocational qualification in the education structure – namely Upper Secondary Vocational qualification, Further Vocational Qualification, and Specialist Vocational Qualification and Training. According to the Finnish National Board of Education (2010), these comprise the suite of vocational institutions, adult education institutions, and apprenticeship training under VET. They are used to guide the vocational training system and ensure that there is compliance across the nation.

Legislation and policies for VET fall under the General Education Policy which was designed through the Finnish Parliament. Budgetary allocations are also determined by Parliament. The Government then put in place decrees and development plans as well as policies for education and training of which the Ministry of Education and Culture is expected to develop specific education policies and strategies to steer the implementation, qualification framework, and regulations. The Ministry is also responsible for the regional administration of education and specific administrative duties.

The Finnish National Board of Education has responsibility for the

National Core Curricula and qualification requirements as well as for the implementation of development programmes. These are the policy related arms of the Finnish VET system that provide overall support for the National Education and Training Committees, the Qualification Committees, and contacts with the world of work. The operations of the VET programmes are managed by VET providers, local planning and organization of education and training, provision of education and training, local advisory councils for VET, and other bodies (Finnish National Board of education, 2010).

There are similarities between the Finish system and policy framework and the Jamaican system, but there are also differences. The Finnish system is more centralized with more structured legislation than the Jamaican TVET system. This is evident in the legislation that supports TVET as well as the governance structure in place for funding and support. The overarching legislation and focus are determined by Parliament for implementation by the government and the Ministry of Education and Culture. The policies of Finland to support TVET education are far more advanced than those that exist in Jamaica. Finland has the Vocational Education and Training Act, the Vocational Adult Education Act, and the Act on the Financing of the Provision of Education and Culture. Jamaica currently has a policy on TVET, but although the Education Act and Code of Regulation cover vocational education it does not do so in any great details. The legislation in place for Finland perhaps is an indication of the success they have been able to attain over the years where over 60% of the school population pursue vocational and technical education (Finnish Board of National education, 2010). Their Acts place specific emphasis on TVET and hence allow for greater support to be provided for implementation. The Finish Act on financing the provision of Education also allows for focus as it demonstrates government support and private sector support for education in a coordinated and structured way.

The overarching policy for VET within the Jamaican context is determined through the Ministry of Education, Youth and Information for approval by the Government. This has its disadvantages, as in some cases the investment opportunities are not fully linked to the education system and hence in some cases the preparation for the investments lag. This then result in the country having to import labour in scarce skills which defeats the overall purpose in the first place of attracting investments. The creation, however, of an Economic Growth and Job creation Ministry as well as an Economic Growth Council under the office of the Prime Minister allow for greater coordination of the sectors in tapping in on investments and allows for more targeted preparation of skilled workers to meet the demands of the workforce.

The Government of Finland according to the National Board of Education (2010) funds VET up to 43%. There are also different kinds of subsidies that adult learners, employers and apprentices can also receive to assist them in their training pursuits. The HEART Trust/NTA within our context provides funding for TVET training. This, however, needs to be broadened to support areas that are in demand, and not just only programmes that are offered through their institutions. There is also the need for a more coordinated source of funding for all levels of the system for TVET training.

The Finnish system has a core of training providers who carry out training on behalf of the Government. These providers are paid based on the number of students and the areas that they are offering. In some cases, there is a performance-based incentive that can benefit employers. Jamaica also has a core of training providers, but funding support is not provided in the way it is provided for the providers in Finland. Some institutions are supported in Jamaica through the HEART/NSTA Trust, some are funded directly by the Government while there are others that are self-financing. This structure does not sufficiently allow for the sector to be effectively coordinated, making the argument for a new structure for improved coordination.

Finland has a very mature system that has resulted in a larger percentage of their students entering upper vocational education as against upper general secondary education. According to Brown Ruzzi (2005), 65% of Finnish students go on to higher education with two-thirds of this amount entering Polytechnics and 43% entering the vocational institutions. This has resulted in a more positive perception of vocational education and indeed a more skilled workforce. Overtime the Jamaican TVET system will be further enhanced as greater awareness is created and more effort is made to support adults and the out of school population. The impending mergers and strategies such as the National policy on work supported by a National Apprenticeship system, will allow for greater structure and coordination. There will also be changes in the legislation of various entities that will create greater alignment.

Impact of Policy Development on the Performance of the Education System

The policy development process in Jamaica has certainly had a significant impact on the integration of TVET within the education system. Over the last 40 years and significantly within the last 10 years, noteworthy strides have been made regarding the implementation of strategies to support the established policies and directives relating to TVET development. The move to incorporate TVET in the system from early childhood has started off successfully and greater strides are being made to allow students to learn the fundamentals at each stage. At the upper levels, more and more students are pursuing TVET programmes and the results from these programmes continue to be above the national average of all examinations (Ministry of Education, Youth and Information Report, 2016).

The HEART/NSTA Trust is re-organized to further support the integration of TVET within the system. A part of this support includes the provision of capacity building for teachers and the auditing of systems within institutions with a view to assisting the Ministry to take the corrective measures as necessary. STEM is currently being used to rebrand TVET as a part of the implementation of the curriculum. This has seen greater support being provided by industry personnel through industry exposure and the provision and use of applicable equipment and tools in different areas. All TVET areas currently must use the application of science, technology, the engineering design process, and mathematics principles in instruction and demonstration to students.

Perhaps a most significant impact is the ability of the education system to offer customized education based on industry needs as well as to provide work experience/apprenticeship programmes for students. This approach has allowed for more applicable programmes to be offered and students to be ready to move into the world of work, creating their own employment or into further education. The introduction of the Centre of Occupational Studies, responsible for the development of Occupational degrees and the commencement of the Occupational associate degree is an indication that the system of mainstreaming and fully integrating TVET in Jamaica is advancing.

PLACING JAMAICA ON A SOLID PATH OF TVET INTEGRATION

As Jamaica moves into the future, greater effort now needs to be made to place Jamaica on the cutting edge of technology and to invest further in research and innovation. This will lead to the creation of original and better products and services to serve the Jamaican people as well as patents for products and services in other countries. As the education system re-creates itself to prepare qualified and competent workers who are fit for the Jamaican workforce, the country needs to seek opportunities for further investments for more persons to become engaged in the workforce. The ability to train adequate number of workers in sector adaptable skills is indeed a plus for the Jamaican education system, and if it continues in the same trajectory it is expected that there will be greater improvement in the economy and indeed the quality of life for all Jamaicans.

The global market has opened up making it very easy to access information and to establish trade arrangements in neighbouring countries as well as those that are farther afield. This is therefore creating greater opportunities for attracting investments to Jamaica. The education system must continue to re-invent itself and to keep abreast with the changes and trends taking place while repositioning itself to serve the student population.

Industry, Government, NGOs, parents and other stakeholders must come on board to support the development of young people and change the general perception of TVET across the country. Career development also serves a major role in educating parents and children on the choices available and areas of growth in TVET. The Government should also continue to support companies with incentives to invest and fund secondary level education including the payment of examination fees for students, especially those who live below the poverty line. Jamaica will continue to adopt and adapt international best practices in reviewing and formulating new policies that will allow for ease in the continuous integration of TVET within the system.

BIBLIOGRAPHY

Apprenticeship Act. (1957). Kingston, Jamaica. http://www.moj.gov.jm/laws/apprenticeship-act-0

Atchoarena, D., & McArdle, T. (1999). Reforming training governance: The Jamaican experience. http://unesdoc.unesco.org/images/0011/001176/117647E.pdf.

Bennell, P., & Segerstrom, J. (1998). Vocational education and training in developing countries: Has the World Bank got it right? *International Journal of Educational Development, 18* (4), 271–287.

Billett, S., & Seddon. T. (2004). Building community through social partnerships around vocational education and training, *Journal of Vocational Education and Training, 56* (1), 51–68.

Bjørnavold, J., & Coles, M. (2008). Governing education and training: The case of qualifications frameworks. *European Journal of Vocational Training, 42/43*, 203–235.

Brown Ruzzi, B. (July 2005). Finland Education Report. National Center on Education and the Economy New Commission on the Skills of the American Workforce.

Caribbean Examination Council (2012). Draft TVET Policy. St Michaels, Barbados.

CARICOM Secretariat. (2012). The CARICOM Regional TVET. Guyana.

Finnish National Board of Education. (2010). Vocational education and training in Finland: Vocational competence, knowledge and skills for working life and further studies. http://old.adapt.it/adapt-indice-a-z/wp-content/uploads/2014/08/finish_nationaledu.pdf

Goh, C. B., & Gopinathan, S. (2006). The development of education in Singapore since 1965. In Fredriksen, B. & Tan, J. P. (Eds.), *Development practice in education: An African exploration of the East Asian education experience* (pp. 80–108). Washington, DC: The World Bank.

Goleman, D. (1998). Working with emotional intelligence, London Bloomsbury Publishing.

Green, F., Ashton, D., James, D., & Sung, J. (1999). The role of the state in skills formation: Evidence from the Republic of South Korea, Singapore and Taiwan. *Oxford Review of Economic Policy, 15* (1), 82–96.

HEART Trust/NTA. (2000). Annual report. Kingston, Jamaica.

HEART Trust/NTA. (2007). Annual report. Kingston, Jamaica.

HEART Trust/NTA. (2011). Annual report, 2011. Kingston, Jamaica.
HEART Trust/NTA (2003). Return on investment study. Kingston, Jamaica
HEART Trust/NTA. (2000). Strategic plan. Kingston, Jamaica.
HEART Trust/NTA. (2006). Try-a-skill concept document. Kingston, Jamaica.
HEART Trust/NTA. (2007). Try-a-skill manual. Kingston, Jamaica.
HEART Trust/NTA. (2004). WorldSkills concept document. Kingston, Jamaica.
International Labour Office. (2008). Skills for improved productivity, employment growth and development. (International Labour Conference 97th session). http://www.ilo.org/wcmsp5/groups/public/.../wcms_092054.pdf.
International Labour Office. (2010). Increasing the employability of disadvantaged youth. Skills for employment Policy Brief. http://www.ilo.org/wcmsp5/groups/public/---ed_emp/---ifp_skills/documents/publication/wcms_167168.pdf.
International Labour Organization. (n.d.). The changing role of government and other stakeholders in vocational education and training. ILO.
International Organisation of Employers (IOE). (2002). Employers' handbook on HIV/AIDS: A guide for action (UNAIDS/02.17E). Retrieved from http://www.unaids.org/en/media/unaids/contentassets/dataimport/publications/irc-pub02/jc767-employershandbook_en.pdf.
Kuruvilla, S., Erickson, C. L., & Hwang, A. (2002). An assessment of the Singapore skills development system: Does it constitute a viable model for other developing countries? http://digitalcommons.ilr.cornell.edu/articles/214/.
Lasonen, J. (n.d). *Reforming technical and vocational education and training in Finland.* Institute for Educational Research University of Jyväskylä.
McArdle, T. (2002). Planning in technical and vocational education and training. HEART Trust/National Training Agency.
McArdle, T. (2006). Investment in the HEART TRUST/NTA. HEART Trust/NTA.
Ministry of Education. (2010). *Career advancement programme (CAP) concept document.* MOEYC, Jamaica.
Ministry of Education. (2013). *National standard curriculum conceptual framework.* MOEYC, Jamaica.
Ministry of Education. (2010). *Career advancement programme framework.* MOEYC, Jamaica.
Ministry of Education. (2012). *Career advancement programme report.* MOEYC, Jamaica.
Ministry of Education. (1993). *Caribbean plan of action for early childhood education, care and development [ECECD].* MOEYC, Jamaica.
Ministry of Education Competence. (2009). *Based transition policy document.* MOEYC, Jamaica.
Ministry of Education. (2005). *Early childhood taskforce report.* MOEYC, Jamaica.
Ministry of Education. (2012). *TVET policy.* MOEYC, Jamaica.

Ministry of Education. (2010). Education system transformation programme document. MOEYC, Jamaica.
Ministry of Education. (1973). *Education thrust report.* MOEYC, Jamaica.
Ministry of Education. (2001). *Education white paper.* MOEYC, Jamaica.
Ministry of Education. (1973). *Jamaica education assessment.* MOEYC, Jamaica.
Ministry of Education. (1990). *Jamaica five-year development plan.* MOEYC, Jamaica.
Ministry of Education. (2012). *National strategic plan.* MOEYC, Jamaica.
Ministry of Education. (1966). *New deal for education.* MOEYC, Jamaica.
Ministry of Education. (2015). *Occupational degrees concept paper.* MOEYC, Jamaica
Ministry of Education. (2016). *Youth and information CXC report.* MOEYC, Jamaica.
Ministry of Education. (2010). *Reforms in education.* MOEYC, Jamaica.
Ministry of Education. (1991). *Ministry of education report.* MOEYC, Jamaica
Ministry of Education. (2000). *Ministry of education report.* MOEYC, Jamaica.
Ministry of Education. (2003). *Ministry of education report.* MOEYC, Jamaica.
Ministry of Education. (1993). *ROSE concept document.* MOEYC, Jamaica.
Ministry of Education. (1965). *The education act 1965.* MOEYC, Jamaica.
Ministry of Education. (2008). *The development and state of the art of adult learning and education (ALE): National report of Jamaica.* The Jamaican Foundation for Lifelong Learning.
Ministry of Education. (2008). *USAID Country Plan, 2009–2013.* Ministry of Education, Jamaica.
Ministry of Education, Youth and Culture. (1995). *The ROSE secretariat. Planning and building together: Options for upper secondary education in Jamaica.* MOEYC, Jamaica.
Molebash, P. (n.d.). Technology and Education: Current and future trends. http://itari.in/categories/futuretrendsineducation/FutureofEdu-Tech.pdf
Morris, R. R. (2011). *Post-Independence Education Sector Report, s1962–2012.*
Morris, H. A. (1998). Technical and vocational education at the secondary level. *Institute of Education Annual, 1,* 110–127.
OECD. (2010). *Strong Performers and Successful Reformers in Education: Lessons from PISA for the United States.* https://www.oecd.org/pisa/46623978.pdf
Shanghai TVET Declaration. (2012). UNESCO. Final Report of International Congress on Technical and Vocational Education Shanghai, China.
UNESCO. (2000). *Pillars of learning.* http://www.unesco.org/delors/fourpil.htm
UNESCO. (2012, May). *Transforming technical and vocational education.* Third International Congress on Technical and Vocational Education and Training, Shanghai, People's Republic of China, 13–16 May. http://unesdoc.unesco.org/images/0021/002160/216065e.pdf
UNESCO/ILO. (2001). *Recommendations on TVET for the 21st Century.*
UNICEF. (2008). *Education statistics: Singapore.* Division of Policy and Practice,

Statistics and Monitoring Section. http://www.childinfo.org/files/IND_Singapore.pdf

Wee, J. (1997). Singapore Productivity and Standards Board. *SPRING Singapore*. National Library Board Singapore of Singapore.

CHAPTER 7

Technical and Vocational Education and Training at the Tertiary Level in Jamaica:
Achievements, Challenges and Impacts

HALDEN MORRIS

THE LANDSCAPE OF TERTIARY LEVEL EDUCATION IN Jamaica has changed significantly during the last three decades because of increased recognition and influence by important stakeholders in a dynamic technological global market. The education system must adjust to facilitate growth and development and strive to satisfy the needs of the economy. The inception of the Caribbean Single Market and Economy (CSME) and the continued removal of restrictions for accessing international markets have challenged the Jamaican education system to deliver quality personnel to marshal what can now be viewed as non-traditional high demand professional education and training.

The importance and value of Technical and Vocational Education and Training (TVET) is also being increasingly recognized in the context of lifelong learning in a globalised world by the United Nations Educational Scientific and Cultural Organization (UNESCO), and other national, regional and global stakeholders in education and national development. At the tertiary level, TVET is becoming more prominent and is increasingly becoming a viable choice for students, if they are convinced that they are receiving high quality education. In this regard and according to Morris (2015, p.119), "with the growing momentum and interest in

TVET at the tertiary level, quality is currently regarded as an essential component in the provision at this level and type of education."

This chapter provides a brief synopsis of TVET at the tertiary level in Jamaica prior to 1970 and a comprehensive account of what took place after 1970. The chapter will focus on new developments in TVET at the tertiary level and attempt to provide relevant information on the implementation of processes and practices which significantly impact the delivery of TVET at this level in Jamaica. The challenges, outcomes, impacts and the present status of TVET at the tertiary level in Jamaica will also be discussed.

BACKGROUND

Technical Vocational Education and Training (TVET) is referred by the 2001 United Nations Educational Scientific and Cultural Organisation and International Labour Organisation (ILO) general conference on TVET, as a discipline which covers,

> those aspects of the educational process involving, in addition to general education, the study of technologies and related sciences, and the acquisition of practical skills, attitudes, understanding and knowledge related to occupations in various sectors of economic and social life. (UNESCO and ILO 2002, 7)

In recognition that TVET can better enable individuals to participate in social, economic and technological innovation processes, it is imperative that efforts are made to embed TVET into regional and national innovation structures to stimulate economic performance and social development of countries. Over the last two decades several countries introduced TVET subjects at their universities and have subsequently developed complete tertiary level TVET programmes. Among these countries are China, Malaysia, Indonesia, Malawi and Jamaica. Partly, they already existed in German speaking countries and in Scandinavian countries. Other international initiatives include the Commonwealth of Learning (COL) partnership with local organizations, to establish and support the Commonwealth Educational Media Centre for Asia (CEMCA). The COL initiative has also strengthened the Pacific TVET network in association with the Open Polytechnic of New Zealand. This network organizes and coordinates educational and training programmes in the technical/vocational area including the training of technical/vocational teachers. The Hangzhou declaration of 2004 also emphasized this point and suggests implementation of more TVET subjects in more universities (UNESCO-UNEVOC, 2004).

In addition to universities, tertiary level TVET includes curricula pursued in technical institutes and colleges. These institutions deliver courses and programmes geared at attaining advanced qualifications and professional certification in technical and vocational areas. It must however be understood that not all TVET curricula pursued in these institutions can be classified as "tertiary level TVET". At the tertiary level, a clear distinction is that students are exposed to advanced knowledge, skills and understanding that are required to address critical developmental issues, usually leading to at least an associate degree or its equivalent (Mishra, 2006). According to Mishra (2006), higher education

> develops the student's ability to question and seek truth and makes him/her competent to critique on contemporary issues. It broadens the intellectual powers of the individual within a narrow specialization, but also gives him or her a wider perspective of the world around. (p.5)

According to Navaratnam, and O'Connor (1993) in Morris (2015), tertiary level TVET provides the basis for scientific and technological advancement and economic growth of a country. It provides opportunities for lifelong learning which allows persons to upgrade their knowledge and skills, ensuring currency in industry practice. It also facilitates access to training in other linked areas as needed by the individual or the society, upgrades leadership skills to provide quality leadership in areas of specialization and promotes quality and social justice by focusing on the values and attitudes needed for developing individuals and the society.

It is evident that sustainable development of a society cannot be achieved when students have limited access to tertiary education. Limited access in developing nations in particular, will perpetuate continuous reliance on the delivery systems of developed countries to provide personnel to satisfy their TVET leadership demands. It has become necessary for institutions to rethink their policies and reconfigure their operations to deliver education and training to address leadership and technical needs to facilitate critical developments of nations. One may argue that the institutions in developing countries are neither equipped nor prepared to deliver this type of education, however, a modest start must be made in order to achieve capacity building. UNESCO-UNEVOC (2004) suggested that it would be unwise to start with a large number of vocational disciplines, since institutions offering these new programmes will have to develop their own profile and at the same time compete with already established academic disciplines.

According to Clarke (2005, p. 51), "one of the most fundamental aspects of the mission of tertiary education should be its participation in the development and improvement of education at the other levels of the education system." He also claimed that tertiary education should have an impact on the content and quality of the work being done at the early childhood, primary, and secondary levels. This should not only include the training of teachers, but also personnel in the various sectors. Technical and vocational education at the tertiary level must aim at providing a platform for research and providing advanced education and training for technical and vocational educators, practitioners and administrators. It is anticipated that this education will consolidate technical and vocational disciplines and serve as a catalyst for further developments in the field. Universities and colleges in most developed and some developing countries have recognized the importance of TVET and have made deliberate attempts to provide access to tertiary level education for a wide cross-section of persons in the field.

To ensure that TVET at the tertiary level is not left to chance, the government of some countries have provided funding by way of grants and or creative taxation measures for institutions to access, primarily to facilitate the implementation of vocational disciplines and the delivery of programmes to support these disciplines. Unfortunately, the funding provided is chiefly for the lower levels of the system, and in many cases no funding is provided for the tertiary levels. This revelation begs the question, are tertiary level TVET disciplines considered critical and important for nations? UNESCO-UNEVOC (2004) outlined three main reasons for implementing vocational disciplines at this level:

1. Vocational disciplines constitute the framework for subject-area oriented research-based development of TVET.
2. Vocational disciplines can form the basis of contents of technical and vocational education and training, which is common to several occupational profiles. This part of subject-related contents can be taught for different occupations.
3. Vocational disciplines are what TVET teachers must study in order to be able to provide subject-related technical and vocational education and training for a restricted group of occupations.

The reasons put forward by UNESCO-UNEVOC embrace three primary areas of focus for tertiary programmes, namely research, specialization core content and programme specific courses for the various occupations. These areas of focus are congruent with programme offerings by most universities. Approaches such as that used in Germany could be utilized to make TVET less complex in terms of delivery, organisation and administration. According to UNESCO-UNEVOC (2004), Germany introduced so-called occupational areas. This was done essentially to identify various sets of occupations, for which a particular basic education and training was defined to be identical. Hence, the concept of basic education for the whole occupational field was introduced. This meant that for all occupations, the first year of the 3/4 years was identical. Curriculum development work had only to be done once for each occupational field, also the implementation of education and training for this first year was easier in terms of concepts and equipment for the institutions as well as for industries that participated in TVET. This concept proved quite successful for the occupations which were multi-disciplinary but was less favourable in more recent times where technological development imposed a much more interdisciplinary shape on the major occupational profiles (UNESCO-UNEVOC, 2004).

This concept could be adapted for delivery of tertiary level technical and vocational education and training programmes in general. It is evident that organizational and management courses could be delivered to satisfy education and training needs at the tertiary level without compromising quality using this approach. Programme efficiency could be enhanced by placing emphasis on entry qualifications to ensure that an acceptable level has been attained in the technical and or vocational field before candidates are accepted into these programmes.

EARLY TERTIARY LEVEL TVET INITIATIVES IN THE CARIBBEAN

Tertiary level TVET is a relatively mature concept in the Caribbean. According to Evans and Burke (2007), "the 'idea of higher education' in the West Indies began with the proposals by Bishop Berkeley in the eighteenth century" (p.8). Berkley, regarded the University as 'a place of contemplative solitude in which minds untainted by the corrupt world dwelt with a love of truth and honourable regard' (Brathwaite, 1958, p.3). A later proposal for a nondenominational higher education institution was made by the Jamaican Baptist missionary James Phillippo for a college for secular studies in 1843. This plan would ensure 'intelligent and aspiring youth should have the means of assembling in halls of their own' (Brathwaite, 1958; Evans & Burke, 2007). This college was to be modelled on the newly established University College in London with an objective to 'train young men immediately before entering upon the business of active life' (Brathwaite, 1958; Evans & Burke, 2007). In the early twentieth century, Marcus Garvey also proposed a private high level Technical Institute in Jamaica based on the Tuskegee Institute established by Booker T. Washington in the USA.

Although the qualifications of skilled workers and technicians are regarded as a key for the competitiveness of companies and economies all over the world, technical and vocational education at the tertiary level is still considered scarce commodity in the Caribbean and many developing countries. Despite the call for this type of education by political leaders, industries, commerce and the public in general, very little has been done to provide access to this education in many developing countries. Up to 2007 there are only a handful of institutions in the Caribbean which offer significant technical and vocational education and training programmes at the tertiary level. Among these are the University of Technology, Mico Teachers' College, and the Vocational Training Development Institute (VTDI) located in Jamaica. Sir Arthur Lewis Community College (SALCC) located in St Lucia, St Vincent and the Grenadines Community College (SVGCC), the Samuel Jackman Prescod Polytechnic (SJPP) located in Barbados, the Southern Caribbean University and the University of Trinidad and Tobago (UTT), located in Trinidad. These institutions experience severe limitations, consequently, access is limited to only a small fraction of persons desirable and eligible to enter these institutions. With Jamaica being the most prolific in TVET programme offerings at the tertiary level, the country served as the main source of tertiary TVET training for the Caribbean. As a result of lack of places and programmes for tertiary TVET in the Region, many Caribbean nationals access this type of education in developed countries such as United States, Canada, Germany, Australia, New Zealand, England, and Russia. It is evident that developing countries benefit most from Caribbean persons equipped with technical and vocational education since many of those who were trained in developed countries remain there to work after training.

As the Caribbean embraces the Caribbean Single Market and Economy (CSME), more is placed on the TVET system since this area of education is considered critical in national and regional development. As evidenced in research conducted by Morris in 2007, the need for personnel who are capable of operating at advanced levels will drastically increase, especially in the area of leadership, standard setting, and quality assurance. It was also abundantly clear that institutions need to retool and revise their programme offerings to provide personnel to fill these important positions. The importance of making these provisions cannot be overemphasized as indicated by the UNESCO-UNEVOC International Centre for Technical and Vocational Education and Training (2005) that stated, "having a pool of skilled and knowledgeable people within the TVET industry is as important to the TVET industry as it is to the industries TVET serves." Delivery of tertiary level TVET in the Caribbean and Jamaica has provided necessary leadership capacity in various technical and vocational fields. This has led to the development of policies, systems, and mechanisms to assist in advancing TVET training in the region.

HISTORICAL SYNOPSIS OF TERTIARY LEVEL TVET PROGRAMMES IN JAMAICA

The term tertiary education presented by Roberts (2001) is considered to be the third stage of the educational experience that builds upon secondary education completed, which is often indicated by possession of credentials such as the Caribbean Examinations Council's Secondary Education Certificate (CSEC). Tertiary is a level and not a type of education and it can be engaged in not only colleges, universities and polytechnics, but also in schools ... (p. 20).

Evans and Burke (2007) provided a review of the first phase of tertiary education in Jamaica which took into account the introduction of tertiary level TVET programmes which were very minimal or could be considered practically non-existent. They claimed that the need for tertiary education in Jamaica became a pressing one after emancipation in 1834 and documented the scenario that once it was accepted that the ex-slaves would receive some form of rudimentary education or training, it was recognized that local teachers had to be provided. Education was undertaken mainly by the religious denominations who were interested in converting the ex-slaves to Christianity, and there was keen competition among the various religious denominations to establish some form of teacher training. The Moravians, for example, established an institution as early as 1832. The Anglicans, the Church Missionary Society, the Baptists, the Presbyterians, and the Wesleyans followed soon after with development of their institutions (D'Oyley, 1963). Most of these institutions were short lived because of problems of financing, and differences of opinion about the curriculum. Teachers colleges and model schools were later established by the government when it became obvious that the churches could not provide a sufficient number of teacher training institutions to satisfy the need for teachers. These, however, were also short-lived. One of the early teacher education institutions that has survived over the years is The Mico College – established in 1835 with proceeds from the Negro Education Grant given by the British government for the religious and moral education of the ex-slaves. A sum of £5000 was secured from this grant for the preparation of teachers and most of this money was given to the Mico Trust which at the time operated the largest number of schools in Jamaica. Other teachers colleges established in the nineteenth century and still currently exist are: Bethlehem Moravian Teachers College, established in 1861; Shortwood Teachers College, established in 1885; and St Josephs Teachers College, established in 1897" (Evans and Burke, 2007, p.11). This constituted the first phase of tertiary education in Jamaica which was embraced until 1963.

Following the first phase, TVET gained more prominence in the tertiary level education landscape. This began with the granting of a charter to the regional University of the West Indies. According to Evans and Burke (2007), this phase was "characterized by a dramatic increase in the number and types of higher education institutions, and an expansion in the objectives and scope of existing colleges. These institutions included schools of nursing, physical therapy, occupational therapy, pharmacy, radiology and medical technology, technical colleges, business colleges, colleges of agriculture, colleges of physical education and sports. The four Schools of Art, Drama, Music and Dance were established and operated as separate tertiary teacher/artist training institutions until they merged to form the Edna Manley College for the Visual and Performing Arts in 1987. Two new teachers colleges were created and single purpose institutions such as the Jamaica School of Agriculture merged to form multi-purpose institutions" (p.11). The Jamaica Institute of Technology (JIT) was established in 1958 with a mandate to focus on technical training. One year later, the name of this institution was changed to the College of Arts Science and Technology (CAST). The Vocational Training Development Institute (VTDI) was established in 1970 with the aim of preparing technical and vocational education and training instructors, managers and technicians. Private institutions also responded to the need for access to tertiary education (Evans & Burke, 2007).

Significant among these, as it relates to tertiary TVET, was CAST where a diploma in technical teacher education programme was developed and implemented by the College in collaboration with the Ministry of Education. The programme was initiated with a pilot group of six students specializing in mechanical technology and six specializing in business education. It was later expanded with funding from the Canadian International Development Agency (CIDA) during 1973–1978. This fund provided buildings, furniture, equipment, technical support inclusive of lecturers to develop and teach the programme. CIDA funding also provided fellowships to prepare Jamaican scholars to replace the Canadian staff at CAST. In addition to mechanical technology and business education, the expanded programme prepared teachers in the specializations of Electrical Technology, Construction Technology, Information Technology and Home Economics and produced an average of 100 technical teachers on an annual basis. Quality assurance for these programmes was provided by the Joint Board of Teacher Education (JBTE), an entity which was created as a tri-partite arrangement between Ministries of education, teachers colleges and the University of the West Indies to provide certification and quality assurance for all teacher training programs in the English speaking Caribbean.

The 1970s also ushered in the creation of community colleges, the first of which was established in 1974. These colleges developed strong part-time evening programmes which facilitated access to tertiary TVET for the benefit of many working people. They provided continuing education after grade 11, for various middle level occupations and continuing education for persons who wanted to enter certain professions, occupations, higher education institutions or the world of work, and to respond to the needs of the community (Walsh, 2005; Evans & Burke, 2007). Significant among these was Excelsior Community College, which offered a wide variety of TVET programmes such as nursing, industrial technology education and business education.

In the 1980s, a number of teachers colleges began offering bachelors degrees in affiliation with foreign universities. During this period a wide variety of affiliations, articulation, and franchising arrangements were developed between colleges and universities outside and within the region. In the late 1980s CAST introduced its first TVET bachelor's degree programme to upgrade the qualifications of teachers who earned diplomas. This was accomplished by delivering a one-year programme over three summers. A special programme was developed (BEd – General Technology) for the industrial arts diploma graduates of the Mico Teachers college or equivalent diplomas from other teacher training institutions.

In 1996, the Task Force on New Directions in Teacher Education declared that colleges should begin to prepare teachers at the Bachelors degree level within a five year period. These degree granting colleges continued to offer diploma programmes since this certification would continue until the degree programmes were in effect in all colleges (Evans & Burke, 2007). In 1995, CAST was renamed the University of Technology, Jamaica. This renaming was accompanied by a phased development and implementation of bachelor's programmes in TVET among other disciplines across the institution. The first phase constituted continuation of the upgrading of three-year diploma to a bachelor's degree in a joint agreement with the Ministry of Education. The second phase consisted of restructuring the technical teacher education diploma programme into a four-year bachelor's degree programme for all specializations. Parallel to this development was the introduction of graduate level TVET programmes. Table 7.1 shows the number of tertiary level programmes that were offered in selected institutions in Jamaica in 2006. Notwithstanding, during 2005, most teachers' colleges offered at least one TVET programme. The programmes offered by these institutions were limited to business education, information technology education and home economics/ home and family life education (HFLE). Since 2006, the number of institutions which offer tertiary level TVET programmes has increased significantly. The Mico University College now offers bachelors' degrees and the remaining seven teachers' training colleges in Jamaica offer bachelor's degrees in collaboration with UWI. Two institutions, the University of the West Indies and the University of Technology, Jamaica are currently offering masters and PhD programmes which focus on TVET Leadership.

Table 7.1: Tertiary Level TVET Programmes Offered in Jamaica (2006)

Institution	Diploma	Bachelors'	Masters'	Doctorate
University of Technology, Jamaica	1(7)	1(11)	2	0
Vocational Training Development Institute	7(3)	3	1	0
Mico Teachers College	1(6)	0	0	0
University of the West Indies	0	0	0(1)	0

Note: Number in ( ) represents courses/specializations
Source: Morris, 2007 & 2012

GRADUATE LEVEL TVET EDUCATION IN JAMAICA

Although it has been established that vocational disciplines are considered to be of great importance to society, decision makers and institutions often are reluctant to implement many technical and vocational programmes because many of them are not regarded as programmes which lead to fully recognized academic disciplines even in countries where they exist for a long time. According to UNESCO-UNEVOC, 2004, the academic communities fear to damage their high status if too many – in their eyes "low quality" – subjects exist at their universities. Furthermore, more traditional academic oriented subjects such as physics, aeronautics, material sciences, etc. bring higher reputation and usually more money to institutions. They suggested that it might be unwise to start with too many vocational disciplines, then needing to build up their own profile in order to compete with already established academic disciplines. On the contrary, the World Bank (2000) indicates that the world economy has been changing, as knowledge supplants physical capital as the source of present and future wealth. As knowledge becomes more important, so does higher education. This has resulted in a greater demand for higher and adult education internationally. Rapid technological advances and the global trend in the liberalization of services, in addition to the quest for knowledge and certification, have resulted in an even greater demand for higher education in an ever-increasing competitive environment such as that which exists in Jamaica. In addition to local public institutions, local private tertiary institutions are offering their services and have contributed to the expansion of access in the region. Overseas colleges and universities registered in Jamaica are also offering programmes. Despite all these developments, the demand for tertiary education is still not completely filled. The target set by CARICOM of 15 percent of the 18–24 age cohort gaining access to tertiary education has already been surpassed in the case of Jamaica.

According to UNESCO-UNEVOC (2004), 60% to 80% of the workforce worldwide are trained and educated in institutions for TVET for the intermediate employment sector. Recent trends have shown that internationally there is a pipeline of students who will expect to pursue upper secondary and tertiary education (Marope, Chakroun, & Holmes, 2015). Marope et.al (2015) claimed that the expansion of secondary education and growing concern about the school-to-work transition is producing changes in the general education curriculum. They further claimed that "as opportunities for lower education have increased, the movement of vocational studies has progressed into upper secondary education. In countries where upper secondary education is readily available, technical and vocational studies have progressed into post-secondary education" (p.41).

Graduate level TVET education in the Caribbean was practically non-existent until 1986 when in Jamaica, CAST introduced a master's degree in Workforce Education in collaboration with Southern Illinois University (SIU), a United States university. This development was facilitated through a memorandum of understanding between SIU and CAST developed and implemented by Halden Morris in 1982. Following the upgrading of CAST to university status in 2006 and renamed the University of Technology, Jamaica (UTech), and through the School of Technical and Vocational Education, the Faculty of Liberal Studies and Education, the institution adopted the programme as its first post graduate offering. The university continues to be aggressive in forging ahead with development of graduate programmes in technical and vocational education for the Caribbean Region. Notwithstanding these developments, it is evident that limited access to graduate programmes in TVET remains a challenge in Jamaica and the Caribbean region because of cost and the unavailability of places to pursue programmes of this nature.

TVET GRADUATE DEGREES AT THE UWI

In 2009 the School of Education in the Faculty of Humanities and Education, UWI, Mona Campus launched a Master of Arts degree in Leadership in TVET and Workforce Development. In 2012, UWI, St Augustine Campus adopted and delivered this programme to a cohort of over 30 students. Following these developments, the UWI School of Education at the Mona campus developed and launched its MPhil/PhD programme in this discipline in 2016.

In formulating the role of TVET in national development, Tobias (2012), indicated that new programs in TVET are introduced to meet labour market skills needs and changing workplace requirements. The TVET graduate degrees at the University of the West Indies (UWI) were designed with this view in mind. The concept of graduate level TVET programme at UWI was first introduced with the development and implementation of a course entitled "Administration of TVET Programmes (ED63G) by Halden Morris in the Masters' in Education (MEd) programme in the School of Education in 1996. The extensive demand for this course in the Med programme led to a concept paper entitled *"Graduate Studies in Technical and Vocational Education and Training (TVET) in the Caribbean – Whose Responsibility?"*, authored and presented by Halden Morris at the Ninth Schools of Education Biennial Conference held in 2007 in Trinidad. The proposed programme aimed at building on the undergraduate programmes delivered by the other tertiary institutions in the region and from elsewhere in the world, was developed based primarily on research conducted in Jamaica prior to 2007 (Morris, 2007). The proposed programme offering was multidisciplinary and focused on professional development in the field. Under the leadership of Professor Halden Morris, and in collaboration with Dr Moses Peart and Dr Disraeli Hutton, a complete set of courses was developed for the proposed Master of Arts in Leadership in Technical and Vocational Education and Training and Workforce Development programme. The strategic objectives and commitment of the University of the West Indies, to the progressive development of education in the Caribbean under the leadership of Professor Nigel Harris, former Vice-Chancellor of UWI and Professor Gordon Shirley, former Principal of the Mona Campus UWI, led to its acceptance and implementation in 2012.

Recognizing that TVET is considered a major component in sustainable economic and social development of any nation, it was of critical importance for the University to make a contribution in this area. According to Gordon Shirley at the launch of the programme, "the success of this programme will be accomplished through informed engagement with TVET educational theory, policy and practice." The degree takes the form of a Lifelong Learning Model (LLM) which is increasingly becoming a feature of the educational landscape and is becoming the day-to-day responsibilities for professionals across all sectors of the economy. It was designed for those working in education and training in schools, colleges, universities, training organisations; for those working in training departments of industries and commercial enterprises; and for those working with disadvantaged sections of the population and socially excluded groups.

The UWI, School of Education, Mona having worked for more than forty years with Teachers Colleges (TC) and other Tertiary Level Institutions (TLI), was deemed best suited to engage learners and researchers at this level to bring to the fore a new and progressive cadre of committed TVET planners and educators. The UWI, having implemented a successful on-line course delivery system maximized the experience and expertise of international professionals in TVET education in planning, developing and reviewing the programme in order to ensure that it adequately reflects the educational needs of industries and the social, cultural and political context in which they work.

CAREER/EMPLOYMENT OPPORTUNITIES FOR TVET GRADUATES

Graduates of TVET programmes in general are currently in great demand. Increasingly, the demand for persons with tertiary level training in TVET has become critical. According to the Ministry of Education (2015),

> The integration of technical and vocational education (TVE) into the education system ensures that the system prepares fully rounded students equipped with the skills and competencies necessary for a globalized workforce. The small number of entries for the technical and vocational subjects in the regional examination (CSEC) is a reflection of the low premium that the society in general, places on these subjects. The thrust of the Ministry of Education is that all students should exit the secondary level with at least one technical or vocational subject. (p.22)

It is evident that persons with tertiary TVET will be in demand to support the education and training system if this objective is to be realized. Persons with this qualification will satisfy positions in organizations which develop and implement technical and vocational education programmes for institutions across the Caribbean. Industrial organizations that develop and offer their own technical and vocational programmes would also benefit from these persons. In general, organizations that cater for life-long learning such as universities, teachers colleges, community colleges, business and industry, community service agencies, training agencies, military services and governmental bodies will benefit enormously from this programme.

Programme Objectives

The objectives of the Master of Arts programme in Leadership in TVET and workforce development is as follows:

1. To satisfy the demands of CARICOM region for new TVET leaders who can design, manage and support TVET and workforce development programmes.
2. To encourage, facilitate and guide new quality research and development activities in TVET to inform policy and workforce development.
3. To provide a professional development track for TVET practitioners to improve their leadership capacity.
4. To provide qualified instructional leaders with new skills and capabilities to improve the quality of existing TVET programmes and to enhance the quality and performance of TVET institutions in the region.
5. To prepare candidates for doctoral studies in the areas of TVET and WFD.
6. To develop researchers in the field of TVET and WFD.

Specifically, the programme delivers a curriculum that caters to principles of research-led teaching, critical inquiry into the development of technical and vocational education while exposing students to current TVET theories and principles. Students are engaged in self-directed learning, collaborative learning and reflective practice and encouraged to develop a learning culture among themselves that would assist them in acting critically and competently in a variety of educational contexts. These students are provided with opportunities to engage in high quality, rigorous, scholarly research which will enable them to acquire a good understanding of TVET and of the cultural, political, and historical contexts in which it occurs. It is anticipated that these students will engage in the continuous development of TVET in the Caribbean as practitioners/trainers. The programme was designed with a balanced menu of courses to expose TVET professionals to the rudiments of tertiary level TVET. The programme consisted of six major elements:

1. TVET and WFD core courses
2. Applied science courses
3. Elective courses
4. Research
5. Structured field experience
6. Seminar series

Students are required to complete five core courses which include Philosophical Foundations of TVET and WFD; Workforce Analysis; Management of TVET and WFD programmes; Comparative Studies of TVET and WFD in Developed and Developing Countries; Budget Planning and Financial Management. Elective courses are selected by students to support their area of specialization or special interest needs. Students are also required to participate in three pre-approved TVET related conferences, workshops or seminars.

A critical aspect of this programme is research. Students are required to conduct research and complete a research paper which focuses on a particular aspect of TVET or a workforce development issue. Students are also required to complete an industrial attachment engagement, working as a shadow manager for a stipulated period.

This development synchronizes with the outcomes of the UNESCO International Meeting on Innovation and Excellence in TVET Teacher/Trainer Education, held in Hangzhou (China) from November 8 to 10, 2004, where participants agreed on standards and a framework curriculum for a university-based master degree for teachers and lecturers in TVET. The meeting defined 12 vocational disciplines that they claim would facilitate the international exchange of students and lecturers, which was previously impossible because of highly diverse traditions and modes of the education of TVET teachers and trainers. International co-operation in TVET research and development will likewise draw benefit from this UNESCO initiative. According to Runner and Dittrich in INWENT & UNESCO-UNEVOC (2004), representatives of both developing and developed countries emphasised the importance of the Hangzhou conventions. Developing countries anticipate involving their academic elites in research and development in TVET by initiating relevant masters' degree programmes at universities.

RESEARCH IN TVET IN JAMAICA

The UNESCO-UNEVOC International Centre for Technical and Vocational Education and Training (2005) outlined the importance of research in TVET. They pointed out that at the very centre of quality TVET is an effective interaction between teacher/trainer and learners. Indeed, an overall improvement in vocational skills for employability and citizenship can only be realized if there is an improvement in the quality, effectiveness, and relevance of teaching. This UNESCO-UNEVOC claim can best be realized through rigorous research. In recognition of the important role TVET plays in equipping individuals with relevant skills and knowledge, many persons, both in the developed and developing countries, are increasing the emphasis they place on improving the capacity of their TVET systems through research.

Governments in the Caribbean and developing nations in general have been calling for data to be used as the basis for making decisions in just about all sectors. Graduate level TVET education will provide a solid base for research in the field and hence necessary data. Worldwide, approximately two thirds of the workforce perform jobs that require a skill level which usually is associated with vocational education and training. Considering that workforce-development is one key issue for a country's overall development, it is necessary that the best minds – which usually gather in academic communities – carry out research and provide empirical data for use in the decision-making process. There are only a few countries in the world where such "vocational disciplines" are implemented at universities.

The University of the West Indies, a research focused university, is committed to providing opportunities for appropriate research to guide national and regional policy. To this end, a primary objective of this graduate studies programme is to carry out research in TVET. The Master of Arts and MPhil/PhD programmes are designed as a platform for satisfying the TVET related research needs in the Caribbean Region. Consequently, UWI, Mona Campus awarded its first PhD in Education with a focus on TVET and Workforce Development in 2014 to Dr Carole Powell whose research was titled "Towards a Model for Engaging the Jamaican Secondary Schools in Efficient Delivery of Technical Vocational Education and Training (TVET)." Likewise, the University of Technology, Jamaica, the Northern Caribbean University, the University of Guyana and other universities in the Caribbean are expanding their curricula to provide platforms to carry out research in TVET.

As a mechanism for dissemination of research, UWI in collaboration with the United Nations Education Scientific and Cultural Organization (UNESCO) and partners such as the Ministry of Education – Jamaica, the HEART Trust/NTA, the University of Technology – Jamaica and CANTA, staged a series of international conferences which focused on TVET in the Caribbean. The first conference was held in 2012 and embraced the theme "TVET and Human Capacity Development in the Caribbean." The second conference, held in 2015 was expanded to include additional partners under the theme "STEM Education in TVET: Imperative to National and Regional Development." Cumulatively, these conferences attracted over 200 technical papers, several of which disseminated research findings. It is anticipated that this conference will be staged biennially and will provide a sustainable mechanism for disseminating and sharing best practices in TVET.

QUALITY ASSURANCE FOR TERTIARY LEVEL TVET

According to Morris (2015), TVET at the tertiary level is not static; therefore, quality assurance mechanisms must assure ongoing improvement in the institutions' operations as they seek to produce quality outcomes while strategizing to satisfy emerging trends in the society. During the process of improvement, quality needs be at the forefront. All stakeholders must make quality a key priority, know and perform their roles and responsibilities, and adhere to established quality assurance principles. Morris also claimed that the establishment of an effective quality assurance process for tertiary level TVET can be a major challenge, since this requires commitment from all stakeholders to the process. The institution will have to make considerable commitments with respect to the provision of management and resources that are required to attain and maintain the standards that are acceptable to both industry and the educational institution. Additionally, he asserted that it may be necessary to develop a customized quality assurance process that is relevant and feasible for the specific nature of the TVET programme and the conditions found in the institution.

While a dedicated quality assurance mechanism has been established for TVET at the post-secondary level in Jamaica through the National Council on Technical and Vocational Education and Training (NCTVET) from as early as 1994, no dedicated quality assurance mechanism was established for tertiary level TVET. The Joint Board of Teacher Education established at the University of the West Indies was charged with the responsibility of providing certification and quality assurance services for all teachers colleges in the English speaking Caribbean, as such, quality assurance for TVET teacher training programmes was provided through this mechanism. Additionally, the University Council of Jamaica (UCJ), established by an Act of Parliament in 1987 in Jamaica was charged with the responsibility of providing quality assurance for all tertiary level programmes and institutions in Jamaica. This organization also provided quality assurance services for tertiary TVET programmes in Jamaica. As noted on the UCJs website, this institution was established "as the national quality assurance body for tertiary education to ensure quality through the adoption and improvement of educational standards. Today, the UCJ functions as a statutory body and is currently under the portfolio of the Minister of Education." The Council is governed by persons whose membership is drawn from the public and private sectors, professional bodies and societies and academic institutions, appointed by the Minister of Education with whom the portfolio resides.

The UCJ maintains a list of recognized (registered) higher education institutions. The Council registers institutions that have met minimum tertiary educational standards with respect to scope, level, appropriateness and educational value of institutional programmes and experiences; qualifications and competence of staff; rigor and strategy for assessing student performance; adequacy and suitability of physical facilities with regard to student enrollment; adequacy of resources, library, computers, laboratories, to support the programmes; and other operational factors. The UCJ also maintains a list of recognized (accredited) higher education programmes. The UCJ accredits degree and specialized programmes by establishing standards and applying criteria for the accreditation of tertiary educational programmes and courses of study; assisting registered institutions in the improvement of their educational programmes; and encouraging and facilitating programmes related to national needs. This body is the pace setter in the Caribbean as it relates to quality assurance for tertiary level institutions and programmes and provides quality assurance services for several tertiary level institutions in the Caribbean.

Other quality assurance initiatives include the Association of Caribbean Tertiary Level Institutions (ACTI) which was formed in 1992 to develop a mechanism for accreditation, equivalency and articulation within the Caribbean (ACTI, 2000). Also formed was a Joint Committee for Tertiary Education. Tertiary Level Institutions Units were established on each campus of the University of the West Indies, and a Tertiary Education Project Unit was initiated on the Mona campus of the University.

CHALLENGES OF TERTIARY TVET IN JAMAICA

Despite the remarkable gains that TVET at the tertiary level in Jamaica has achieved during the last century, especially during the last three decades, there are significant challenges that need to be urgently addressed. In addition to challenges identified earlier in this chapter, the lack of philosophical foundations, misunderstood TVET concepts and unawareness of the value of TVET at this level continue to be major challenges. Jamaica, and indeed the rest of the Caribbean, continue to be inundated with erroneous information about TVET, as such, many persons are inclined to avoid accessing TVET at the tertiary level. Although several efforts have been made to increase the cadre of trained professionals to deliver TVET programmes, both at the secondary and post-secondary levels, shortages continue to be a challenge. Studies have shown that highly trained technical persons are attracted to higher paying jobs in industries rather than in education both locally and abroad (Morris, 2007). There is need for TVET at the tertiary level in Jamaica to embrace a philosophy which is aligned with the developmental needs of the nation as well as that of individuals. Qualifications offered should not only reflect individual performance levels but aligned to critical development benchmarks such as social, economic, and political targets.

The quality of training facilities for tertiary TVET continues as a major challenge. Effective TVET require state-of-the-art equipment and facilities which are very expensive. Unfortunately, these become obsolete in a short time and will require continuous funding to maintain relevance. Curriculum which is aligned to the needs of industry and commerce continue to be a challenge. Successive governments are not prepared to make this investment, in spite of the fact that adequate continuous and sustainable funding mechanisms through the HEART Trust/NSTA have been established to avert this challenge. Inadequate number of appropriate training places and curriculum for tertiary TVET continues as major challenges. Despite numerous calls from both public and private sectors to provide more highly skilled personnel and highly trained TVET professionals, tertiary institutions continue to implement mainly soft TVET programmes such as business education and information technology which do not require significant capital investment.

Under-qualification and inexperience of directors and management personnel of tertiary TVET institutions continue as a significant challenge. Most directors and managers possess advanced qualifications at the master and doctoral levels, however, several have no exposure in the TVET area, as such leadership is compromised. Invariably, decisions are made which are not congruent or aligned to achievement of success in TVET. Attempts are made by some institutions to avert this challenge by implementing customized short-term courses or training seminars, however these are usually quite expensive and invariably inadequate since the training is in many instances carried out by persons who are themselves unaware of the requirements of TVET.

Lack of support from the industrial and commercial sectors continues as a major challenge. Many industries claim that their support in the form of tax collected by the HEART Trust/NSTA is adequate for providing appropriate training of personnel. They also claim that TVET institutions fail to include them in their curriculum development and delivery plans and that they are called on only when they need financial support. Personnel from some industries are invited to be members of boards and advisory bodies of secondary and non-tertiary, post-secondary TVET institutions, however, this endeavour is inadequate at tertiary levels (Morris, 2015). According to Morris (2012), the core business of a TVET institution is to provide on-the-job learning opportunities for its students so that they can better fit into the world of work. Establishing relationships with stakeholders will facilitate placement of learners in industries which will impact positively in a significant way on the learning process. All constituents will get a better understanding of the training system and will be better able to make recommendations for its improvement. Additionally, relationships will facilitate personnel familiarization with institutional policies and practice. This will also enhance professionalism; these interactions help in raising awareness among students, trainees, and faculty of challenges of professionalism, and provide opportunities that help to build critical evaluation skills that reinforce high individual standards, norms, and behaviors.

Relationships may also promote policies that facilitate scholarships or provision of other educational funds from industry. Importantly, relationships provide opportunities for curriculum content validation. The TVET curriculum is quite dynamic and should be frequently adjusted to meet the needs and requirements of industries and, by extension, society. An obsolete curriculum is a major source of discontent for employers since such curricula are not aligned to the needs of industries and major retraining must be undertaken to produce graduates that are more effective when employed (Morris, 2015).

Research in TVET continues to be a major challenge. Although funding for TVET programmes are generated through a tax mechanism in

Jamaica, dedicated funding for carrying out research in TVET is unavailable. As a result, the education system and tertiary TVET in particular, does not have access to empirical data to support decisions. It is evident that research conducted by various sectors through their data gathering mechanisms does not provide information that is necessary to inform TVET. Implementation of masters' and PhD programmes in TVET at UWI, UTech, and other local universities are poised to improve this situation. According to Morris (2012), programmes of this nature embody the importance of critical inquiry and field research of a participatory nature. It provides students with enhanced concepts and competencies in designing, implementing, and evaluating TVET programmes for a variety of public and private educational settings. Additionally, these programmes will provide students with an understanding of how educational, social, political, and economic systems interface with communities. It seeks to develop individuals who are capable of delivering world class TVET programmes.

CONCLUSION

Tertiary TVET in the Caribbean is not a recent phenomenon. The need for tertiary education in Jamaica became pressing after emancipation in 1834. It was recognized that local teachers had to be provided and this education was undertaken primarily by the religious denominations among which keen competition existed to establish some form of teacher training. Our current social context points to the need for a cadre of educators capable of tackling the complex issues related to globalization, Caribbean Single Market Economy (CSME), national TVET policy development, economic growth and adult education for development, including mobilization, participation, and empowerment of individuals in creating civic societies. TVET is increasingly being dubbed as a primary feature for the economic stability of developing nations. It is evident that professionals across all sectors of the economy; those working in education and training in schools, colleges, universities, training organizations; those working with voluntary organizations, trade unions and community groups; those working with disadvantaged sections in the population and socially excluded groups are increasingly becoming aware of the importance of TVET. Efforts of the Ministry of Education in Jamaica to mainstream TVET in the primary and secondary curriculum is an indication of the value placed on TVET.

Tertiary level Technical and Vocational Education and Training will give prospective and existing practitioners a conceptual and practical understanding of TVET within the education system. It must be recognized that much of TVET takes place in non-institutional settings with adults whose experience of compulsory education may not have been positive. This education should give persons the confidence to become reflective practitioners with the necessary teaching and facilitating skills to enable adults to learn in a variety of settings including work with educationally disadvantaged adults. Post graduate programmes in TVET at the University of the West Indies and the University of Technology, Jamaica are configured to meet these requirements.

Tertiary level TVET programmes embody the importance of critical inquiry and field research of a participatory nature. It provides students with enhanced concepts and competencies in designing, implementing, and evaluating TVET programmes for a variety of public and private educational settings. Additionally, persons trained at this level will develop an understanding of how educational, social, political, and economic systems interface with communities. Inclusion of appropriate research components in the tertiary programmes offered in the Caribbean will facilitate meaningful research activities which will no doubt provide empirical data which can be used to inform the TVET decision making process.

Although substantial progress has been made in the development and delivery of tertiary level TVET in Jamaica during the last century, and more specifically during the last three decades, it is evident that significant challenges still exist. In order to progress smoothly in the future, efforts must be made to eliminate or take actions to reduce the impacts of these challenges.

BIBLIOGRAPHY

Clarke, S. (2005). *Tertiary Education in a Changing World, Revisiting Tertiary Education Policy in Jamaica: Towards Personal Gain or National Good* (R. Holding & O. Burke, Ed.). Ian Randle Publishers.

Marope, P. T. M., Chakroun, B., & Holmes, K. P. (2015). Unleashing the Potential: Transforming Technical and Vocational Education and Training. UNESCO Publishing.

Ministry of Education. (2015). Jamaica Education for all review 2015. http://unesdoc.unesco.org/images/0023/002300/230020E.pdf

Sanjaya, M. (2006). *Quality Assurance in Higher Education: An Introduction.* National Assessment and Accreditation Council (NAAC) & Commonwealth of Learning.

Morris, H. (2015, May 13–15). *Strategies for Enhancing Relationship of TVET Institutions with Industry* [Conference Session]. Second International Conference on TVET in the Caribbean. Montego Bay, Jamaica.

Morris, H. (2015). "Quality Assurance for Tertiary Level Technical and Vocational Education and Training for the Caribbean". In *Quality in Higher Education in the Caribbean*. Ed: A. K. Perkins. UWI Press.

Morris, H. (2012). "Tertiary Technical and Vocational Education and Training (TVET) In the Caribbean: A call for Engagement in Higher Education in the Caribbean". In A. Ezenne (Ed.). *Research Challenges & Prospects.* Information Age Publishing Inc.

Morris, H. (2007). *Graduate Studies in Technical and Vocational Education and Training (TVET) in the Caribbean – Whose Responsibility?* Proceedings of the 9th Biennial Conference of the UWI's Schools of Education, St Augustine, Trinidad

Powell, C. (2013). *Towards a Model for Engaging the Jamaican Secondary Schools in Efficient Delivery of Technical Vocational Education and Training (TVET).* [Unpublished Doctoral Dissertation] University of the West Indies, Jamaica.

Tobias, O. (2012). *TVET National Development Jamaica: The role of technical and vocational education in national development.* Ministry of Education, Jamaica. http://www.academia.edu/8946663/TVET_National_Development_JAMAICA

UNESCO National Report – Jamaica. (2008). Jamaica Foundation for Lifelong Learning. http://www.unesco.org/fileadmin/MULTIMEDIA/INSTITUTES/UIL/confintea/pdf/NationalReports/Latin%20America%20-%20Caribbean/Jamaica.pdf

UNESCO-UNEVOC. (2004, November 8–10). *Skills Development for Employability and Citizenship: The Southeast European Experience within a Global Context.* UNESCO International Meeting on Innovation and Excellence in TVET Teacher/Trainer Education. Hangzhou, China. www.unevoc.unesco.org/publications/meetings/Hangzhou-MeetingReport.pdf

UNESCO-UNEVOC. (2004, November 8–10). TVET Teacher/Trainer Training: Prospects.
UNESCO International Meeting on Innovation and Excellence in TVET Teacher/Trainer Education. Hangzhou, China. http://unesdoc.unesco.org/images/0014/001480/148003eo.pdf
INWENT (Capacity Building International/Germany) & UNESCO-UNEVOC. (2006). *TVET Teacher Education on the Threshold of Internationalization.* Frank Bunning & Zhi-Qun Zhao (Eds) Hangzhou, China. http://www.unevoc.unesco.org/fileadmin/user_upload/pubs/TVET_Teacher_Education.pdf
UNESCO-UNEVOC. (2004, November 8–10). International framework curriculum for a master degree for TVET teachers and lecturers. UNESCO International Meeting on Innovation and Excellence in TVET Teacher/Trainer Education. Hangzhou, China. Hangzhou, China, http://www.unevoc.net/fileadmin/user_upload/pubs/Hangzhou_International_framework.pdf
UNESCO-UNEVOC. (2006). UNESCO-UNEVOC in action: Report on activities 2004–2005; 2006 technical and vocational education and training (TVET) http://unesdoc.unesco.org/images/0014/001493/149333e.pdf
UNESCO & ILO. (2002). *Technical and Vocational Education and Training for the Twenty-first Century: UNESCO and ILO Recommendations.* UNESCO-UNEVOC Publications. http://unesdoc.unesco.org/images/0012/001260/126050e.pdf.

CHAPTER 8

The University of Technology, Jamaica
Reflecting on a Model Institution for Workforce Development

HOPE MAYNE AND RAYMOND A DIXON

THIS CHAPTER AIMS TO ORIENT READERS TO the impact a historically framed polytechnic university has on workforce development. The University of Technology, Jamaica (UTech, Ja.), formerly the College of Arts Science and Technology (CAST), originates from a polytechnic educational model which prepares individuals for the local, regional and the global workforce. The chapter begins with a brief history of the university as it transitions from a national and regional college, to become the second major university in Jamaica. It provides a description of its programmatic achievements as highlighted at the university's 50-year celebration of institutional existence, followed by specific programmatic development in response to workforce needs after it transitioned from a college to a four-year degree granting university. An interview with a foundational member and past president provides insight on how UTech, Ja. has contributed to the workforce development. Finally, the chapter describes the role that UTech can play as an entrepreneurial university to address the impact of workforce competency required for a knowledge-based society.

A BRIEF HISTORY

The University of Technology, Jamaica, is the only public university in Jamaica and one of two technological universities in the English-speaking Caribbean, which prides itself on offering outcome-based programmes built on a polytechnic model. It offers over 100 programmes at the certificate, diploma, undergraduate and postgraduate degree levels, including several programmes offered nowhere else in the English-speaking Caribbean – e.g. Architecture, the Health Sciences, and Technical and Vocational Education (Jamaica Foundation for Lifelong Learning [JFLL], 2008). The university was started in 1958 under the name, The Jamaica Institute of Technology. In 1959 the name was changed to the College of Arts, Science and Technology (CAST). Historically, the institution's focus was to prepare students to impact social and economic development. By expanding secondary education with the addition of Grades 10 and 11 to the Junior Secondary Schools, the Manley regime in the 1970s provided a direct path for students to exit the high school system with both a general and technical education background, and access post-secondary education and training in a technical area at CAST where they would earn a diploma or certificate. One of the primary considerations for the expansion of the technical and vocational education programme was the need to provide skills that were compatible with the occupations required by the productive sector. The occupational areas where training were provided included carpentry and cabinetmaking, plumbing, construction, auto-mechanics, machine shop and welding, electrical installation, home economics, secretarial, and principles of business (Hutton, 2009). Students would sit external examinations based in England, such as The City and Guilds, and General Certificate Exams (GCE or O'Levels) such as Cambridge and the Association Examination Board (AEB). Passing a number of these exams would allow students to gain the prerequisite to enroll in programs at CAST. Later GCE was gradually replaced with the Caribbean Examination Council (CXC) and passes in CXC subjects became the prerequisite to enter programs at CAST.

CAST was upgraded to a university in 1995 and its name was change to the University of Technology, Jamaica. It has served as a model institution in the Caribbean for polytechnic universities by combining active classroom experiences with on-the-job training (Evans & Burke, 2006). The curricula are framed on the English polytechnic system, and as such there is much emphasis on work-based learning and professional linkages. The university acknowledges that the use of technology is critical to developing the requisite skills students need to contribute to the workforce. Combining the arts, humanities, science and technology is key to producing a productive workforce and the curriculum at UTech bridges these knowledge domains to meet workforce needs.

The university stands as a major national institution and boasts a student population of over 10,000. It offers more than 50 programmes at certificate, diploma and degree levels. The philosophy of the University of Technology highlights why its graduates today are still sought after by service, manufacturing, and business enterprises.

> The University is committed to the total education of the individual as a social being and seeks to develop the whole person in terms of personal well-being and social and intellectual competence. It promotes life-long learning, personal development and service to the community.

Through five faculties; Engineering and Computing, The Built Environment, Business and Management, Health and Applied Science and Education and Liberal Studies; it offers postgraduate degrees in Architecture, Workforce Education, Educational Leadership, Business Administration and Engineering Management (Jamaica Foundation for Lifelong Learning, 2008). Addressing some of the unique features of UTech's programs the JFLL articulated:

> One important feature of UTech's programmes is that they expose students to real-world learning experiences through internships, study tours, field exercises, site visits, work-related and community related projects. In keeping with global trends in education, in 2002 the office of Continuing Education and Distance Learning (CEODL) was established with the mandate to facilitate the expansion of learning opportunities, increase enrolment through flexible access to diverse lifelong learning options and multimodal delivery options, including offerings by open and distance learning and continuing education. (p. 43)

According to the *Report on Higher Education in Jamaica*, UTech, Jamaica was accorded the status of a bicameral system of governance, a council and an academic board. The Governing Council is the supreme University body that has legal responsibility for all University appointments, promotions, resources and the maintenance of standards within the University. There is a Chancellor who chairs the Council and Pro-Chancellor who acts as chairperson in the absence of the Chancellor. The President of the University is responsible to the Council. The Academic Board is the highest authority with respect to academic matters and is responsible to the Governing Council. In addition, there are various committees and boards that report to the Academic Board that are guided by various governing instruments, ordinances and regulations that relate to the function of the institution (Evans & Burke, 2006).

EDUCATION AND TRAINING FOR THE WORKFORCE AFTER 50 YEARS OF OPERATION

UTech's graduates continue to be graduates of choice for the workforce, especially in the technical areas, by many businesses in Jamaica. After one half century of existence and about eleven years as a university, the University's 2006–2007 annual report revealed the following accomplishment of the five faculties.

Engineering and Computing

The degree programmes in the School of Computing & Information Technology (SCIT) were being restructured to a new BSc in Information Technology (BScIT), and a BSc in Computer Science. The Master of Science programme in Engineering Management being offered jointly by the Faculty of Engineering and Computing (FENC) and Florida International University (FIU), received its first cohort in September 2006. A bachelor's degree in Agricultural Engineering was developed in collaboration with the College of Agriculture, Science & Education (CASE) to be offered in 2008. A Bachelor of Industrial Engineering programme was scheduled for implementation in the academic year 2008–2009. An Associate Degree in Engineering, the product of partnership between The School of Engineering and the island's Community Colleges was set to be offered by the Community Colleges commencing September 2007. On completion of the associate degree students would be eligible to enter the School of Engineering's degree programmes at Year 2 (Utech Jamaica, 2007).

By September 2008, Utech's School of Computing & Information Technology (SCIT) completed the restructuring of its degree programmes and offered a new Bachelor of Science Degree in Computing with majors in Information Technology and Computer Science. The Computer Science major was offered only to full-time students, while the Information Technology major was offered to both full-time and part-time students. Information Technology major is designed to serve students who desire a computing career that features a mix of technical and business/social issues rather than a focus on technology only. The aim is to produce graduates who possess the right combination of knowledge and practical hands-on expertise to take care of both an organization's information technology infrastructure and the people who use it. Students pursuing this major are required to complete a required mix of management, organization, and human/technology modules. The Computer Science major is designed to serve those students who wish to proceed as generalists in computing or who aspire to graduate study, research positions, or cross-disciplinary innovation. Graduates of this major are expected to possess the required skills to design and implement software, devise new ways to use computers, and to develop intelligent systems. Students pursuing this major were required to complete a set of modules that concentrate on computer theory, mathematics, and science. The Information Communication and Technology Division (ICT) successfully implemented online testing for students enrolled in Information Technology (Utech Jamaica, 2008).

The School of Engineering (SoE) launched the new Bachelor of Engineering in Industrial Engineering with options in Manufacturing and Engineering Management in September 2008. The Computing Option in Electrical Engineering is available to students entering their third year of study since September 2008 (UTech, Jamaica, 2008).

Education and Liberal Studies

The Faculty of Education and Liberal Studies (FELS) partners with its sister faculties to provide the highest quality programmes in support of disciplines in education, business and management, engineering and computing, architecture and sciences. The aim is to provide the Caribbean region with technical-vocational educators of the highest level of competence and professionalism. The faculty continues to develop its flagship B.Ed. TVET programme and to improve participation in the post-diploma B.Ed. programme. In November 2006, eight students from St Kitts graduated with the Special Diploma in TVET teaching, offered in collaboration with the Commonwealth of Learning (COL) using distance education methodologies. The School of Technical and Vocational Education (SOTAVE) in FELS collaborates with the HEART Trust/NTA through the Vocational Training Development Institute (VTDI) in the delivery of the B.Ed. TVET. The faculty celebrated the success of the first batch of 13 students to complete the MSc Workforce Education and Development (WED) Programme (Utech, 2007).

Business and Management

According to the 2007 report, in keeping with a time-honoured tradition of creating unique partnerships with industry to meet the needs of the nation, the School of Business Administration collaborated with the Continuing Education Open and Distance Learning (CEODL) unit to provide a new opportunity for tertiary training for members of the Jamaica Constabulary Force (JCF). The new pilot course in Police Studies and Management was created in response to a request from the JCF in pursuit of its own imperative of upgrading the nation's security force. The course was delivered in an accelerated mode so contact hour requirements can be completed in one year, instead of two. On completion of the course of study, candidates are awarded an associate degree.

An eighteen-month Master's in Business Administration Degree was developed and commenced in August 2007 (Utech Jamaica, 2007). In 2008, The Faculty of Business and Management (FOBM) launched its Master of Business Administration degree. The programme integrates a sound balance of theory and practice and offers students a choice of five concentrations: general management; finance; entrepreneurship; marketing; hospitality and tourism management. Classes for the programme were held in two locations, Kingston and Montego Bay. A total of

112 students were accepted for the first cohort and over 220 applications were received for the second cohort.

Health and Applied Science

During 2007, The Faculty of Health and Applied Science placed emphasis on the accreditation of courses and the development of post-basic and post-graduate courses of study. Attention was also placed on providing special training routes and professional development for workers in the public and private sector. This operational plan was developed to ensure the delivery of quality education and training in the health-related and applied science disciplines, and also generated additional income for the faculty. Of importance is the faculty's sensitivity not only to national manpower needs, but to regional needs as well. Two new academic courses were implemented, Master of Philosophy (MPhil.) in Pharmaceutical Technology, which was offered to students who completed the didactic part of the course and are currently conducting research on the potential of Ackee oil in pharmaceutical and industrial manufacturing. The other, Associate Degree in Health Information Technology, is offered as a two-year full-time course or as a post-basic course at two levels. The first cohort of 12 students graduated in November 2006 with a Level 2 associate degree. The Bachelor of Medical Technology – both 4 year and post-diploma – received accreditation from the University Council of Jamaica for a period of 4 years effective May 1, 2006. The self-study for accreditation of the Bachelor of Science in Environmental Health (Public Health Inspection Option) and the Post-basic B.Sc. in Public Health Nursing was submitted to the University Council of Jamaica. Letters of Intent were submitted for the Bachelor of Science in Applied Statistics and Community Rehabilitation and Disabilities Studies (Utech Jamaica, 2007).

In 2008, two new academic courses were implemented. The Bachelor of Science in Nursing was offered as a 4-year full-time course. It had an intake of 75 students for its first cohort, forty-four (44) students at UTech and thirty-one (31) at the Cornwall School of Nursing campus. The Bachelor of Applied Statistics gained approval from the University Academic

Board as a course of study to be offered from the Department of Science and Mathematics in academic year 2008/2009 (Utech Jamaica, 2008).

The Built Environment

The Caribbean School of Architecture and the School of Building and Land Management, which both constitute the Faculty of the Built Environment, depend heavily on external partners and stakeholders for patronage, internship placements and advisory services, as well as on internal collaboration and support. The school offers Bachelor of Arts in Architectural Studies (BAAS), Bachelor of Science in Urban and Regional Planning, Bachelor of Science Construction Management (Post Diploma), Bachelor of Science in Surveying and Geographic Information Sciences, Bachelor of Engineering in Construction Engineering, Bachelor of Science in Quantity Surveying, Bachelor of Science in Land Economy and Valuation Surveying, and Bachelor of Arts in Architectural Studies. Associate degree is offered in Surveying and Geographic Information Technology (SGIT) and diploma in Construction Management and Structural Engineering. Masters of Science degrees are offered in Geomatics/Geographic Information Sciences, Urban Design, Construction Management and Land Management.

The name of the Bachelor of Construction Engineering Management (BCEM) degree programme was changed to Bachelor of Construction Management (BCM). A Master of Science in the Built Environment was developed for offering in September 2007. Study tours remain an integral part of the architectural curriculum. Lecturers accompanied students from Years 3 and 4 on study tours to Barbados, Trinidad and Tobago, and Cuba.

Programmatic Development to address Workforce Needs

UTech, Ja., continues to make significant contributions to the workforce seven years after its 50th anniversary through several program development and collaborative initiatives. According to the Planning Institute of Jamaica [PIOJ] (2014), there were several programmatic achievements that were of note. These included the launching of the School of Humanities and Social Sciences in the Faculty of Education and Liberal Studies; the establishment of the Brian Silvera Refrigeration and Air Conditioning laboratory in the School of Engineering; the graduation of the first cohort of the Civil Engineering and Information Systems Management programme; and the diversification of the undergraduate courses of study in new disciplines such as Bachelor of Science Degree in Entrepreneurship, Post-Diploma Bachelor of Pharmacy, Pharmacy Technicians Certificate and Bachelor of Arts in the Communication Arts and Technology (PIOJ, 2014).

In response to internal and external labor market demands, several courses of study were revised. These include Bachelor of laws (LL.B), Bachelor of Business Administrations, Bachelors of Science in Child and Adolescent Development, Bachelors of Science in Critical Care Nursing, Dialysis Technicians Certificate (part-time) and Bachelors of Science in Pharmaceutical Technology. Graduate courses of study were developed in Engineering, Mathematics Teaching (MPhil), Workforce Training and Education, Dental Therapy, Nurse Anesthesia, Science in Trauma Studies, Integrative counseling and a Doctor of Philosophy in Educational leadership and Management (PIOJ, 2014).

The university also extends its distance learning courses to 10 Caribbean countries, and the College of Health Sciences commenced its first online course of study. The Child and Adolescent Development (ChAD) course of study initiated a Minor in disability study in January 2014. According to the report,

> A unique element of this course is that it is taught by persons with disabilities. Students are required to spend time in the Shelly-Ann Fraser Assessment Centre where they observe a trained care giver. Additionally, they are permitted to administer supervised care. (pp. 22.32)

Collaborative partnership in research intensified with partnerships from countries such as the UK, Spain, Sweden, Switzerland, Dominican Republic, Cuba, Suriname, Belgium, Finland, Germany, Denmark, Austria, Barbados, and Trinidad & Tobago.

The enrollment at UTech in 2013/14 was at 13,150 students (58.1 percent female) compared with 13,034 (58.8 percent female) in 2012/13. The

Table 8.1: Enrollment and Graduation at the University of Technology, Jamaica: 2011–2014

Total Enrollment and Graduation at the University of Technology Jamaica, by Faculty/Colleges						
	No. Enrolled 2011–2012	No. Graduated 2011–2012	No. Enrolled 2012–2013	No. Graduated 2012–2013	No. Enrolled 2013–2014	No. Graduated 2013–2014
Faculties	Total	Total	Total	Total	Total	Total
College of Health Sciences	1,973	440	1,541	331	1,582	259
Faculty of Education Liberal Studies	1,169	253	1,156	214	1,171	220
Faculty of the Built Environment	1,071	242	1,058	259	1,025	246
College of Business and Management	5,385	1,020	5,182	880	5,086	696
Faculty of Engineering and Computing	2,333	420	2,270	360	2,384	370
Faculty of Law	632	159	601	103	560	109
Faculty of Science and Sport	448	13	619	31	732	84
College of Oral and public Health Sciences	–	–	597	168	610	182
Grand Total	13,011	2,547	13,034	2,346	13,150	2,166

Source: Planning Institute of Jamaica

total number of graduates in 2013/14 was 2,166 (62.6 percent female) a decline of 7.7 percent compared with the previous academic year (See Table 8.1). The College of Business and Management and the Faculty of Engineering and Computing accounted for 56.8 percent of total enrollment and 49.2 percent of output respectively.

CONTRIBUTIONS TO WORKFORCE DEVELOPMENT

In 2016 an interview was conducted with a former president of CAST/UTech, Ja. to ascertain his perspective on the institution's contribution to workforce development before and since it became a university. Three broad themes framed his perspective of the institution's contribution to workforce development. These are, movement from diploma status to degree status, enhancing skills/competencies through experiential programs and the significance of rural background context for workplace skills. Firstly, he categorized the movement of CAST/UTech from diploma to degree status and highlighted the issue about its credit rating. He stated:

> CAST before it became UTech spent ten years giving degrees. Some twenty-three degrees were in place. On September 1995, then Minister of Education, Burchell Whiteman, pronounce that CAST was going to become UTech. The Faculty of Education and Liberal Studies (FELS), pioneered by Mr Christian, was the leader in developing the conceptual credit rating and building on a diploma in order to offer a degree . . . If you had a diploma in education or engineering, and across the road U.W.I had similar diplomas, they regarded the Diploma offered at CAST with some sense of scorn. There was a legitimate question in terms of its credit rating.

He acknowledged that the students who earned a diploma at CAST could easily attend a university in the USA and complete the Baccalaureate degree in less than two years. This adds legitimacy to the quality of the diplomas that were being offered at CAST.

> The same students, studying engineering could go abroad to America and complete the degree in a year and a half because they got the credit rating that is worthy of the course. So once that principle was established and understood, we said ok, fair enough, we will hike to the credit that they need to have to get a degree.

To offer degree programs, some departments adopted the credit model while others used other models. Eventually CAST was offering over 23 degree programs across several Schools and Faculties.

> We did not have to start from scratch . . . All the different departments, including Building, Engineering, all started their own degree program with different models. Some adopted the credit model whilst some did other models, but as I say we had over twenty degree programs in place when CAST became UTech.

Enhancing skills/competencies through experiential programs

He highlighted the contributions that UTech made to workforce development by specifically referencing some programs instituted to help to complement the academic curriculum and develop the holistic worker required by employers. The first he addressed was the summer work experience program.

> If students want to work in a business they need to think about what it is I need to have, that I can go there and fit in and not have to start from scratch. Teaching and the students' aspiration, therefore, are meshed in respect to providing a curriculum . . . that essentially was geared to fitting the student in the world of work. In fact, one of the programs that we developed was the educational work experience program, where students were placed in the workforce industry in the summer. In this regard students in their pre-final year would then know when I go to work in that sugar factory, or when I go to that engineering firm, or that surveying firm, I learn the kind of things that I need to know. So when I graduate I am a step ahead in respect to the expectations of what the world of work is demanding.

Another program he referenced that contributed significantly to the development workforce competencies was the earn and study program. He reflected:

> The Earn and Study Program was essentially geared to help students in college to have a widened sense of workplace skills. Attaching students to learn a particular skill, for example business studies, is not only restricted to accounting but more business in its widened sense. You could be a top tier surveyor or civil engineer or whatever, so attachment to the skill led to that student's expectation of the world of work. What he or she would find when he's finished is he would not be starting from scratch because he had gained significant experience in that work attachment, he had gained significant experience not only in the technology of the business but also in the attitudes to dealing with fellow employees and issues associated with management and issues associated with performance and integrity. In other words, you are not going to try and cut corners, you are going to give a full day's work for a full day's pay. So, there are a full set of values that I listed that essentially make for the preparations for going into a job. In fact, employees appreciated this because often the student who have done a work experience in Kingston Industrial Garage or whatever they would say I want you to come back when you graduate.

Rural background a conduit for developing technological skills

He drew on the significance of students' background and noted how it was essential to leverage. The good work ethics that many students from rural areas have needed to be harnessed and channel into the technological skills that they were learning. Students needed to appreciate or continue to appreciate the legitimacy of work.

> So many of the students came from humble beginnings, from parishes in the poor country areas that boy or girl would have been accustomed to subsistence farming. The pickaxe and the hoe were significant to them, so that when they came to a technological institution, the idea of the pickaxe and the hoe was something else you wanted them to leave behind. In other words, somehow the pickaxe and the hoe were symbols of slavery, of poverty, and wanting to get out of that. It was not attitudes that had to be changed, essentially there's the dignity in the pickaxe and the hoe, and it is the dignity of work. As any kind of work done honestly, done competently, has legitimacy. I, for example have used this principle to look after the campus work Study.

Polytechnic institutions such as UTech demonstrate a model for partnership and collaboration with industry as is shown through the field experience programmatic format described by the past president. These work-related experiences promote skill development, prepare a more holistic student for professional or occupational fields, hence creating a demand for UTech graduates in the workforce.

The polytechnic model was highly recognized before CAST became a university. The institution was recognized for producing students who were highly skilled and an asset to workforce. Employers often requested "the CAST graduate." The transformation from CAST to UTech, Ja., has opened doors to other areas such as forensic science, law degree, nursing, public health etc.

UTech is built on a polytechnic model which is embedded in its pedagogy, methodology, and curriculum design. The model has been strengthened with the advancement of technology, partnership with industry, programmes such as work experience, earn and study and community service. Skills and competences are harnessed not only through academics but through the provision of real-world experience.

PARTNERSHIP AND COLLABORATION TO STRENGTHEN WORKFORCE EDUCATION AND TRAINING

Besides gradually increasing its menu of courses offered at the Baccalaureate and graduate levels, UTech has also progressively increased the number, quantity and quality of partnerships with various enterprises, national and international, to enhance and professionalize the experience of its students. For example, according to the PIOJ (2010) report, a new partnership was established with the MARMICMON (a Canadian marketing company) and the College of Health Sciences resulting in two accelerated dental auxiliary courses of study, the BSc. in Dental Hygiene and the Diploma in Dental Assistance. The courses were of the same quality as the Canadian accredited Dental Auxiliary courses. Completers who are successful in the Canadian Board of Examination, are assisted by MARMICMON to secure employment in Canada.

In 2011 Utech's continued collaboration with the Jamaica Institute of Management (JIM), School of Advanced Management resulted in the establishment of a trading room equipped with the Blooming Trading Platform, which provided students majoring in finance with real-time trading experience (PIOJ, 2011). Work on the expansion of the School of Hospitality and Tourism Management (SHTM) began in March 2012. The expansion included the building of a hotel for teaching at UTech's campus in Papine, St Andrew. Also, in 2012 a memorandum of understanding was signed between UTech and the Child Development Agency. This agreement will allow students in the Child Health Adolescent Development (CHAD) programme to assist the CDA in the areas of assessment and field investigations. CDA sites became practicum places for CHAD students (PIOJ, 2012). UTech also became a part of the wide network of Diploma de Espanol Como Lengue Extranjera (DELE) examination centres across the world allowing language students to have access to the Virtual Spanish Classroom, and books and audio resources for use in the teaching and learning of Spanish.

The School of Engineering and the Armstrong Atlantic State University, USA collaborated on students' team summer research initiatives. Teams comprising of four students from each institution, designed a portable air conditioning unit that was low cost, environmentally friendly and utilized locally available biomaterials as well as alternative power sources. The Biomedical Unit of the School of Engineering in collaboration with the School for Therapy, Education and Parenting (STEP) of children with disabilities embarked on a project to provide affordable, comfortable and appropriate ambulatory devices to children with physical challenges. In addition, the School of Computing and Information Technology (SCIT) formalized an MOU with Toon Boom Animation Inc. to collaborate in the provision and use of Toon Boom Inc's license animation software products and the integration of Toon Boom curriculum (animation and digital content) into the school's multimedia programme (PIOJ, 2012). The university through grant funding from the African, Caribbean and Pacific Group (ACP) and the European Union (EU) launched in October 2012 its research project entitled "The application of Solar-Powered Polymer Electrolyte Membrane (PEM) electrolytes" for the sustainable production of hydrogen gas as fuel for domestic cooking. The funding supports collaborative work led by a team in the School of Engineering at UTech with persons from Brunel University, London; the University of the West Indies; the Ministry of Science, Technology, Energy and Mining (MSTEM); and the Bureau of Standards Jamaica (PIOJ, 2013). The Faculty of Engineering and computing (FENC) collaborated with MSTEM to build an information system, the Energy Database and Management Information System (EDMIS). The EDMIS enables the capture, process and use of energy-related data to enhance decision-making capabilities in the MSTEM.

So UTech continues to demonstrate strong levels of collaboration and partnership to strengthen the quality of their programme and the caliber of students available to the workforce. The economic and social survey of 2014 shows that the level of partnership and collaboration continues to grow, standing at about 14 countries regionally and internationally. Countries include Spain, Sweden, Switzerland, UK, Dominican Republic, Cuba, Suriname, Belgium, Finland, Germany, Denmark, Austria, Barbados, and Trinidad & Tobago (PIOJ, 2014).

ROLE IN A KNOWLEDGE-BASED ECONOMY

The University's role as a higher education institution and the strategies it embraces to effectively address the development of workforce competencies in a knowledge-based society must continue to be transformed in order to properly address Jamaica's unique socio-economic needs. Merely seeing itself as the premier "Polytech" university in the Caribbean can result in fixedness on curricula, programs, research, collaboration and outreach that fits outdated labour and industry needs and movement and does not meet the demands to generate the quality workforce required to function in a knowledge economy and global competitive labour market. More than ever before the quality of higher education plays a crucial role in determining wealth as well as poverty of nations (Task Force on Higher Education and Society, 2000). It's therefore necessary that higher education institutions do not merely replicate what other universities are doing at a process level; but self-reflect and restructure internal programs and processes and external partnerships to respond to the needs of a 21st century workforce.

With less financial support from the government, UTech will have to become more entrepreneurial. By entrepreneurial we mean as Davis (1987) and Clark (1998) suggest, a university which is adaptive and innovative to the needs of the outside world, actively seeking ways to innovate how it goes about its business, while maintaining its core functions as a university. Being entrepreneurial involves putting the necessary infrastructure, support, and resources in place to encourage faculty consultation, university-industry collaboration, intellectual property protection, and technology transfer (Rothaermel, Agung, & Jiang, 2007). To achieve this, it is necessary to move beyond research or knowledge production that is single-disciplined focus and which "regard the cognitive and social norms that govern basic research and academic sciences, implying the absence of practicality in nature" (Sam & van der Sijde, 2014, p. 897; Gibbons et al. 1994). On the other hand, trans-disciplinary knowledge production that engages stakeholders from other disciplines, industry, and the community and which is carried out within an application context will be more relevant in developing workforce competency that drives sustained economic growth. According to Sam and van der Sijde (2014), this mode is a more complex system of knowledge production which involves specialists from various disciplines to work cooperatively on problems guided by cognitive and social practices. In such an approach, scientific and technological knowledge is not produced only within university but even beyond the university boundary, closer to the real-world problem.

While universities that are entrepreneurial differ, according to Yokohama (2006), universities that are entrepreneurial implement organizational changes to properly respond to changing demands internally and externally. Naturally this would encompass a change in the culture at UTech. He also goes on to add that these universities strive toward self-support and autonomy. Invariably, this necessitates corporation formation, partnership with the private sector, change in academic organization, and curricula that are driven by technical, professional, and entrepreneurial competencies required by a knowledge society. So, in entrepreneurial universities, "students are exposed and subjected to a conducive (study) environment in which they can take risks, explore responsibilities in a project (a protected environment, but in the "real" world) and identify business opportunities" (Sam & van der Sijde, 2014, p. 902; see also Laine 2008). Entrepreneurial concepts, processes, and competencies also permeate the university curricula. So, as the university produces human capital through its teaching – research, enterprise incubation, private sector partnerships, government partnerships, and community outreach provide essential contextual learning for students and faculty. This produces an educational framework for the development of workforce competencies with the necessary innovative and entrepreneurial competencies to develop the Jamaican economy in a global, competitive, knowledge base society.

CONCLUSION

There is no question that UTech, Jamaica continues to play a crucial role in the development of workforce skills for the Jamaican (and the Caribbean) economy. As the Jamaican economy struggles with growth, the university must take on a greater role in producing the type of human capital that is capable of innovative thinking and producing new product, services and new businesses. To do this UTech, Jamaica, needs to continually reexamine and re-imagine how it teaches, research and collaborate with the private sector, government and the community. The structural changes that are required for this type of strategic focus necessitate changes in internal structures, and external collaboration that see the university taking on roles; encompassing industry, government and community; to assist new firm formation in incubator facilities, provide consultation, and foster entrepreneurship. Through these collaborative structures the curricula will be constantly informed about critical and changing workforce competencies and needs that must be addressed in curricula and programmes, to the end of producing a workforce that is always competitive regionally and globally.

BIBLIOGRAPHY

Clark, B. R. (1998a). *Creating Entrepreneurial Universities: Organizational Pathways of Transformation*. Pergamon for IEU Press.

Davies, J. L. (1987). The entrepreneurial university. *International Journal of Higher Education Management*, 11(1), 227.

Evans, H., & Burke, O. (2008). National report on higher education in Jamaica. UNESCO-IESALC. www.iesal.unesco.org.ve/dmdocuments/.../national_report_jamaica.pdf

Gibbons, M., Limoges, C., Nowotny, H., Schwartzman, S., Scott, P., & Trow, M. (1994). *The New Production of Knowledge: The Dynamics of Science and Research in Contemporary Societies*. SAGE Publications Ltd.

Hutton, D. (2009). "Preparing the workforce for the 21st century: The Jamaican experience". *Caribbean Journal Education*, 31(1), 21–51.

Jamaica foundation for Life Long Learning. (2008). The development and state of the art of adult learning and education (ALE): National report on Jamaica. http://www.unesco.org/fileadmin/MULTIMEDIA/INSTITUTES/UIL/confintea/pdf/National_Report s/Europe%20-%20North%20America/Slovenia.pdf

Laine, K. (2008). A Finnish Concept for Academic Entrepreneurship: The Case of Satakunta University of Applied Sciences. *Industry and Higher Education*, 22 (1), 19–28 https://doi.org/10.5367/000000008783877002

PIOJ, (2010). *Economic and Social Survey of Jamaica*. Planning Institute of Jamaica

PIOJ, (2011). *Economic and Social Survey of Jamaica*. Planning Institute of Jamaica
PIOJ, (2012). *Economic and Social Survey of Jamaica*. Planning Institute of Jamaica
PIOJ, (2013). *Economic and Social Survey of Jamaica*. Planning Institute of Jamaica
PIOJ, (2014). *Economic and Social Survey of Jamaica*. Planning Institute of Jamaica
Rothaermel, F. T., Agung, S. D., & Jiang, L. (2007). University entrepreneurship: A taxonomy of the literature. *Industrial and Corporate Change, 16* (4), 691–791. https://doi.org/10.1093/icc/dtm023
Sam, C., & van der Sijde, P. (2014). Understanding the concept of the entrepreneurial university from the perspective of higher education models. *Higher Education, 63*, 891–908. https://www.jstor.org/stable/43648761
Task Force on Higher Education and Society. (2000). *Higher education in developing countries: Peril and promise*. The International Bank for Reconstruction and Development/The Word Bank.
UTech, Jamaica. (2007). Partnership and Service for Development. Annual Report 2006–2007. http://www.utech.edu.jm/about/pdfs/AnnualREPORT2006_7.pdf
UTech, Jamaica. (2008). Partnership and Service for Development. Annual Report 2008–2009. http://www.utech.edu.jm/about/pdfs/AnnualREPORT2006_7.pdf

CHAPTER 9

Workforce Training Readiness

RAYMOND A. DIXON

TECHNOLOGICAL CHANGES ALONG WITH GLOBALIZATION HAVE RAPIDLY reshaped the landscape of work. The kind of work that most people do has changed dramatically over the years, with the service sector displacing agriculture and manufacturing sectors as the main source of jobs in many economically developed countries, the Caribbean and in Jamaica. The change in work marked by the evolution of technology and business practices, is described by Lynn and Salzman (2010) as the third generation of globalized knowledge work. In 1994 after the World Trade Organization (WTO) was formed, it led other organizations in establishing a group of policies termed the Washington Consensus. To gain the benefits of trade "emerging economies had to dismantle barriers and extend more protection to foreign business and investors" (Lyn & Salzman, 2010, p. 63). Policy changes permitting joint ventures in India, for example, encouraged the inflow of investment and technology from North American, Europe, and Japan. By the turn of the century, many firms in the USA, Canada and Europe sought help from software engineers in India to cope with widely feared Y2K problems (Salzman, 2000; Salzman & Biswas, 2000). China became more open and "started welcoming foreign firms, often pressuring them to form local joint ventures in exchange for market access and requiring them to share some of their core/propriety technology as a further cost for doing business in China" (Lyn & Salzman, 2010, p. 63). In time, and with the returning of many expert scientists and engineers who worked with Multinational Enterprises (MNEs) to their country, the R&D in many emerging economies gradually grew and improve in quality, making them more attractive as outsourcing destinations. Consistent with this, MNEs from North America, and Europe tried to find ways to outsource technology development, following the conventional business wisdom that outsourcing save money. The then state of technology and the impact it had on the workforce is captured in Lyn & Salzman (2010) statement:

> Technology increasingly crossed traditional boundaries of industrial expertise, and it seemed that no firm, no matter how large, could possibly master every relevant technology. In fact, it became a management truism that large firms could not keep pace with innovation that, it was thought, increasingly came from start-ups and small firms. With the increase mobility of people and companies and radically improved means of storing and moving information, knowledge flow far more rapidly and supported collaboration more tightly linked but globally dispersed. (p. 64)

The outsourcing of operations and movement of companies to emerging economies was not without consequence to many countries in the Caribbean. Because of high production and wage costs and the lack of policies to reduce them, thus making investments in the economy less attractive and increased competition from other economies, many manufacturing and other types of industries either closed or relocated to other countries where production and labour cost was cheaper. The foregoing economic dynamics modified the labour trends and demands in Jamaica and have led some national leaders and educators to ask questions about the type of training system that is required to produce a workforce with the essential skills for the country to be competitive globally. In this chapter an argument is made for the type of educational framework required to deliver the type of competencies for workforce in Jamaica (and similar constituents in the Caribbean) to be innovative and competitive globally – situating Jamaica as a leading country that produces a 21st century workforce.

RE-IGNITING THE VALUE OF TVET

It is appropriate at this point to define Technical and Vocational Education and Training (TVET) and expound its strategic importance to the workforce in Jamaica and the Caribbean region. The World Bank and the European Finance Association (EFA) use the following definition for TVET:

> TVET is a comprehensive term referring to those aspects of the educational process involving, in addition to general education, the study of technologies and related sciences, and the acquisition of practical skills, attitudes, understanding, and knowledge relating to occupants in various sectors of economic and social life... Technical and vocational education is further understood to be:
> (a) an integral part of general education
> (b) a means of preparation for occupational fields and for effective participation in the world of work
> (c) an aspect of lifelong learning and a preparation for responsible citizenship
> (d) an instrument for promoting environmentally-sound sustainable development
> (e) a method of facilitating poverty alleviation (UNESCO & ILO, 2002, p. 7)

The term TVET is still widely used in many European, Eurasian, African, Asian, and Caribbean countries (Dixon, 2016). In many developing countries, the primary goal of TVET is to prepare youth with occupational skills for the workforce, making it a primary part of the educational agenda. This focus is consistent with the original aim of TVET. Hutton (2008), however, made a salient point about TVET in the context of Jamaica, stating that the purpose often emphasized is to provide an alternative to those in the education system who have failed to cope with the general education programme. This view of TVET of course is antithesis to the evolved perspective that many countries have of TVET, seeing it as equally essential as general education. In fact, in countries such as Australia, New Zealand, Singapore, China, and South Korea, TVET is integrated throughout the education system in response to the global technological revolution which demands higher levels of education and technological skills for the 21st century (Fawcett, El Sawi, & Allison, 2014).

While globalization is prompting governments to take renewed interest in TVET in some countries, including Jamaica, it is often seen as second-class education (Ochtet, 2005; Hutton, 2008). Recent trends – particularly the emphasis of integrating science, technology, engineering and mathematics (STEM) systemically in the education system in order to develop 21st century competencies – have moved some to begin scrutinizing the integral role TVET can play in the learning of these competencies. Often overlooked, is the fact that TVET not only promote the learning of practical occupational competencies, but also the sciences that undergirds these occupational areas. Therefore, as a pedagogical paradigm, it concretizes, operationalizes, and bring alive abstract scientific concepts and mathematical models.

The Economic Rationale

There is strong economic rationale for having a viable TVET system in any country. Boodhai (2010) indicated that because of having TVET systems that are well structured, the output from such a system in countries such as Germany, Singapore, Canada, Australia, and Japan cause those countries to become leaders in all aspects of their enterprise within a very short space of time. Marope, Chakroun and Holmes (2015) in a UNESCO publication reported:

> Technical and vocational education and training (TVET) is steadily emerging as a winner in the race to the top' of global debates and government priorities for education and national development agendas. TVET also features high in strategic and operational priorities of regional economic communities (RECs) such as the African Union, the Caribbean Community (CARICOM) and the European Union; of other multinational groups such as the G20, the Organization for Economic Co-operation and Development (OECD), and of multilateral organizations such as the International Labour Organization (ILO) and UNESCO.

In the present global competitive context, TVET systems are seen as a strategic force to contribute significantly to "the development of the skilled, knowledgeable and technology-savvy people required to support higher value-added productivity; accelerated, sustained and shared growth; global competitiveness; and potentially global peace and stability through a better balance of economic power" (p.14).

TVET can prepare youths with the competencies – knowledge, skills, and attitudes – to gain or produce fruitful employment and become lifelong learners. The fact is youths are three times more likely to be unemployed than adults. In 2010, one in six of the world's population were young people (aged from 15 to 24 years) and one in eight of them were unemployed (ILO, 2012a). Some 621 million youth suffered multiple disengagement from schooling, training, jobs, and job-seeking. Lack of opportunities to acquire skills for employability is one of the key reasons for high youth unemployment as well as for poor-quality and low-paying jobs (Marope, Chakroun, & Holmes, 2015). In a more recent press release by the World Bank (2023), deep concerns are raised about TVET in medium and low-income countries. In the context of rapidly changing labour markets and evolving skills needs due to globalization, technological progress, demographic transformation, and climate change, the need for well-performing TVET is even greater to ensure smooth job transition. This is especially critical as global youth unemployment stands at 16 percent in 2022, much higher than the overall unemployment rate.

TRAINING AND WORKFORCE READINESS ISSUES

Two factors that mitigate Jamaica producing the quality of workers required to effectively address innovation and increase productivity and competitiveness of businesses are the insufficient technical and tertiary level education of skilled workers, and the quality of the education system at all levels (UNCTAD/UNDP, 2002). In fact, according to the STATIN 2005 report, only 22 percent of the Jamaican workforce reported that they received any form of formal training for the jobs in which they were employed. Such high levels of non-training or training that lacks appropriate rigor for specific job areas or which fails to address occupational standards appropriately, points to the failure of the education system to adequately target competencies required for the present workforce. The Jamaica Education Transformation Commission (2021) stated,

> The country is at an intermediate stage of demographic transition with its youth, 15–29, representing 29 percent of the total population and 42 percent of its working age population. In spite of recent declining unemployment, the youth population still experiences high rates of un- and under-employment. Those youth who are employed are mainly in informal jobs, only a quarter in formal

work. At the same time, the economy is greatly in need of skilled labor. This mis-match is a major brake on economic development. One obvious solution is the provision of technical and vocational training. (p. 36)

The evidence shows that with the establishment of the HEART Trust/NTA (now HEART/NSTA Trust) the number of programmes from their institutions has been expanding and the number of graduates from their programmes has been increasing over the years. Hutton (2009) purported that in 1998 the HEART Trust/NTA Corporate Plan expected that the number of persons accessing training was expected to be 30,453 by the year 2002, with a steady increase beyond. However, by 2007 the HEART Trust/NTA Annual Report said:

> ... with the new training platform, there has been an increase in training in all sectors and the overall enrolment moved from 35,000 in 2002 to 87,037 in 2006/07. This represented an increase of 147 per cent over the period of four years. For the same period, certification moved from 22,949 to 76,275, representing an increase of 283 per cent. (p.24)

According to the 2021–2022 Heart Trust/NSTA annual report, the number of trainees enrolled at the various training entities of the Heart Trust/NSTA stood at 112,320. While this was less than the pre-pandemic peak enrolment (143,321 in 2019), it represents a recovery from the previous decline in 2021.

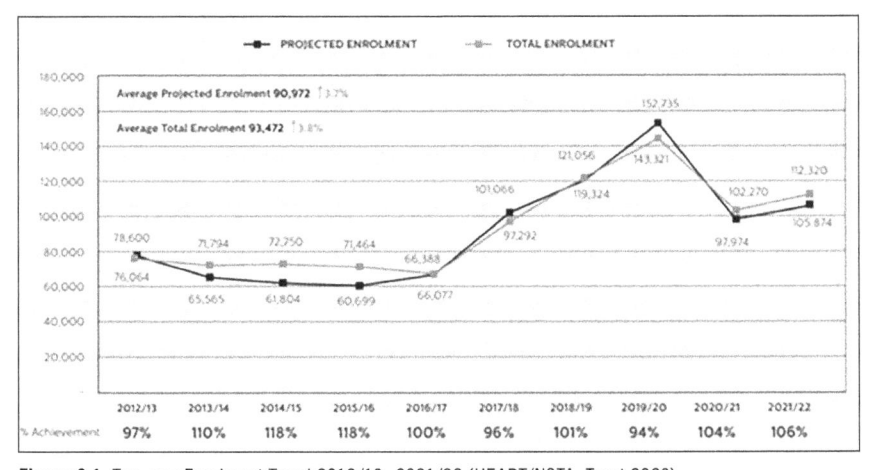

Figure 9.1: Ten-year Enrolment Trend 2012/13–2021/22 (HEART/NSTA, Trust 2023)

This might not, however, show a complete picture of the total numbers being trained in TVET. Previously, Hutton (2009) offered pointed reasons for the discrepancy between the reported training that has been provided by HEART Trust/NTA and the reported number of persons who are trained in their current jobs. Some of the reasons given were:

- Labourers, especially those in the areas of agriculture and construction, are not impacted by the training system because the tasks they do are basic and can be learned by simple coaching/instruction provided by an experienced worker, on-the-job training, or trial and error learning, so there is no need for the training agency to play any meaningful role as far as direct skills training is concerned.
- Even if training is being done in the occupations or industry areas, the overwhelming focus of the agency is on training school leavers.
- Only a small portion of those already in the workplace are affected by the offerings of the training agency.
- Only the apprenticeship and on-the-job training could be directly associated with the workplace.

The present lack of training, particularly in technical and vocational areas, are reasons for concern because of the long-term effects this will have on the pool of qualified talents for the workforce. This will in turn affect investments, production quality, wages, and the competitiveness of business. The secondary education system, which is a feeder to post-secondary institutions and businesses, are not producing the number of students with the technical and vocational background to meet this critical country need. According to the 2015 report of the PIOJ on students' performance of the CSEC exams of the previous year,

> ... the Technical and Vocational subjects recorded the highest average pass rate, 83.2 per cent compared with 82.6 per cent in the previous academic year. Physical Education & Sports (97.2 per cent), Food and Nutrition (92.6 per cent), and Home Economics Management (90.2 per cent) recorded the highest proportion of passes. Electrical and Electronic Technology recorded the lowest proportion of passes, 56.3 per cent. Performance in the four business-related subjects had an average 78.7 per cent pass rate compared with 84.0 per cent in 2013. Principles of Business had the highest pass rate, 82.5 per cent, followed

by Office Procedures, 79.5 per cent. The average pass rate for the Arts and Language subject group was 67.0 per cent (69.5 per cent, 2013). The subjects with the highest performance in this group were French (79.6 per cent) and Music (78.5 per cent). (p. 22.19.)

While the passes reflect reasonable progress, the overall number of students that are being outputted into society with technical and vocational skills is still low – except for information technology, business and accounting. In fact, this has had serious implications to economic growth to the point where Prime Minister Holness made the disclosure in 2023 during the opening ceremony of the May Pen to Williamsfield leg of the Southern Coastal Highway Improvement Project (SCHIP) on September 14, ". . . we have a good thing going with employment, but we now have a new challenge a new problem. We cannot fill skilled workers . . ." (McKenzie, 2023). The Capri Report (Blake, 2023), however, added another dimension explaining,

> The decline in unemployment, and the associated growth experienced, however meagre, is a positive development in the Jamaican economy. Growthless jobs is an area of significant policy concern because, as the country approaches full employment, the Jamaican economy is in reach of its productive limits. The level and quality of workers' human capital is the critical variable in understanding Jamaica's growthless jobs phenomenon. The policy options available to Jamaica are centred around increasing the quantity and quality of human capital through improving education . . . (p. 5)

ADDRESSING WORKFORCE READINESS

For Jamaica to be competitive globally, the educational system must produce workers whose level of attainment is comparable with graduates from similar institutions in developed countries. While this may seem like a daunting task, higher education institutions such as the University of Technology, and the University of the West Indies are known to produce graduates of very high quality. Therefore, it is within the country's institutional capability to accomplish this outcome. Jamaica's educational system outcomes must benchmark with competencies that are validated as critical for global citizenship and national employability.

The U.S. Department of Labors' influential 1991 Secretary's Commission on Achieving Necessary Skills (SCANS) report identified the following competencies that are essential for the 21st Century Workforce.

- Creativity/innovation
- Critical thinking
- Information literacy
- Problem solving
- Decision making
- Flexibility and adaptability
- Learning to learn
- Research and inquiry
- Communication
- Initiative and self-direction
- Productivity
- Leadership and responsibility
- Collaboration
- ICT operations and concept
- Digital citizenship
- Media literacy

These generic competencies must be the outcome of all graduates from secondary and post-secondary institutions who are entering the workforce. Being competitive also involves the ability to perform different activities from competing companies or performing similar activities in different ways (Porter, 1996). This means that businesses will need to find innovative ways to perform common processes – necessitating the need for close collaboration with the educational system and strong structured on-the-job training programs. Finegold and Notabartolo (2010, p. 34) pointed out that "research suggests that the way in which competencies are developed – particularly whether employers are cooperating with educational institutions – may be as important as the competencies themselves." They emphasized that trends in education support the approach of aligning students' skills with industry needs because of the integral role this plays in the success of individuals in the labour market. Such insight, by extension, points to the benefits of structured on-the-job training, internships and apprenticeships, experiential learning programs that allow students to develop skills specific to particular occupations.

The reality is, we cannot afford to delay the exposure of students to workforce competencies until grades 10 and 11. This will result in delay in the development of expertise. Work and college "ways of knowing and doing" must be integrated throughout the various levels of the educational system. The more time spent acquiring these "ways of knowing and doing", the more time will students have in developing their "expertise" and the more likely they will be creative and innovative workers. Hutton (2009) pointed out that of the remaining manufacturing companies in Jamaica, the preferred employees are those who are multi-skilled or competent in a number of related job functions. This points to the need for a manufacturing workforce that has "skill sets ranging from enterprise management related own-account businesses to the technical competence needed to function in a structured business organization" (p. 35). This verify Atchoarena and Caillods (1999) statement years previously that the profile of the Jamaican workforce must be persons who exhibit the mental capacity to acquire both technical and mental competencies.

A caveat is the danger of overproducing qualified people. In other words, there must be jobs to absorb the qualified people – the output of the educational institutions. Murray, Owen and McGaw (2005) cited in Finegold and Notabartolo (2010, p. 41) speaks to such danger in the skills mismatch by saying "despite the strong associations between skills and economic outcomes . . . there are significant proportions of workers who have medium to high levels of skills but who nevertheless occupy low-paying jobs. In such a case the worker will likely to be less motivated and less productive in view of the underutilization of their skills. So as more energy is put into producing more skill workers, equally more jobs must be available to absorb them.

Knowledge Economy and Workforce Skills

The four types of knowledge identified for the workforce of any entity are General Knowledge, Occupational specific knowledge, Firm- or agency-specific knowledge, and Industry-specific knowledge (Lepak & Snell,

2003). General Knowledge is acquired primarily through formal schooling and include academic knowledge such as analytic skills, written and oral communications, critical thinking etc. Occupational specific knowledge is acquired through formal schooling, training, on-the-job experience, or a combination of these. Firm- or agency-specific knowledge may result from a combination of formal schooling, training and on-the-job experience and is unique to the firm. Industry-specific knowledge can also be acquired through experience and formal schooling related to a number of industries, usually over several years of experience and advance schooling (Schurman & Soares, 2010).

The problem that developing countries like Jamaica face is the architecture for acquiring this knowledge is still based on the mass-production economy, rather than on a knowledge-based/information economy, without a strong systematic linkage between the post-secondary entities and experiences that result in the acquiring of all four knowledges. Schurman and Soares (2010) suggests that:

> The emerging knowledge economy creates both a major challenge and opportunity for postsecondary education. Knowledge-based work reduces the disparity between some academic and vocational competencies but introduces new ones. For example, the analytic, critical thinking, and problem-solving skills traditionally attributed to liberal arts education are important to knowledge-based firms along with other foundational skills of the academic curriculum, including quantitative reasoning, writing, information literacy, and demonstrated mastery of major subject. However, knowledge work also places a high premium on collaboration and the ability to apply such skills when working in teams on real problems – skills not taught in many undergraduate liberal arts education. (pp. 139)

All four areas of knowledge need to be integrated and linked strongly at all levels of post-secondary institutions. Admittedly, to have competitive advantage there must also be an accompanied change in the organizational structure of companies that are operating in a knowledge/information-based economy. The intent is to enable workers to focus their specialized knowledge and mental capacity on arriving at creative and innovative solutions (Schurman & Soares, 2010). This sometime requires businesses moving to flatter organizational structures to allow for quicker and more efficient information flow, without which innovation is often stymied. There is also the need to tap into creative and innovative ideas and solutions that can be generated from a diverse workforce.

In Jamaica, more women are graduating from colleges and universities with baccalaureate and advance degrees. Yet their overall participation in the workforce lags behind men by about 15 percent. The disproportional involvement of women in the workforce is reflected globally. According to the International labour Organization (2014b), approximately 47.1% of women were employed, as compared with 72% of men. Not only do women enjoy above 50% or more education in 160 of 206 countries surveyed, they also graduate with more higher degrees globally then men (Bierma, 2016). Despite their educational advancement, Bierma admitted that the number of women in the workforce is less than men, and they are even less in leadership positions. Yet "women leaders have been shown to bring improve performance and profitability to organizations, infuse leadership teams with innovation and fresh perspective, and inspire vision among employees" (p. 120). Their abilities and academic accomplishments must not be overlooked as critical human capital that will endow companies with competitive advantages. More women must be encouraged to enter fields of work that were formerly dominated by men.

INTEGRATIVE STEM, TVET AND WORKFORCE READINESS

The recent upsurge in the Caribbean regarding the importance of STEM education offers a unique opportunity for TVET. It is obvious that the traditional ways of teaching without much connectivity between other knowledge domains will not produce the quality of students who will exhibit higher *thinking* and *doing* that is essential for businesses to be competitive. New ways of *doing* that result in innovative breakthrough for companies are often the embodiment of interdisciplinary collaboration and application of knowledge; thus, the movement to integrative STEM pedagogy, a pedagogy whose strategy is teaching with a deliberate effort to connect across knowledge domains and provide the experiential engagement that reinforces these connections.

As identified previously, Schurman and Soares (2010) explained that the type of competencies required for the 21st century cannot be acquired sorely through the type of education engagement offered through the liberal arts education – but only through a converging of academic and vocational ways of *knowing* and *doing*. Integrative STEM education (or STEAM where the A stands for the Arts) allows this reality because as explicated by Sanders (2009) integrative STEM education is grounded in the tenets of constructivism and the findings of three decades of cognitive science. The types of cognitive themes which permeate integrative STEM education are:

- Learning is a constructive not a receptive process.
- Motivation and beliefs are integral to cognition.
- Social interaction is fundamental to cognitive development.
- Knowledge, strategies, and expertise are contextual.

There is growing evidence that integrative instruction enhances learning (Hartzler, 2000). Not only is integrative STEM education student-centered and knowledge-centered, but it also "provides a context and framework for organizing abstract understandings of science and mathematics and encourage students to actively construct contextualized knowledge of science and mathematics, thereby promoting recall and learning transfer" (Sanders, 2009, p.23).

Integrative STEM pedagogy is not the teaching strategy norms in Jamaica, although commendably there have been many efforts to address this paradigm of instruction. Ironically, many of the strategies that have come to be associated with integrative STEM education have always been strategies used in TVET. These include project-based learning, teamwork, and experiential learning. Most of the knowledge areas in technology, business, family and consumer sciences draw upon knowledge from mathematics, science, and engineering. So, STEM is implicitly built into TVET *ways of knowing*.

Schurman and Soares (2010) articulated very convincingly the need for the four-knowledge associated with work to be integrated and connected at the post-secondary level. That being the case, I will hasten to say that Jamaica does not have the "luxury" or time to wait until students reach the secondary level to expose them to integrative STEM education and TVET. Integrative STEM teaching must be done from the primary level and the types of engagement and activities to which students are exposed must bear some linkage or connections to the core occupational areas associated with TVET. For Jamaica to become competitive in a global market, general education must be integrated with TVET. Literacy must also encompass an understanding of the nature of technology (technological literacy) and every student from primary to secondary levels must be exposed to systematic, age-appropriate curricula that allow this to be achieved (Dixon, 2013). At the national level, standards for technology – which draw from the major occupational areas such as energy, manufacturing, hospitality and agriculture – should be developed for both primary and secondary levels of the school system and these standards should be cross-mapped to the relevant mathematics and science standards or concepts. The aim is to provide core concepts in science, technology, and mathematics that initiate students at the primary level in STEM literacy or thinking, stir their interest in the STEM fields, and develop their STEM competencies in preparation for work. This can be achieved through a thematic curriculum that is driven, but not limited, by themes from major occupational areas and which engage students through discovery-based and problem-based learning (see Figure 9.2).

The technology concepts (and procedures) that students will be exposed to will deliver foundational technical knowledge that they will need later in their secondary and post-secondary school years, as they pursue courses in TVET or in the individual STEM fields. Through technological design, students will be introduced to basic engineering design concepts from primary schools. They will also be able to relate science and mathematics to technological products and understand basic biological and technological systems. Students should be engaged in problem solving activities that require them to use math, science, and technology concepts. They should be taught how to communicate their solutions through reports and other communication tools. This emphasizes the importance of the arts and the development of skills that are important for entrepreneurship. According to Dixon (2013), the numerous computer-assisted educational software and low cost and low maintenance equipment and apparatus

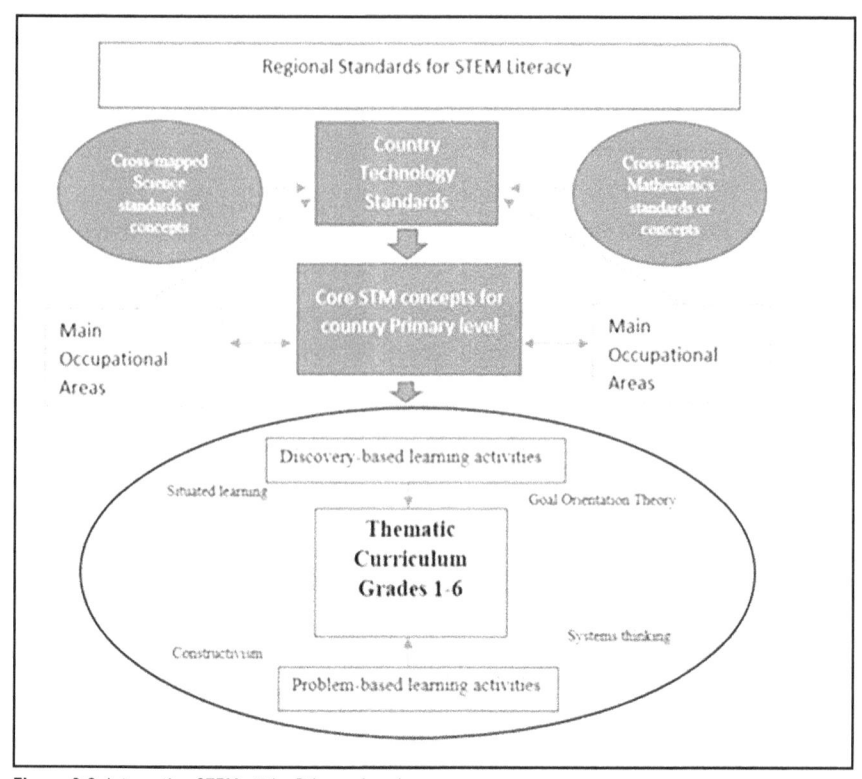

Figure 9.2: Integrating STEM at the Primary Level

that are available, can enrich the learning of STEM at the primary level through discovery, inquiry and problem-based learning.

Integrative STEM at the Secondary Level

Every student should be exposed to the intellectual domain of technology in both their primary and secondary education along with science, mathematics, and the arts. Technology standards for secondary level must include a progression in the development of engineering outcomes relating to engineering principles, engineering design, and engineering/material science (Dixon, 2013). At the early secondary level, particularly at grades 7–9, students will necessarily complete individual curriculums in mathematics, science, and technology to achieve the required depth and breadth in the respective knowledge domain. There must, however,

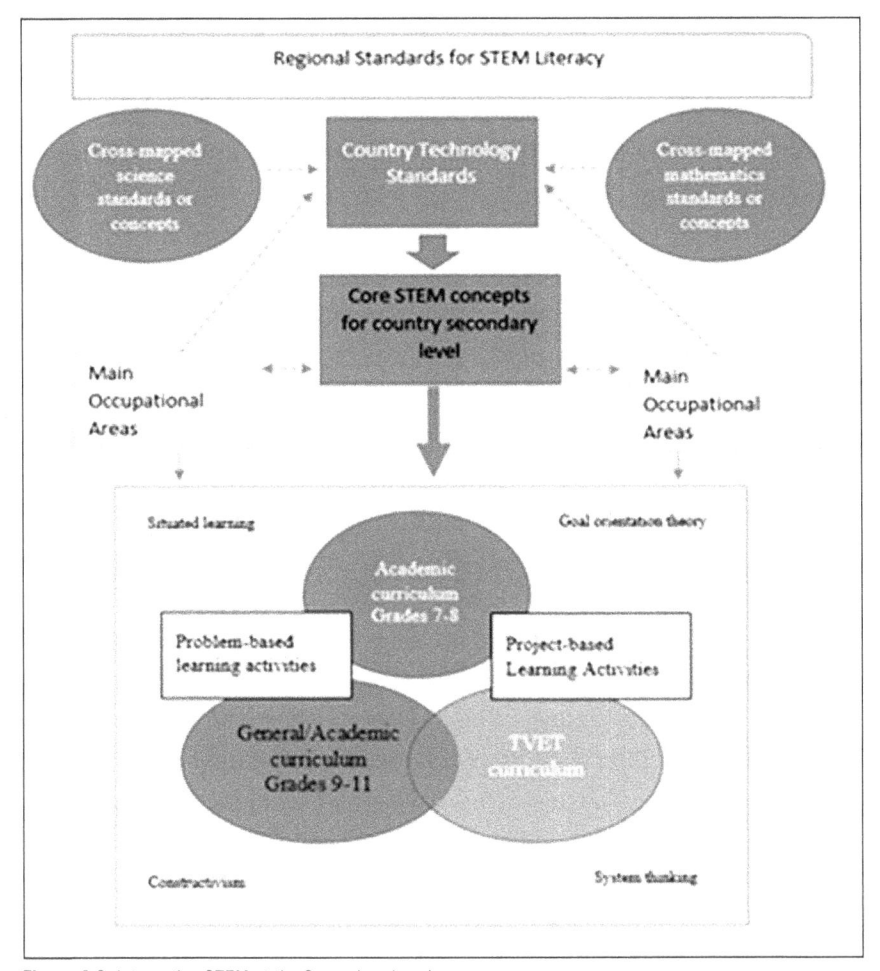

Figure 9.3: Integrating STEM at the Secondary Level

be culminating experiences, whether through problem-based or project-based activities, that require students to collaborate in the solving of authentic problems relating to the occupational areas, and which require the application of STEM concepts. Standards in technology that are cross mapped with standards in science and mathematics should encourage more collaboration between teachers across the STEM disciplines to achieve this outcome.

From grades 9–11 the academic curriculum should be integrated with TVET curriculum from the National Service Training Agency to ensure that students are not only prepared for college but are also prepared with the necessary competency for entry into various occupations. Through this integrated curriculum, students will acquire specific job competencies at the appropriate proficiency while they are still in secondary school and also develop interest in STEM related careers which they can pursue in college (see Figure 9.3).

It is important that the National Training Agency partners with secondary schools to integrate the early levels of key TVET programs into high school curriculums. Through this collaboration, schools can expose students to STEM professions, business and entrepreneurship, internships, problem-based and project-based activities that require the application of STEM concepts and procedures learnt throughout their high school years. (UNESCO, 2005; 2011; Lewis, 2007).

CONCLUSION

According to the PIOJ (2015), the Ministry of Education in Jamaica focus to improve education include the producing of a high-quality education product to all Jamaicans 3–18 years so as to equip them to become productive contribution citizens. This reflects the deficiency that was highlighted in the Vision 2030 (2009) report that there is still inadequate science and technology education at the primary, secondary, and tertiary levels and secondary school examination pass rates are particularly low in subjects that are critical for technological progress, including mathematics and sciences. The report also mentioned that there is a low capacity for enquiry-based approaches to learning, and scientific enquiry which are core components of teacher training. Interestingly, the Capri Report (Blake, 2023) indicated that seven years of significant employment growth has failed to deliver commensurate economic growth because of declining productivity and productivity declined most in sectors with the greatest job growth such as construction and business services. It posits a salient point,

> The majority of workers gaining employment between 2015 and 2022 were semi-skilled workers, bumping up their share of employed labour. The skilled labour that has not emigrated is almost fully employed. This means that the most productive groups of workers are already operating at full or near-full

employment levels. Growth prospects are bleaker in a less skilled workforce . . ." (p. 33)

The Jamaica Education Transformation Committee report (2021), often referred to as the Patterson Report, recommended that TVET should be fully integrated into the secondary school curriculum and rebranded in a well-coordinated and aggressive marketing strategy to effectively promote TVET programs as a viable career path for national development. It also recommended that training institutions should be retooled, and teachers/instructors should be retrained to improve the quality of instruction. In addition, TVET should be repositioned to facilitate and strengthen capacities for entrepreneurial development.

Fundamental to accomplishing these goals – and essential for the development of a 21st century workforce that is competitive – are needed actions to address the *"ways of knowing and doing"* from the primary level through to the post-secondary level. To accomplish this, targeted energy must be invested in research in workforce development and learning in Jamaica by the various universities. Business and community groups must be integrally involved in the curriculum especially at the primary and secondary levels. These curricula must be aligned with the STEM and TVET competencies for the core occupational areas. Learning environments must be structured to cultivate creative thinking, expression, and problem-solving – using proven teaching strategies. Business and industry cannot be side players but need to become key players in driving the curriculum and providing experiential activities, thus orientating students to the *"ways of doing"* in particular occupational areas. The knowledge economy is dynamic and requires quick responses not only in business but also in how we position students to the various ways of "knowing and doing" if we are to be competitive. The volition must be there, however, to change when we need to, and not to hold on to paradigms of *"knowing and doing"* that do not align with the knowledge economy that characterizes the norm in today's business operation.

BIBLIOGRAPHY

Bierma, L. L. (2016). Women's leadership: Troubling notions of the "ideal" (male) leader. *Advances in the Developing Human Resources, 18* (2), 119–136.

Blakes, R. (2023). Growthless jobs the paradox of rising employment and stagnant output. Caribbean Policy Research Institute (CAPRI). https://www.capricaribbean.org/document/growthless-jobs-paradox-rising-employment-and-stagnant-output

Boodhai, N. (2010). Concept paper for the development of a CARICOM strategic plan for vocational education services in the CARCOM Single Market and Economy. Port of Spain, Trinidad and Tobago: National Training Agency.

Hartzler, D. S. (2000). *A meta-analysis of studies conducted on integrated curriculum programs and their effects on student achievement.* Doctoral dissertation. Indiana University.

HEART Trust/NTA. (1998). *Corporate plan 1998–2002.* Kingston, Jamaica: TVET Media Services.

HEART/NSTA Trust. (2023). *2021–2022 Annual Report.* https://www.heart-nsta.org/wp-content/uploads/2023/09/Annual-Report-2021-2022_compressed.pdf

Hutton, D. M. (2008). Re-affirming the role of technical vocational education and training in the development of the Jamaican economy. *Journal of Education and Development in the Caribbean, 10*(2), 71–92.

Hutton, D. M. (2009). Preparing the workforce for the 21st century: The Jamaican experience. *Caribbean Journal of Education, 31*(1), 21–45.

Fawcett, C., El Sawi, G., & Allison, C. (2014). *TVET models, structures and policy reforms: Evidence from the Europe & Eurasia region.* Washington, DC: USAID. http://pdf.usaid.gov/pdf_docs/paoojzsw.pdf

Finegold, D., & Notabartolo, A. S. (2010). 21st century competencies and their impact: An interdisciplinary literature review. In D. Finegold, M. Gatta, H. Salzman, and S. J. Schurman (Eds.), *Transforming the US Workforce Development System: Lessons from Research and Practice.* Urbana-Champaign, IL: Labor and Employment Relations Association.

International Labour Organization. (2010a). Key indicators of the labour market. Geneva, ILO. http://www.ilo.org/empelm/what/lang--en/WCMS_114240

International Labour Organization. (2014b). *Global employment trends 2014: Risk of a jobless Recovery.* http://www.ilo.org/global/research/global-reports/global-employment-trends/2014/WCMS_233953/lang--en/index.htm

Lynn, L., & Salzman, H. (2010). The globalization of technology development: implications for U.S. skills policy. In D. Finegold, M. Gatta, H. Salzman, and S. J. Schurman (Eds.), *Transforming the US Workforce Development System: Lessons from Research and Practice.* Urbana-Champaign, IL: Labor and Employment Relations Association.

Lepak, D., & Snell, S., (2003). Managing the human resource architecture for knowledge based competition. In S. Johnson, M. Hitt, and A. DeNisi (Eds.), *Managing knowledge for sustained competitive advantage: Designing strategies for effective human resource management* (pp. 127–153). San Francisco, CA: Jossey-Bass

Marope, P. T. M., Chakroun, B., & Holmes, K. P. (2015). *Unleashing the potential: Transforming technical and vocational education and training.* UNESCO Publishing

McKenzie, V. (September, 2023). PM: Shortage of skilled workers a threat economic growth, *Vison.* https://our.today/pm-shortage-of-skilled-workers-a-threat-economic-growth/

Murray, T. S., Owen, E., & McGaw, B. (2005). *Learning a living: First results of the adult literacy and life skill survey.* Organization for Economic Co-operation and Development and Statistics Canada.

Ochtet, A. (2005). Vocational education: Technical and vocational education and training has fuel phenomenal economic growth in some countries and fallen short of expectation in others. *Education Today, 13,* 107. http://www.unesco.org/education.

Planning Institute of Jamaica. (2009). Vision 2030: Jamaica national development plan *Economic and social survey Jamaica 2014.* Planning Institute of Jamaica. https://www.pioj.gov.jm/wp-content/uploads/2019/08/Vision-2030-Jamaica-NDP-Full-No-Cover-web.pdf

Planning Institute of Jamaica. (2015). *Economic and social survey Jamaica 2014.* Planning Institute of Jamaica.

Porter, M. E. (November–December, 1996). What is strategy? *Harvard Business Review, 74*(6), 61–78.

Salzman, H. (2000). *The information technology industries and workforces: Work organization and human resource issues.* Report for the National Academy of Sciences Committee on Workforce Needs in Information Technology.

Salzman, H. & Biswas, R. R. (2000). *The Indian IT industry and workforce.* Report for the National Academy of Sciences Committee on Workforce Needs in Information Technology.

Schurman, S. J. & Soares, L. (2010). Connecting the dots: Creating a postsecondary education system for the 21st century workforce. In D. Finegold, M. Gatta, H. Salzman, and S. J. Schurman (Eds.), *Transforming the US workforce development system: Lessons from research and Practice.* Urbana-Champaign, IL: Labor and Employment Relations Association.

STATIN. (2005). *The labour force survey.* Kingston, Jamaica: Author

The Jamaica Education Transformation Committee, (2021). *The reform of education in Jamaica,* 2021 – Report. https://nationwideradiojm.com/wp-content/uploads/2022/01/2021-8-JETC-Patterson-Report.pdf

World Bank. (2023, July 2). Improve Technical and Vocational Education and Training (TVET) to meet skills and labour mismatch. Press Release NO: 2024/004/EDU. https://www.worldbank.org/en/news/press-release/2023/07/12/improve-technical-vocational-education-training-tvet-meet-skills-labour-mismatch#:~:text=Improve%20 Technical%20and%20Vocational%20Education,meet%20 skills%20and%20labour%20mismatch

CHAPTER 10

Funding Strategies in TVET
Implications for Performance

DISRAELI HUTTON

THE FINANCING OF TECHNICAL AND VOCATIONAL EDUCATION and Training (TVET) must be seen from the standpoint of the value and worth of TVET, now and in the future, and its implication for the Jamaican education system and the workforce. Palmer (2018) said, "The financial resources allocated or spent on all TVET programmes reflect the country or region's priorities and, when combined with outcomes, the system's efficiency, as well as its policy priorities and trade-offs" (p. 3).

Further, the Sustainable Development Goal 4 on education presented by the United Nations Educational, Scientific and Cultural Organization (UNESCO) specifically highlighted the importance of TVET by targeting that, by 2030, both women and men will have equal access to TVET up to the university level. This will ensure that youths and adults can obtain relevant training for entrepreneurship and employment in jobs with liveable wages and remove "gender disparities in education and ensure equal access to all levels of education and vocational training for the vulnerable, including persons with disabilities, indigenous peoples and children in vulnerable situations" (United Nations, 2015, p. 19). As noted by the UNESCO-UNEVOC (2017) virtual conference, "Technical and vocational education and training (TVET) is considered a powerful tool to prepare youth for the labour market and provide lifelong learning opportunities to adults" (p. 4). It is therefore the opportune time for governments, along with the major participants in education and training, to recognize the ways they can benefit from the investment options available for training.

MODELS AND APPROACHES TO THE FUNDING OF TVET

The issue of the funding of TVET has been a major concern of both developed and developing countries. It is even more pressing for developing countries which must make a variety of choices on how their limited resources are spent among contending priorities including security, health, and education beyond that of TVET. Palmer (2018) points to the fact that among countries "the policy debate is increasingly focused on raising the level of financing through diversification, and on enhancing efficiency while maintaining equity" (p. 4). The diversification of financing would incorporate individuals who are engaged in the training and also those who are the direct beneficiaries of training, such as companies and enterprises that employ persons who received training. Targetted sources of funding would include local and international sponsors along with philanthropic sources, and through public-private partnerships (PPP), which represent a collaborative approach involving the private sector (Palmer, 2018).

In presenting his broad overview of the financing of TVET in Latin America and the Caribbean, Hanni (2019) identified three categories which should be considered. These include the public sector, private sector, and the rest of the world, which would underpin most, if not all, viable models of funding TVET in the region – and possibly for developing countries and emerging economies worldwide. For the public sector, there is the centralized model in which the state is singular in determining the TVET needs of the country and the required financing. This approach is associated with the formal education system. The model usually highlights the number of participants completing the programmes and not the outcomes or effects of the training delivered. The role of the market is limited in this model of financing TVET. The other major model is wholly market driven and the market forces involved determine the supply and demand of TVET. The participants in this model would include companies which need trained workers, individuals requiring training, banks which would provide loans for prospective trainees, and non-governmental organizations, among others. This mixed model would comprise aspects of both models, thus the market forces would include players from both the private and public sectors.

For the private sector, both households and firms are involved in funding TVET and education. Households play an important role in funding TVET and education, in general, for a number of countries in the region. Hanni (2019) indicated that "... expenditures by households account for more than 20% of total spending. Within the regional context, there is a wide variety of situations with households contributing exceptionally large amounts in El Salvador (47%), Peru (37%) and Colombia (30%) ..." (p. 45). It should not be surprising that firms provide non-formal training in technical vocational education in the Latin American and Caribbean region, which is assessed to be significantly higher than other regions and even better than the average for other countries.

The third category of financing, the rest-of-the-world model, comprises (a) bilateral Official Development Assistance (ODA) (b) ODA by multilateral institutions, and (c) private-sector financing. The bilateral ODA, even though it is steadily declining, has targeted technical vocational education, especially between 2008 and 2017. The main providers of this type of aid to the region include Germany, France, the United States, Spain, and Canada. ODA by multilateral institutions include the European Union institutions, the Inter-American Development Bank, and the Caribbean Development Bank. These institutions provide funding support for TVET programmes which were experiencing serious problems with remaining viable.

Addressing the "optimal model for structuring and partnership-based training funds" (p. 10), Walther and Uhder (2015) identified three main categories of training funds in a study of countries carried out by the Association for the Development of Education in Africa (ADEA). These were classified as pre-employment, continuing, and equity. (See Table 10.1.)

Increasingly, these approaches to funding are being adopted by both developed and developing countries alike in order to address the issues such as relevance and needs which are related to both the enterprise and

Table 10.1: Categories of Training Funds Applied for TVET Countries in Latin American and African Countries

Pre-employment Training Funds	Continuing Training Funds	"Equity Training Funds
Designed to increase the supply of skilled labour to the labour market	Aimed at increasing the competitveness and productivity of businesses through the training of their employees	Whose purpose is to strengthen the skills of vulnerable people (the unemployed, young people, informal sector workers, etc.)

Note. Adapted from *Financing TVET: Main issues for an effective policy in development cooperation* by R. Walther and C. Uhder, 2015, Association for the Development of Education in Africa (ADEA) and Professionals for Fair Development (GRET).

the individuals. This is especially true because of the spotlight being placed on vulnerable populations such those with disabilities, skills deficiency, women, and informal workers.

UNESCO-UNEVOC International Centre for TVET (2017) presented three main approaches which are being implemented by different jurisdictions. (See Figure 10.1.) It should be noted that the budget-oriented funding approach is the traditional input-driven model which focuses on factors such as the number of trainees targeted, overhead costs, training materials and instructor costs. This approach falls in line with the funding practices for TVET in Jamaica. Underpinning the new approaches is the emphasis on quality and relevance. The three main approaches which are highlighted in Figure 10.1 include (a) the trainee-centred funding approach which allows the trainee to select their own training provider utilizing payment of the training using vouchers, loans and scholarships, (b) the contract-based approach, which allows training providers to tender for training programmes, and the selected provider would be based on set criteria including costs, effectiveness, etc. and (c) providing funding to training providers based on targets including achieving output indicators such as employment rates of graduates, and adhering to quality indicators namely industry experience by TVET instructors and industry participation in institutional governance.

Palmer (2018) posited that it "is important for TVET financing to distinguish between sources of funds and how these funds are allocated and subsequently used. In other words, the distinction should be made between resource mobilization, resource allocation and resource

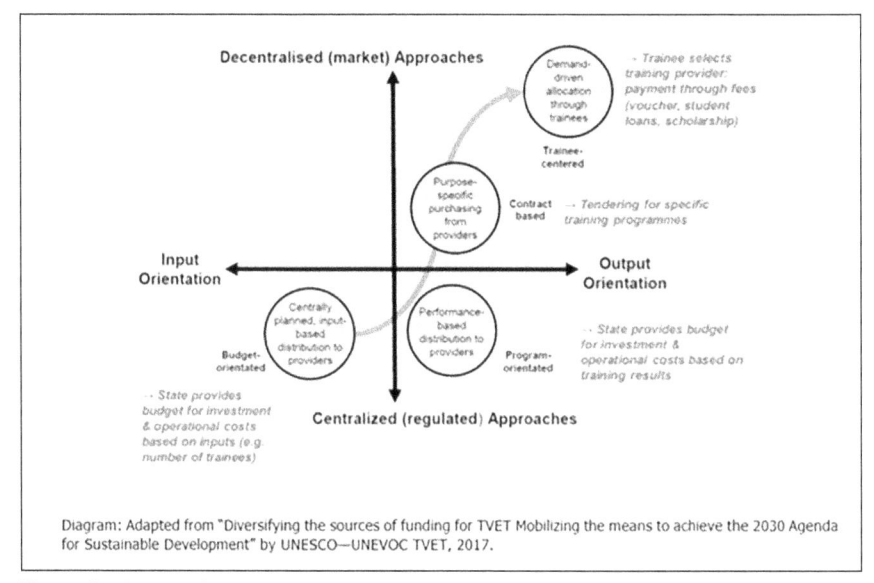

[Figure 10.1 diagram: Sources of funding for TVET — axes showing Decentralised (market) Approaches vs Centralized (regulated) Approaches, and Input Orientation vs Output Orientation. Quadrant labels and descriptions:
- Demand-driven allocation through trainees / Trainee-centered: Trainee selects training provider: payment through fees (voucher, student loans, scholarship)
- Purpose-specific purchasing from providers / Contract based: Tendering for specific training programmes
- Centrally planned, input-based distribution to providers / Budget-orientated: State provides budget for investment & operational costs based on inputs (e.g. number of trainees)
- Performance-based distribution to providers / Program-orientated: State provides budget for investment & operational costs based on training results

Diagram: Adapted from "Diversifying the sources of funding for TVET Mobilizing the means to achieve the 2030 Agenda for Sustainable Development" by UNESCO—UNEVOC TVET, 2017.]

Figure 10.1: Sources of funding for TVET

utilization" (p. 4). Palmer identified three types of funding sources: (a) Pre-employment type, which involves both public and individual sources, (b) In-service type, which is broken down into initial job training and apprenticeship and the sources are both enterprise and individual; updating workforce for which the source is enterprise only; and upgrading workers for which the sources are both enterprise and the individual, and (c) Active labour market programmes, which are broken down into upgrading low or unskilled workers, youth transitioning to the labour market, and adults transitioning between jobs. In all three subtypes the source of funding is the government, but enterprise is also involved in the funding of adults transitioning between jobs.

Walther and Uhder (2015) itemized the multi-dimensions in terms of costing, budgeting, financing and funding which must be incorporated in the planning and delivery of training in order to realize effectiveness. As pointed out in Table 10.2, the how questions "have a number of commonalities, as they unveil similar cross-cutting issues, which are linked to governance (who are the key stakeholders? what are the channels or schemes?) and to scientific methods and tools (what are the calculation methods?)" (p. 7).

Table 10.2: Multi-Dimension Questions Regarding the Efficient and Effective Implementation of TVET

1.	How the cost of measures and policies envisaged are estimated in order to inform policy making: This is the costing dimension.
2.	How the budget is planned to cover the cost of TVET policy: This is the budgeting dimension.
3.	How the money is raised in order to fund the TVET system (including where it comes from): This is the fundraising, also commonly called financing dimension.
4.	How the money is distributed within the TVET system (including where it goes to): This is the funding dimension.

Source: *Financing TVET: Main issues for an effective policy in development cooperation*, by R. Walther and C. Uhder (2015).

FUNDING WORKFORCE EDUCATION AND TRAINING IN THE US

The role and success of all types of training and education in North America is well documented. In fact, developed countries have taken full advantage of training to ensure that quality and efficiency are constantly emphasized in their economic activities. The quality of data provided for training and education are extensive and generally can be readily accessed. This situation seems to not exist in many developing countries, and Jamaica is no exception. The Training Industry Report Training Magazine (Freifeld, 2016–2023), for example, has provided comprehensive information about training over the past 30 years, with data covering almost all aspects of the training function. This basic training data is shared so that steps can be taken by both the government and private sector to share data in order to better track performance. Additionally, the information will allow both the government and the private sector to better plan and effect the delivery of training and avoid unnecessary challenges and concerns when vital information is unavailable to decision-makers.

Table 10.3 provides basic data on training conducted in US for the period 2016 to 2023. The data focus on the overall expenditure annually and some of the training costs of organizations based on their size. For the 2018 Training Report, the sample size was presented as small companies – 100–999 employees, 36%; medium sized companies – 1,000–9,999 employees, 41%; and large companies – 10,000 or more employees, 23%. Medium sized companies represent the majority of companies in the US, thus the justification for the sizable sample size. The overall expenditure

Table 10.3: Training Expenditure in the United States of America Based on Company Size

Types of Companies	Training Period							
	2016	2017	2018	2019	2020	2021	2022	2023
All Companies	$70.64B	$90.6B	$87.6B	$83B	$82.5B	$92.3B	$101.6B	$101.8B
Small	$376,200	$1.00M	$355,700	$367,500	$506,800	$341,500	$368,897	$459,177
% Expenditure	2.42	5.13	1.61	1.89	2.17	1.78	1.75	2.54
Medium	$870,000	$1.50M	$2.10M	$1.70M	$808,400	$1.3M	$1.5M	$1.5M
% Expenditure	5.60	7.69	9.48	8.59	3.47	6.79	7.12	8.31
Large	$14.3M	$17.00M	$19.7M	$17.7M	$22.0M	$17.5M	$19.2M	$16.1M
% Expenditure	92.98	87.18	88.91	89.54	94.36	91.43	91.13	89.15
TOTAL (Average Spending)	15,546,200	19,500,000	22,155,700	19,767,500	23,315,200	19141,500	21,068,897	18,059,178

Note. Adapted from eight training articles titled "Training Industry Report" published in the Training Magazine, edited by L. Freifeld, 2016 to 2023.

on training ranged from US$70.6B to US$101.8B, an increase of 43.7%. For small companies, the average expenditure on training ranged from US$376,200 in 2016 to US$506.8M in 2020. In the case of medium-sized companies, the average spending on training ranged from US $870,000 in 2016 to US$808,400 in 2020. For large companies, the expenditure ranged from US$14.3M in 2016 to US$22M in 2020. For small and large companies, 2020 represents the largest spending year, which seems to be associated with the COVID-19 pandemic. As would be expected, the largest average spending was done by the largest companies whose average spending for the period was US$17.94M. The second highest was the medium-sized companies with an average spending of US$1.41M and then small companies with average spending of US$471,972.

FUNDING APPROACHES FOR THE CARIBBEAN

The level of financing has been a central factor impacting the performance of TVET, not only in the Caribbean but in the rest of the world. As King (2011) indicated, "the drive to mobilize finance for TVET is much weaker than efforts to raise resources for academic schooling or higher education; there is no fast track initiative for TVET" (p. 5). The factors affecting the ability of developing countries to attract funding include (a) pressure to make budgetary allocation based on competing priorities, (b) failure to demonstrate the importance of TVET to national development, and (c) a conviction that TVET will not be able to attract the level of support as in the case of general education (King, 2011). So the overall factors could be summarized as a lack of understanding of the scope, importance and need for national development. Of the 15 countries which currently make up the Caribbean Community (CARICOM), only three have funding mechanisms which allow for some level of sustainability in the implementation of the TVET programme. Ndahi (2011) identified them as Barbados, Trinidad and Tobago, and Jamaica. The level of payroll ranged from 0.5% to 3% and they have been maintained despite the economic constraints facing these countries. But for even those with funding, the decline in economic activities would have depleted the potential amount of funding they would have received from the tax levies.

In addition to funding raised through the tax mechanism, the CARICOM Secretariat (1990), in its Regional Strategy for TVET document, spelled out several strategies which could be considered for addressing the funding issue. These include (a) projectizing of TVET activities to match the financing available, (b) development of income-generating capacities which will utilize the earning to further enhance TVET, (c) establishing financial partnerships between the government and the private sector in order to share the cost of implementing TVET, (d) maximizing the use of available resources including staff, space, equipment and facilities, and (e) rationalizing the inputs of bilateral and international agencies to reduce duplication and increase effectiveness. As the strategy document pointed out, these funding options were to complement the substantive arrangements in place by member states. For the revised CARICOM Strategy document of 2013, a combined local and regional approach to the implementation of TVET means that the funding would be anchored to a platform of public- private partnership involving "government, education and industry in areas of sectoral economic development [thus providing] . . . a great opportunity for TVET to be funded as part of major economic development initiatives undertaken by broad based partnerships of regional and national sectoral bodies and various government departments" (CARICOM/CANTA, 2014, p. 21).

The issue of funding has been a challenge to TVET for decades. One of the factors at play is the cost of implementing some TVET programmes. Adams et al. (1993) said that "governments could not afford vocational programmes with average unit costs twice those of academic secondary education" (p. 3). This is especially true of those programmes related to manufacturing and production-type operations which require a heavy outlay of funding to establish viable training. This was compounded by the fact that the economic climate helped to reduce the funding available, and those who were able to obtain training could not access suitable jobs. This view is supported by Adams et al. who pointed out that between the 1970s and early 1980s vocational graduates were unable to find jobs due to the "economic stagnation, rising levels of public debt and economic stabilization and adjustment programmes" (p. 3). Many of the Caribbean countries are currently facing the same type of problems with the implementation of the TVET programme. As a result, quality programmes cannot be sustained because of (a) reduction of governments' funding support, (b) the cost of implementing training, and (c) low level of employment among graduates from these programmes. The countries which have been able to maintain the implementation of TVET have been those with a funding mechanism based on a payroll tax regime.

With the financial constraints being faced by Caribbean countries (some more than others) creative approaches are being identified. For example, the Ministry of Science, Technology and Tertiary Education (MSTTE, 2010) of Trinidad and Tobago outlined its own approach to the issue of the funding of TVET. The emphasis is being placed on sustainable funding, which was never seriously contemplated and implemented by governments in the past. Specifically for TVET, the Trinidad and Tobago government has proposed the introduction of the National Training and Development Fund. This fund will benefit from seed money from the state which will be supplemented by "taxes on revenue from alcohol and gambling, a national education tax, or the issuance of treasury bonds" (MSTTE, 2010, p. 41). In addition, the initiatives being undertaken by the different sectors to provide sustainable funding for tertiary education and TVET will be enhanced by assisting institutions "to diversify revenue streams through innovation and entrepreneurship" (MSTTE, 2010, p. 41). Ndahi (2011) also endorsed the idea of sustainable funding and specifically urged governments to move away from the practice of fully funding TVET through the national budget. Instead, Ndahi proposed that governments should take a tripartite approach. This would include the employees and their organizations, employers, and governments who would drive the relationship. The Organization of Eastern Caribbean States (OECS) Reform Unit (2007) indicated that, in addition to supporting the use of levies and other tax options to assist the implementation of TVET, those who exceed the age of government support for TVET should be responsible for a portion of the cost incurred by training. The Guyanese government has made a more radical approach to funding than most other countries:

> Government will shift its public financing away from the providers of training to the demand side of the market, enabling targeted workers to purchase training within a competitive environment of suppliers. One instrument for doing this is through training vouchers to targeted individuals such as the young, unemployed and women. Trained workers will be required to repay Government part of the training costs after gaining employment at the end of training. (National Development Strategy Committee [NDSC], 2000, p. 23)

Although the funding of TVET has always been identified as a major factor that is impacting its viability as an alternative to general education, little attention is given to the efficient use of the financial resources allocated to schools. King (2011) highlighted the fact that the financing of TVET seems to not go through the same level of scrutiny as other areas which received funding from central government or bilateral or multi-national aid:

> Developing countries' governments usually treat the financing of public TVET as they do academic schooling and an input-driven approach is used; institutions often receive budgetary allocations (based on some input-oriented funding formula related to number of instructors, number of trainees, previous year's budget, etc.) that remain the same whether the institution is performing well or not. Financing is not linked to efficiency, attainment of minimum training standards, outputs, or outcomes. A culture of apathy exists in many cases since there are no incentives, or disincentives, for performing well or badly. (p. 6)

Hence, how the issue of funding is addressed will determine the success or failure of TVET in the region. Both the regional and individual strategies employed must be aligned to those that have been successfully implemented by countries such as China, Brazil, South Korea, among others. At the same time, the peculiarities of the regions and the specific country must influence policy-makers to select the best options available to them. The need to continue working with international agencies such as the International Labour Organization (ILO), UNESCO, and the World Bank, is also a necessary requirement for success. The financing of TVET will continue to be a challenge for the CARICOM countries, but national governments must prioritize the allocation of their scarce finances, bearing in mind the significance of TVET to economic growth and development.

THE JAMAICAN TVET SYSTEM

The Jamaican TVET system boasts a mainly formal training model with limited non-formal and informal training, bearing in mind that the three per cent direct tax on companies is spent on training and education based on its TVET policies and programmes. This model is most favourable for TVET in comparison to other developing countries both inside and outside of the region. But skills training is also supported by funds provided by the trainees who seek to acquire skills training from private institutions. Most importantly, private companies provide training for their employees, even though they are making contributions to the Human Employment and Resource Training (HEART) Trust National Training Agency (NTA) fund. The Ministry of Education also spends a significant portion of the teaching budget on skills training, but the anchor to systematic training in Jamaica is the HEART Trust fund which started its intervention targetting school leavers.

HEART/NTA Trust

The funding of TVET and skills training has come to rely significantly on the funds provided by the HEART Trust Act, which was established under the government of Prime Minister Edward Seaga in 1982. The implementation of a stable and consistent funding source for workforce preparation came out of the need to address the low level of worker competence which was one of the main factors inhibiting the economic growth and development of the country. So the aim of the "HEART programme was to provide vocational training across the island, which, in the long run, would have equipped Jamaican workers with the necessary knowledge, skills and attitudes needed for higher levels of productivity" (HEART Trust NTA, p.3, 2014). Since its inception, HEART Trust/NTA (now HEART/National Service Training Agency [NSTA] Trust) has made significant strides in training and certification, and this has been achieved substantially as a result of the three per cent levy on the wage bill of the business sector. And as outlined by the ACT: "Contributions payable by an employer under the Act be at a rate of three per cent of total amount of emoluments paid in any contribution year by such employer to employees in his employment" (Jamaican Parliament, 1982, p. 22). This funding levy is consistent with the traditional budget-oriented funding approach, which has been instituted for over 40 years.

For the first five years of the HEART NSTA Trust, 1982/83–1987/88, it had an enrolment of 59,256. As of 2023, or 40 years since the start of the HEART programme, the organization enrolled over 2.2M trainees. (See Table 10.4.) While this number is impressive, the fact is the completion and certification rate for the period is 1.1M or 50%. Over the past 20 years, significant progress has been made with both enrolment and completion/certification. Regarding enrolment, 1,811,925 or 84% of the trainees were enrolled in the last 20 years, and the pattern is similar for completion/certification. Separating completion from certification, there were 826,130 or 83% completions between 2003/04 and 2022/23 and 829, 889 or 97% certifications between the same period. This means that only 16% of the trainees were enrolled in the first 20 years of the programme. And for completion and certification, one can surmise that either the record-keeping was limited or there was little focus on both. In the last 10 years, the completion and certification rates for the HEART/NSTA Trust are equal to 357,926[1].

Certification is an important indicator of training, so while the number of persons engaged in training seemed high, with only 50% being certified, the effectiveness and efficiency of the HEART programme delivery can be legitimately questioned on these performance indicators. Despite this limitation, what are some of the factors that allowed HEART to increase its enrolment numbers, especially over the past 20 years? This would be an area for further investigation, but these are some of the evident factors. First, in the early 2000s, the organization introduced Unit Certification which has been now replaced by Job Certification. These added tens of thousands of trainees to the HEART training initiative. Second is the expansion of its programme offerings as a result of the demands of business and industry. The third factor is the expansion of special projects and community-based training, which is taking training to the people in both businesses and communities. Fourth is collaborating with services industries such as Business Processing Outsourcing (BPO). Fifth, maintaining the three per cent tax on businesses allowed

Table 10.4: HEART NSTA Trust Enrolment, Completion, and Certification for the Period 1982/83–2022/23

Financial Years	Enrolment	%	Completion/ Certification	%	Certification	%
1982/83–1987/88	59256	3%	31911	3%	–	–
1988/89–1992/93	29783	1%	30853	3%	–	–
1993/94–1997/98	96338	4%	41239	4%	–	–
1998/99–2002/03	166285	8%	83311	8%	27467	3%
2003/04–2007/08	387832	18%	229040	21%	275881	32%
2008/09–2012/13	431707	20%	239164	24%	196082	23%
2013/14–2017/18	383462	18%	126712	13%	126712	15%
2018/19–2022/23	608924	28%	231214	23%	231214	27%
TOTAL	2,163,587	100%	1,013,444	100%	857,356	100%

Note. Enrolment data compiled by the HEART Trust Planning Unit from the following sources: HEART's Annual Reports (1982–1993); HEART's Annual Training Report (1994–2001); HEART's Annual Statistical Reports (2002–2015); HEART's Annual Training Reports (2000-2008); HEART's Statistical Reports (2009–2024); HEART's Annual Reports (1982–1993); HEART's Annual Training Reports (1994–2001); and HEART's Statistical Reports (2002–2024).

HEART to expand instead of contract the delivery of training. Sixth, the removal of all fees to access training is an incentive for those with no economic support to obtain training.

Table 10.5 captures the income and expenditure of the HEART NSTA Trust for the period 2016/17 to 2021/22. Over 90% of its income is obtained from the three per cent levy. The rest of the funding came from finance incomes and institutional business activities. Over the period, the income increased from J$11.08B to J$15.85B which is an increase of 43% or J$4.77B. So despite the pandemic which had its most debilitating effects in the budget year 2020/21, the income flow to the organization remained steady. Expenditure at HEART Trust experienced a steady increase for the reporting period. It moved from J$10.5B in 2016/17 to J$14.87B in 2021/22, an increase of 41.62% over the period. However, there was a decline of 12.94% in expenditure which moved from J$14.48B in 2019/20 to J$12.82B in 2020/21. This represented the period of reduced activities as a result of the effects of the COVID-19 pandemic. Direct teaching represented the highest item of expenditure which ranges between J$7.12B or 55.6% and J$9.08B or 63.0%. The second highest

FUNDING STRATEGIES IN TVET: IMPLICATIONS FOR PERFORMANCE

Table 10.5: HEART NSTA Trust, Income and Expenditure for Operating Period 2016/17– 2021/22

Areas of Income	2021–2022 (J$, 000)	%	2020–2021 (J$, 000)	%	2019–2020 (J$, 000)	%	2018–2019 (J$, 000)	%	2017–2018 (J$, 000)	%	2016–2017 (J$, 000)	%
Employee three per cent contribution	14,818,050	93	12,843,075	92.6	14,015,714	92.20	12,588,868	91.98	11,705,159	92.3	10,076,036	90.92
Finance income	313,408	02	256,808	1.9	219,912	1.44	190,887	1.40	259,563	2.10	279,574	2.52
Institutional earnings	652,262	04	569,300	4.1				5.79				
Property sales	822,395	5.41	781,569	5.70	640,994	5.00	641,788		(2,959)	(.02)	2,778	.03
Other income	63,665	01	200,754	1.4	3,640	.02	2,784	.02	78,155	0.60	81,427	.74
Total	15,847,385	100	13,869,937	100	142,349	.93	122,764	.90				
					15,204,010	100	13,686,872	100	12,680,912	100	11,081,603	100
Expenditure												
Property cost	2,847,524	19.0	2,634,196	20.5	2,673,503	18.5	2,460,181	18.91	2,281,766	19.12	2,057,056	20.47
Administration staff costs	2,944,761	19.8	2,476,881	19.3	2,072,019	14.0	1,754,793	13.49	1,802,245	15.11	1,610,490	16.03
Other operating costs	628,048	4.2	586,827	4.6	660,677	4.5	702,485	5.39	708,723	5.94	493,491	4.91
Direct training costs	8,454,606	57.0	7,128,736	55.6	9,081,635	63.0	8,093,491	62.21	7,139,129	59.83	5,888,268	58.59
Total	14,874,939	100	12,826,640	100	14,487,834	100	13,010,950	100	11,931,863	100	10,049,305	100
Surplus before tax	972,446		1,043,297		716,176		675,922		749,049		1,032,298	
Deferred tax on post-employment benefits	36011		98,648		(114,919)		(164,446)		(178,267)		(225,215)	
Net surplus	936,435		1,141,945		601,258		511,476		749,049		807,083	

area of expenditure is property cost which includes the rental or leasing of property to support the island-wide training delivery activities. This area of expenditure ranges between J$2.67B or 18.5% and J$2.63B or 20.5%. The expenditure for administrative staff, which is usually the highest in most government-type organizations, is similar to the expenditure for property cost and ranges between J$1.75B or 13.49% and J$2.94B or 19.80%. Without the HEART/NSTA Trust budget, the training of the workforce could not be sustained in areas such as hospitality and the accommodation subsector and, increasingly, direct training to organizations and communities is being channelled through the Special Projects & Community Training Interventions unit of the HEART/NSTA Trust.

FINANCING THE SCHOOL SYSTEM: MAINTENANCE AND UPGRADING OF TVET FACILITIES

Initially, Industrial Arts Education was the primary source of skills training, and this programme was aimed at providing an orientation to industry and the world of work primarily at the all-age and junior secondary schools in the country. Over the past six decades, the spending of the central ministry on TVET is a signal of support for preparing the workforce. The introduction of Grades 10 and 11 programmes in 1974 by the Michael Manley regime extended secondary education for an additional two years (Smith, 2012). This ushered in the two-tiered system of TVET and continuing education. The World Bank and other international agencies played a significant role in the funding and overall consolidation of TVET in the Jamaican education system. With some 50 years since the installation of machines, equipment, and facilities generally across the school system, the need for continuous maintenance and renewal is evident. Just as important is the modernization of the TVET system to reflect the needs of the economic activities of the country (National Council on Education [NCE], 2021). Table 10.6 provides some indication of the effort made by the Ministry of Education and Youth (MoEY) to maintain and, in some cases, upgrade the TVET facilities over the three-year period, 2016/17 to 2018/19. The largest expenditures occurred in Region 5 where two primary and junior high schools received over J$19M

Table 10.6: Capital Expenditures for Secondary Schools in the Then Six Regions of the MoEY

Region	No. of Schools	2016–2017 J$	%	201–2018 J$	%	2018–2019 J$	%	Total J$	%
1	21	16,687,711	18.70	14,237,439	14.04	19,402,721	20.87	50,327,871	17.75
2	15	8,397,407	9.41	10,460,082	10.32	10,469,880	11.26	29,327,369	10.34
3	15	13,336,107	14.95	6,563,567	6.47	11,000,000	11.83	30,899,674	10.90
4	27	13,930,102	15.61	16,910,760	16.68	12,300,000	13.23	43,140,862	15.21
5	25	13,883,134	15.56	41,204,209	40.64	34,680,579	37.31	89,767,922	31.66
6	26	22,986,082	25.76	12,008,477	11.84	5,100,000	5.49	40,094,559	14.14
Total	129	89,220,543		101,384,534		92,953,180		283,558,257	100

and J$15M to significantly upgrade their TVET facilities. Of the over 170 secondary schools, 129 or 76% of the secondary schools benefitted from capital expenditure. There was an average of J$94,519,419 spent per year for the three-year period, and the largest amount of J$101.38M was spent in 2017/18. The majority of secondary schools benefit from some financial support to address the immediate need to maintain TVET programmes. The bigger challenge is the modernization of TVET to reflect the requirements of skills training in the 21st century. This will be a significant effort which cannot be achieved with an average spending of less than J$100,000,000 annually.

The spending on the delivery of TVET programmes represents a significant portion of the overall spending on teaching and learning in secondary schools. For some schools, the recurrent spending on the teaching of TVET exceeds the cost of teaching all the non-TVET subjects. While some schools can supplement the MoEY subventions with other sources of income such as their business enterprises, most schools do not have this option. So, the expenditure on both TVET and non-TVET programmes is limited to the MoEY annual subventions. Table 10.7 presents six schools which include four upgraded secondary and two technical schools showing income, TVET and non-TVET expenditure. The schools are not a representative sample, but the data provide some insights into spending on TVET and non-TVET programmes and courses. For example, the data show only one school with recurrent teaching

TECHNICAL VOCATIONAL EDUCATION AND TRAINING IN JAMAICA

Table 10.7: TVET and Non-TVET Expenditure in Selected Secondary Schools

	School/Type	2017/18 (J$)	%	2018/19 (J$)	%	2019/20 (J$)	%	2020/21 (J$)	%	2021/22 (J$)	%	Total (J$)
Income	A-UpG	16,350,000.00		18,900,000.00		18,800,000.00		20,300,000.00		23,300,000.00		97,650,000.00
	B-THC	39,787,821.66		34,655,585		36,990,530		31,247,145		34,483,519.55		177,164,601.00
	C-UpG	115,564,064.29		118,575,192.68		123,562,755.29		106,912,618.00		112,077,620.00		576,692,250.00
	D-UpG	23,500,000.00		22,700,000.00		23,800,000.00		22,600,000.00		23,300,000.00		115,900,000.00
	E-THC	40,768,955.00		34,999,356.84		30,979,628.29		20,209,105.69		29,319,855.29		156,276,901.11
	F-UpG	60,849,150.00		48,991,155.00		43,054,450.00		48,163,150.00		$39,661,300.00		240,719,205.00
TVET Expenditure	A-UpG	1,250,000.00	7.65	2,400,000	12.7	3,600,000	19.1	800,000	3.94	4,360,000	18.7	12,410,000.00
	B-THC	1,919,358.14	4.82	1,267,365.21	3.66	979,832.79	2.65	542,410.75	1.74	1,042,599.40	3.02	5,751,566.00
	C-UpG	1,447,672.89	1.25	1,505,579.81	1.27	1,580,858.80	1.28	1,000,000.00	0.94	1,150,000.00	1.03	6,684,117
	D-UpG	2,985,000.00	12.7	2,784,000.00	12.3	1,845,000.00	7.75	2,380,000.00	10.5	1,693,000.00	7.27	11,687,000.00
	E-THC	2,419,851.18	5.94	1,333,093.90	3.81	664,125.40	2.14	1,681,660.87	8.32	2,668,922.80	9.1	8,767,654.15
	F-UpG	1,253,905.99	2.06	1,352,822.46	2.76	345,600.00	0.8	216,956.68	0.45	$537,531.32	1.36	3,706,816.45
Non-TVET Expenditure	A-UpG	580,000.00	3.55	103,000.00	0.54	98,000.00	0.52	250,000.00	1.23	250,000.00	1.07	1,281,000.00
	B-THS	1,677,222.53	4.22	769,274.48	2.22	1,260,252.67	3.41	210,525.45	0.67	596,148.18	1.73	4,513,423.00
	C-UpG	2,089,514.49	1.8	2,533,094.91	2.14	2,897,494.26	2.34	2,011,051.68	1.88	2,209,276.81	1.97	11,740,432.15
	D-UpG	450,000.00	1.91	240,000.00	1.06	280,250.00	1.18	150,000.00	0.66	285,000.00	1.22	1,165,250.00
	E-THC	1,535,018.11	3.77	2,660,297.53	7.60	3,002,250.89	9.69	1,527,793.24	7.56	1,818,753.81	6.2	10,544,113.58
	F-UpG	179,288.00	0.29	240,300.00	0.49	75,459.00	0.18	56,499.00	0.12	113,924.00	0.29	665,470.00
Combined Expenditure	A-UpG	1,830,000.00	11.2	2,503,000.00	13.2	3,698,000.00	19.7	1,050,000.00	5.17	4,610,000.00	19.8	13,691,000.00
	B-THS	3,596,580.67	9.04	2,036,639.69	5.9	2,240,085.46	6.06	752,936.20	2.41	1,638,747.78	4.75	10,264,990.00
	C-UpG	3,537,187.38	3.1	4,038,674.72	3.4	4,478,353.06	3.62	3,011,051.68	2.82	3,359,276.81	3.00	18,424,543.65
	D-UpG	3,435,000.00	14.6	3,024,000.00	13.3	2,125,250.00	8.93	282,630.00	1.25	1,978,000.00	8.49	10,844,880.00
	E-THS	3,954,869.29	9.70	3,993,391.43	11.4	3,666,376.29	11.8	3,209,454.11	15.9	4,487,676.61	15.3	19,311,767.73
	F-UpG	1,433,193.99	2.36	1,593,122.46	3.3	421,059.00	0.98	273,455.68	0.57	651,455.32	1.64	4,372,286.45

% TVET and non-TVET and combined TVET and non-TVET expenditure as a percentage of income.   *Key:* UpG – Upgraded High School; Tech – Technical High School; Trad – Traditional High School cost amounting to 20% direct recurrent teaching costs. In addition, as a percentage of the school budget, TVET expenditure on average is less than seven percent, which exceeds the spending on non-TVET programmes and courses. The evidence calls into question the view that a significant percentage of the schools' budget is being spent on TVET. Even though there are only two technical schools represented in the table, the evidence suggests that there maybe little difference regarding the recurrent TVET expenditure for the two types of school. There are concerns that the expenditure on TVET has not resulted in the quality workforce that is needed, and the disenchantment with TVET after more than 150 years of experience is troubling. Some secondary schools have moved back to general education as the focus of their teaching and learning. And even with the high spending on TVET, it is not enough to maintain a viable and effective programme in secondary schools. The Jamaica Education Transformation Commission (JETC) (2021) recommended that "TVET should be fully integrated into the secondary school curriculum and rebranded in a well-coordinated and aggressive marketing strategy to effectively promote TVET programs as a viable career path for national development" (p. 261). So, the fragmentation of TVET in many of the secondary schools must be halted if the recommendation of the JETC is to be realized. This also means that the spending on TVET has to be increased dramatically, and this would put the spending on TVET above the spending on non-TVET programmes. Based on the pattern in the spending on TVET, there is little evidence that TVET is being emphasized over non-TVET programme and courses, and the level of spending is driven more by the cost of training materials, especially in the technical areas. The questioning of the effective and prudent use of funding for TVET is difficult to argue when the items purchased are directly related to the delivery of TVET programmes. However, this does not mean that the necessary steps are not taken to ensure that the spending on TVET meets procurement and quality assurance standards along with efficient and effective delivery of TVET programmes.

PRIVATE SECTOR EXPENDITURE ON TRAINING

For the business sector, the emphasis is on training and education, and not just on TVET. As pointed out earlier, of the 17 countries in the English-speaking Caribbean, only Barbados, Trinidad and Tobago, and Jamaica have a levy system in place. Based on preliminary information from some companies, these countries spend an average of 2.5% of their wages on training for the workforce. This is consistent with expenditure on training in the United States of America. What is of interest is that most, if not all, of these companies by law are required to make the 3% contribution to the HEART/NSTA Trust. So they pay the three per cent levy while, at the same time, spend in the vicinity of three per cent of their wage bill on training. It should be noted that HEART/NSTA Trust is increasingly providing direct training support for contributing sectors such as tourism and business process outsourcing. Before, the emphasis was mainly on providing a trained workforce for sectors operating in the Jamaican economy.

CONCLUSION

The approach to the funding and financing of training must be examined to ensure that the labour market is provided with skilled labour. In addition, funding is also critical for developing, maintaining and continuously improving the competitiveness and productivity of the workforce. Without a highly trained workforce, the country will be unable to compete at a global level, especially in areas such as tourism and music, among others. Further, funding of TVET must increasingly include vulnerable populations in the society.

While the three per cent levy on companies has been a mainstay of the financing of TVET for over 40 years, other funding approaches have to be considered. Currently, skills training outside of the formal tertiary institution is viewed as the responsibility of the government. However, there are limits to the amount obtained from the levy to satisfy the needs of individual companies. HEART/NSTA Trust will increasingly find itself in a 'double bind' position where it will have to continue to prepare the workforce while, at the same, time respond to the demands of individual companies to provide specialized training. Furthermore, HEART is constantly being called on to address priorities in its expenditure. The models shared above must be examined because there is no guarantee that the three per cent levy will be lasting. At the same time, TVET, like education in general, is for the public good, so the State has a responsibility to play a significant role in its funding support.

NOTE

1. Up to March 2013, the focus of output was on completion. This involves the number of trainees exiting the system after fulfilling all training and assessment requirements for the duration of the programme, whether they were deemed competent for certification or not. Since April 2013, the focus has shifted from completions to certifications instead, so both completion and certification are subsequently the same for the HEART NSTA training output.

BIBLIOGRAPHY

Adams, A. V., Middleton, J. & Ziderman, A. (1993). *The World Bank's policy paper on vocational and technical education and training.* http://www.greenstone.org/greenstone3/nzdl?a=d&d=HASH010ead3e9fd3a7ebfe56b791.3.np&c=edudev&sib=1&dt=&ec=&et=&p.a=b&p.s=ClassifierBrowse&p.sa=

CARICOM/CANTA. (2014). *Regional TVET strategy for workforce development and economic competitiveness.* https://issuu.com/caricomorg/docs/caricom_regional_tvet_strategy

CARICOM Secretariat. (1990). Regional strategy: Technical and vocational education and training. Author

Freifeld, L. (Ed.). (2016). *Training Industry Report Training Magazine.* https://trainingmag.com/sites/default/files/images/Training_Industry_Report_2016.pdf

Freifeld, L. (Ed.). (2017). *Training Industry Report Training Magazine.* https://trainingmag.com/2017-training-industry-report/

Freifeld, L. (Ed.). (2018). *Training Industry Report Training Magazine.* https://trainingmag.com/2018-training-industry-report/

Freifeld, L. (Ed.). (2019). *Training Industry Report Training Magazine.* https://trainingmag.com/2019-training-industry-report/

Freifeld, L. (Ed.). (2020). *Training Industry Report Training Magazine*. https://trainingmag.com/2020-training-industry-report/

Freifeld, L. (Ed.). (2021). *Training Industry Report Training Magazine*. https://trainingmag.com/2021-training-industry-report/

Freifeld, L. (Ed.). (2022). *Training Industry Report Training Magazine*. https://trainingmag.com/2022-training-industry-report/

Freifeld, L. (Ed.). (2023). *Training Industry Report Training Magazine*. https://trainingmag.com/2023-training-industry-report/

Hanni, M. (2019). Financing of education and technical and vocational education and training (TVET) in Latin America and the Caribbean. https://repositorio.cepal.org/entities/publication/d2853a1a-ca1a-430d-8551-a3ff525ee84a

HEART Trust/National Training Agency (NTA). (2014). *C-EFE/YSD program: Pre-technology Partnerships, country profile and terms of reference*. https://www.collegesinstitutes.ca/wp-content/uploads/2012/08/2_C-EFE-YSD Jamaica-HEART-Profile-TORS-FINAL.pdf

Jamaican Parliament. (1982). *The Human Employment and Resource Training (HEART) Act*. Government Printing Office. https://www.heart-nta.org/wp-content/uploads/heart-act.pdf

King, K. (2011). *Eight proposals for a strengthened focus on technical and vocational education and training (TVET) in the Education for All (EFA) agenda*. https://unesdoc.unesco.org/ark:/48223/pf0000217862

Ministry of Science, Technology and Tertiary Education (MSTTE). (2010). *Policy on tertiary education, technical vocational education and training, and lifelong learning in Trinidad and Tobago*. https://uil.unesco.org/document/trinidad-and-tobago-policy-tertiary-education-technical-vocational-education-and-training

National Development Strategy Committee. (2000). *National development strategy (2001–2010): A policy framework eradicating poverty and unifying Guyana*. Government of Guyana. http://parliament.gov.gy/documents/documents-laid/4968-national_development_strategy_2001_to_2010_a_policy_framework_eradicating_poverty_and_unifying_guyana.pdf

National Council on Education (2021). *National education sector plan: The COVID-19 pandemic and the transformation of the education system*. Ministry of Education and Youth.

Ndahi, H. B. (2011). *Reinvesting technical and vocational education and training in the Caribbean*. International Labour Organization (ILO) Subregional Office for the Caribbean. http://www.ilocarib.org.tt/images/stories/contenido/pdf/TechnicalandVocational/reinventing-tvet-caribbean-may2011.pdf

Palmer, R. (2018). *Financing Technical and Vocational Skills Development Reform*. In: McGrath, S., Mulder, M., Papier, J., Suart, R. (eds) Handbook of Vocational

Education and Training. Springer, Cham. https://doi.org/10.1007/978-3-319-49789-1_42-1

Smith, P. (2012, December 16). The next 50 years – build the education system we need. *The Gleaner.* https://jamaica-gleaner.com/gleaner/20121216/news/news7.html

United Nations. (2015). *Transforming our world: The 2030 agenda for sustainable development.*https://sustainabledevelopment.un.org/content/documents/21252030%20Agenda%20for%20Sustainable%20Development%20web.pdf

UNESCO-UNEVOC TVET. (2017). *Diversifying the funding sources for TVET: Mobilizing the means to achieve the 2030 Agenda for Sustainable Development.* Report of the UNESCO-UNEVOC virtual conference held January 16–22, 2017. Moderated by Christine Uhder Groupe de recherche et d'échanges technologiques (GRET), France. https://unevoc.unesco.org/up/vc_fin_synthesis.pdf

Walther, R. & Uhder, C. (2015). *Financing TVET: Main issues for an effective policy in development cooperation.* Main outcomes and conclusions of the seminar held in Brussels on November 27, 2014. Final Version. https://gret.org/wp-content/uploads/2021/10/Seminar-report_Financing-TVET_GRET-EU.pdf

Biographies

EDITORS

PROFESSOR DISRAELI M. HUTTON is a graduate of The Mico Teachers' College and the College of Arts Science and Technology. He holds an undergraduate degree in Technology Education from Buffalo State College, United States of America (USA); a Master's degree in Supervisory Management and Training and Development; and a PhD in Educational Administration and Supervision in (Higher Education), both from Bowling Green State University, USA. Professor Hutton's work experience spans both the private and the public sectors. At JAMALCO, he was employed as the Training Director and at the HEART NSTA Trust as Chief Technical Director. Professor Hutton also served as Executive Director of the Education Transformation Team which was responsible for the implementation of the transformation programme for the Jamaican education system. Professor Hutton has taught in the public school and tertiary education systems spanning a period of over 40 years, which included CAST, now the University of Technology, Jamaica. He was Acting Director of the School of Education (SOE) and then Director from 2017 to 2019. He teaches and publishes in the areas of educational leadership, financing of education, and TVET. He is currently on a contractual arrangement at the International University of the Caribbean (IUC) as Dean of Graduate Studies, Research and Consultancy. Professor Hutton has over forty publications including journal articles, book chapters, edited books, and a single-authored book. The areas of emphasis include school leadership, financing of education, and technical and vocational education and training. Professor Hutton is the lead editor of the book, *Leadership for Success: The Jamaican School Experience*, and his latest 2021 book publication, in collaboration with colleagues, is *Improving School Leadership and Management: Using Real Cases in Caribbean Schools to Explore*

Solutions, and he is the single author of *Transforming Leadership Practice: Examining Dimensions of Performance in Jamaican School.*

DR HOPE MAYNE is an Associate Professor of Curriculum and Instruction and Acting Vice Dean in the Faculty of Education and Liberal Studies at the University of Technology, Jamaica. Her body of research work lies in curriculum as lived experiences, teacher preparation, decolonizing the curriculum, curriculum implementation and integration, curriculum as social reconstruction and STEM/STEAM TVET methodology. Dr Mayne has been a Teacher Educator for 23 years and taught at the Secondary High School for nine years. She has worked with the Ministry of Education to train teachers in implementing the National Standard Curriculum (NSC) Curriculum. She is the 2019 recipient of a Canada-CARICOM Faculty Leadership Fellowship from the Government of Canada. Her Fellowship focused on conducting research on 21st Century Teaching and Learning with an emphasis on STEM Inquiry Pedagogy. She continues to build this research area in collaboration with Brock University, Canada to strengthen the practice of STEM Inquiry Based Pedagogy in TVET.

RAYMOND DIXON is a Professor of Career & Technical Education, Curriculum and Instruction, and Human Resource Development and former Department Chair of Curriculum and Instruction in the College of Education Health and Human Sciences. He completed his PhD in Human Resources Education at the University of Illinois, Urbana Champaign, master's in technology at the Illinois State University, and Bachelors in Industrial Technology at the University of Technology, Jamaica. He is a former Fellow of the National Center for Engineering and Technology Education (NCETE). His main research areas include STEM integration, Workforce Development, and Design Cognition. He is a former member of the ITEEA/CTETE Leadership institute. He serves as PI and Co-PI NSF funded projects since joining the University of Idaho in 2011. In Jamaica he served as department head and later deputy manager of the National Tool and Engineering Institute (NTEI), Heart NSTA Trust. As a consultant Dr Dixon has conducted several occupational and job analyses for manufacturing, natural resources, hospitality and cyber security in North Central Idaho.

CONTRIBUTORS

RAYMOND A. DIXON, PhD, Professor of Career Technical Education, Curriculum & Instruction and Human Resource Development. College of Education Health and Human Sciences, University of Idaho, USA.

DISRAELI HUTTON, PhD, Professor (Retired) of Educational Leadership; Former Head of the School of Education, University of the West Indies, Mona Campus, Jamaica.

HOPE MAYNE, PhD, Associate Professor of Curriculum and Instruction. She is currently the Acting Vice Dean in the Faculty of Education and Liberal Studies at the University of Technology, Jamaica.

CEDRIC MCCULLOCH, Interim Executive Director of HEART NSTA Trust in 2013; Former Permanent Secretary of the Ministry of Sports and Community Development; Officer of the International Labour Organization of the United Nations assigned to Nigeria and the Caribbean office located in Trinidad and Tobago.

GRACE MCLEAN, PhD, Former Acting Permanent Secretary in the Ministry of Education and Youth, Jamaica; Former Chief Education Officer Ministry of Education and Youth (MOEY), Jamaica; Former Senior Programs Officer, the HEART NSTA Trust.

HALDEN MORRIS, PhD, Professor (Retired), Workforce Development and TVET; Former Director of the Institute of Education, The University of the West Indies; Professional Engineer (PE).

CHRISTOPHER O'COY BRYAN, Capital Projects Manager at the Jamaica Cement Company, Mechanical Engineer, Jamaica Cement Company, Master's degree in TVET Leadership and Workforce Development, The University of the West Indies.

CAROLE POWELL, DPhil, Lecturer: Educational Leadership, University of the West Indies, Mona, Jamaica; Former Director: Rationalization Programme, Ministry of Education and Youth (MOEY), Jamaica; Former Principal St Andrew Technical High School.

MARCIA ROWE-AMONDE, PhD, Senior Director: Standards, Curriculum & Learning Resources Development HEART/NSTA Trust, Jamaica; Adjunct Lecturer, Faculty of Humanities and Education, The University of the West Indies (UWI), Mona.

Milton Keynes UK
Ingram Content Group UK Ltd.
UKHW020920291124
451807UK00013B/1033

9 789768 335043